BEING A LANDLORD

George Denton-Ashley

Published April 2013 by

Spiramus Press Ltd

www.spiramus.com

ISBN 978 1907444 70 8

© George Denton-Ashley 2013

British Library Cataloguing-in-Publication Data.

A catalogue record for this book is available from the British Library.

Printed and bound in Great Britain by Berforts Information Press

CONTENTS

CONTENTS

CONTENTS

CONTENTS

CONTENTS

INTRODUCTION

The UK private residential rental market is a growing sector. There are several reasons for this: high property prices, especially in the south of England, and restricted mortgage lending; growing demand for residential accommodation not being met by supply; first-time buyers unable to get on the property ladder and local authorities turning to the private sector to meet their housing responsibilities.

Being a Landlord aims to be the most useful book on the market for landlords in England and Wales. It breaks down complex legal concepts so that landlords understand their rights and responsibilities and follow the correct procedures in the most common tenancy situations.

This book is written for all private rented sector landlords – from the individual who decides to invest in property to provide an income flow and capital appreciation, or who becomes a landlord by accident (for example, by inheriting a property) to the professional landlord who owns a portfolio of properties.

The guidance in this book will help landlords to avoid problems with tenancies and provides a step by step guide to dealing with such problems should they arise. New legislation and numerous court cases in recent years have made the role of landlord increasingly complicated, with landlords all too often finding themselves embroiled in litigation. The book advises landlords on how to minimise the risk of legal action being taken against them and the circumstances in which they should take proceedings against a tenant.

Being a Landlord, together with the author's website www.balandlord.co.uk, provides a comprehensive combined resource for landlords.

1 THE ASSURED SHORTHOLD TENANCY (AST)

1.1 Introduction to AST

This book deals mainly with the AST as it is the most common form of tenancy in the private rented sector. If a private rented sector landlord:

- orally agrees to rent a property to an individual; or
- let someone stay in a property initially for free but at some point starts accepting rent without having a discussion about a tenancy; or
- agrees a written tenancy that does not stipulate what type of tenancy it is;

it will usually be an AST.

The criteria for an AST are set out in the Housing Act 1988 Sections 1 to 4, Sections 19A to 20A and Schedule 1. If a tenancy does not meet the criteria it will be another type of tenancy. Different legal rules apply to different tenancies therefore it is important from the outset for a private rented sector landlord to know what type of tenancy they have created. The criteria for an AST can be examined under the following headings:-

1.2 The landlord

The landlord can be an individual person or certain specified organisations such as a company or a registered social landlord (Housing Association). There are exceptions such as a local authority or the Government.

Where a landlord is an individual who lives in the same property or in a different property in the same building as the tenant and that building is not a purpose-built block of flats the tenancy will not be an AST. It will be a resident landlord tenancy (see Chapter 5).

1.3 The tenant

The tenant or each joint tenant must be a person and not an organisation, company, government department, or religious body. A letting where the tenant is a company, even if the property is to be used as residential accommodation by someone associated with the company, cannot be an AST. It will be a Company Let as set out in Chapter 23.

1.4 The property

The property must be a dwelling house (i.e. property for someone to live in) that is let as a separate dwelling and includes arrangements where a tenant has exclusive use of a room in a property and share the common parts with other individual(s) who is/are not the landlord or members of the landlord's family. It does not include commercial, business or mixed use (i.e. commercial and residential) premises.

1.5   The rent

Tenancies where the rent exceeds £100,000 per year, or at a very low rent (£250 per year outside London and £1,000 per year in London) or no rent at all, will not be an AST.

1.6   The purpose of the let

The tenant or at least one of the joint tenants must occupy the property as his/her only or principal home.

1.7   Some exceptions

The following will not be an AST:
- tenancies to businesses;
- tenancies of a licensed premises;
- tenancies of agricultural land or agricultural holdings;
- student and holiday lettings;
- arrangements with a relevant organisation where the landlord provides accommodation for asylum seekers.

1.8   Rules applying to AST

A landlord can only unilaterally end an AST by obtaining a court order for possession followed by a bailiffs' warrant to obtain vacant possession (see Chapter 21). There is no other way a landlord can lawfully end an AST without the tenant's agreement.

A tenant can make a written request that a landlord provide them with the basic terms of an AST in writing. The basic terms include:
- the date the tenancy began or came into being;
- the rent and date it is to be paid;
- rent review terms; and
- length of the fixed term.

If this request is made a landlord has 28 days to comply with the requirements. If a landlord fails to comply with the request they can be convicted and be liable to a fine.

An AST can be fixed term, contractual periodic or statutory periodic.

A fixed term AST is one that is agreed to be for a specified fixed period of time such as 6/12/18 months. A periodic AST is one that has no set period of time as it is continually renewed every week, month or quarter as the case may be.

A periodic AST can come about in two ways. One is where the parties agree to a periodic tenancy from the commencement of the tenancy or at the end of a fixed term. This is called a contractual periodic tenancy as it comes about because of a contractual agreement. The other way is where Parliament decides that a periodic tenancy will come into existence. With ASTs the law provides that at the end of the fixed term if no new tenancy is agreed and the tenant remains in the property, the tenancy will become periodic. The period of the tenancy will depend on the frequency of the payment of rent such as weekly/monthly/quarterly. This is called a statutory periodic tenancy.

There are significant different rules that apply to fixed term and periodic ASTs which are set out in this book. An AST cannot be brought to an end by the landlord under the Housing Act 1988 Section 21 Notice procedure in the first six months of the tenancy whether it is a fixed term or periodic AST.

The other tenancies that may be created by a private rented sector landlord that are covered in this book are:
• Company let; and
• Resident landlord tenancy.

Except where specified to the contrary, this book is about the AST.

ASSURED SHORTHOLD TENANCY

2 BEFORE THE TENANCY

A landlord can find a tenant from many sources and this book does not aim to examine them. However, once a tenant is found this book deals with the matters a landlord should attend to before, at the commencement of, during and at the end of the tenancy.

There are several steps that a landlord can take, before signing a tenancy agreement and handing over the keys, to ensure that a tenant is suitable. Some of these steps will deter the wrong tenant and should the wrong tenant obtain a tenancy some of these steps will help the landlord to deal with problems that may arise.

Before signing a tenancy agreement a landlord should obtain certain documents from and carry out relevant checks on a tenant. The types of documents and checks will vary depending on whether a tenant is working or in receipt of benefits or a combination of both.

2.1 Documents to obtain and checks to carry out on a prospective tenant

2.1.1 Documents to obtain from/checks to carry out on a tenant who is working and/or in receipt of Housing Benefit (HB)

1. Photo identification of the tenant – (passport; driving licence, identity card, other suitable picture ID);
2. Bank statements (two to three months);
3. National insurance number;
4. Previous landlord reference (if applicable);
5. Form of authority;
6. Details of property ownership (if the tenant is a homeowner);
7. Next of kin or someone to contact in emergency.

2.1.2 Documents to obtain from/checks to carry out on a tenant who is working

1. A credible reference from an independent referencing agent. (This should include landlord's reference (if applicable), employer's reference, financial background and affordability checks);
2. Wage slips (two months or eight weeks – this will provide proof of earnings, national insurance number, employee's work number/reference and employer's details);
3. Details of their employer (this should be identifiable from the wage slip, or, if they are about to commence employment the letter/email offering them the job).

2.1.3 Documents to obtain from/checks to carry out on a tenant in receipt of Benefits

1. Letter confirming receipt of Income Support, Employment Support Allowance, Job Seekers Allowance, Child Tax Credit and/or other benefit(s) received;
2. Letter confirming previous receipt of HB/Local Housing Allowance (LHA) (if applicable);
3. Details of how much LHA will be paid for a landlord's property (see Chapter 22);
4. Details of the bedroom size property a tenant is eligible for under the LHA rules (see Chapter 22);
5. Details of the amount of LHA a tenant will actually get (see Chapter 22); and
6. A basic tenant reference.

A landlord should use the above requirements as a checklist when considering the suitability of a prospective tenant.

2.2 Photo identification

It is important to get suitable photo identification of a tenant to verify that the tenant is who they say they are. This is the most important document to obtain to ensure that all further documentation and referencing a landlord receives are about the right person. A landlord should keep a photocopy of this document.

Photo identification is important should it become necessary to serve bankruptcy proceedings on a tenant or former tenant (for full details on this process see Chapter 20). It will help a process server identify the tenant who should personally be served with bankruptcy papers.

2.3 Bank details

A landlord should obtain two to three months' bank statement from a tenant. From examining the bank statement a landlord should be able to deduce the following about a tenant:

- the frequency, timing and amount of wages and/or benefits paid into their account;
- their bank details i.e. account number, sort code, branch address;
- the expenditure from their account;
- whether they have savings or an overdraft;
- the address to which statements have been sent (this should in most cases correspond with where they are now living and the property address from which a landlord's reference (if any) is sought).

A bank statement is also very important for enforcing a money judgment for rent arrears or other breach of the tenancy. Should a landlord need to enforce a money judgment against a tenant, they can seek to do so through a "Third Party Debt Order". This is an order of the court freezing a person's bank account so that the money in it can be used to pay a court judgment. For full details on this process see Chapter 18.

2.4   National insurance number

It is important to obtain a tenant's national insurance number. This should be on a tenant's wage slips or letter confirming benefits or tax credit. It can be a very useful tool in identifying a tenant with an employer, benefit office or when seeking to trace a tenant.

2.5   Previous landlord's reference

Where possible a landlord should obtain a reference from a previous landlord or lettings agency. This may be obtained by a written request (letter or email) or a phone call and a fee may be payable. A previous landlord's reference should not be taken at face value but considered in the light of other information that is available about the tenant. Some landlords may give a very good reference to get rid of a very bad tenant and so the reliability of a reference can be compromised.

2.6   Form of authority

This is a very important document to be obtained from a tenant who is working and/or in receipt of benefits. If a landlord needs to acquire information from a third party about a tenant, it is likely that a form of authority will be required by the third party to ensure they comply with the requirements of the Data Protection Act 1990.

A form of authority could be required by an employer if a landlord seeks a work reference for a tenant or by the Department of Work and Pensions or the benefits office if a landlord seeks to communicate with them about a tenant.

2.7   Details of property ownership

Some tenants may own a property and need to rent for various reasons. Details of their property ownership can be valuable to a landlord seeking to recover a money judgment for rent arrears or other liability. In the right circumstances a landlord can obtain a money judgment and secure it against a tenant's property via a charging order (see Chapter 19). This may result in a landlord receiving their money when the property is eventually sold or transferred.

2.8   Next of kin, friend or family's details

A common occurrence when the relationship between a landlord and tenant irretrievably breaks down is the tenant avoiding all contact with the landlord. Having details of a tenant's family, friend or next of kin gives a landlord a point of contact to establish communication with or about the tenant. This contact can save a landlord time and expense in dealing with a tenancy in the following situations:

- death of a tenant;
- abandonment of the property;
- implied surrender of the tenancy;
- end of tenancy matters;
- tenant's unexplained absence from the property for long period(s);
- contact with the landlord being avoided;
- assignment; and
- sub-letting.

2.9   Obtaining a reference from a credible referencing agent

Where a tenant is working it is recommended that a landlord obtains a tenant reference from a credible referencing agent. The referencing agent will normally require a form to be completed (in paper or online).

The tenant can complete a paper form and give it to the landlord. The landlord should make a copy and send the form to the referencing agent. This may be by post, fax or email or the landlord can copy the information to an online form and submit it to the referencing agent.

Alternatively, the tenant can send their completed paper form directly to the referencing agent or complete and submit an online form.

It is ideal that a landlord gets the tenant to complete a paper form and keep a copy. This form will contain valuable information about a tenant should things go wrong during or at the end of the tenancy. The referencing agency will usually require a tenant's personal, employment and financial information in addition to previous address(es) and landlord details.

The referencing report should confirm a tenant's:

- previous address(es);
- personal details;
- outstanding county court judgments (if any);
- landlord reference (if any);
- employer's reference; as well as
- a credit and affordability scoring.

Some referencing agencies can provide rent guarantee insurance and other products based on the result of a tenant's reference report.

Referencing agents can provide a more basic reference for tenants who are in receipt of benefits. This reference should at least confirm the tenant's details and any outstanding county court judgments. It is usually not worth getting a comprehensive reference on a tenant in receipt of benefits as they are unlikely to pass the affordability and credit scoring. However, a tenant on benefits will be able to afford the rent if they are entitled to sufficient LHA.

2.10 Wage slips

If a tenant is working a landlord should obtain at least two months' pay slips if a tenant is paid each month, or eight weeks' payslips where a tenant is paid weekly. The payslips should provide evidence of a tenant's income which should coincide with the income shown in their bank statement. It should have the tenant's national insurance number, employee reference/work number and employer's details. If a landlord obtains a money judgment against a tenant this information can lead to that judgment being enforced by an Attachment of Earnings Order (see Chapter 16 for full details).

2.11 Details of their employer

It is vital that a landlord obtain details of a tenant's employer. This should include the employer's name, website, email, postal address and telephone number for local and head office. This may be obtained from a completed referencing form, employer's reference report, employment contract, wage slip or a copy of a letter to a tenant from their employer.

If a tenant is avoiding contact, has abandon the property, gets into rent arrears or monetary compensation is being sought from them the employer's details could prove invaluable during and after a tenancy. It provides another address to serve papers on the tenant by post or in person and any money judgment obtained by a landlord can be enforced via a tenant's employer by an "attachment of earnings order". This is a court order requiring the employer to deduct a certain sum from the tenant's wages to be paid towards a money judgment. For full details on this process see Chapter 16.

It may also prove to be a valuable address to have if a landlord needs to serve bankruptcy papers on a tenant/former tenant, which has to be served in person, where the tenant's residential address is unknown.

2.12 Letter confirming receipt of benefits

A landlord renting to a tenant in receipt of benefits should obtain a copy of a letter to the tenant, from the Benefits Agency, confirming the benefits they receive. This letter should provide details of:
- the benefit's office (name, phone number and address);
- the tenant's national insurance number;
- reference number with the benefits' agency;
- the correspondence address the benefit office has for the tenant (which should coincide with the address on their bank statement and from which a landlord reference is sought); and
- how much the tenant is getting and how often.

If a tenant in receipt of certain benefits get into rent arrears it is possible for a landlord to request a deduction from their benefits to pay towards the arrears. This will usually be a minimal sum and is called a Third Party Deduction. No court order is required for the deduction to be made. For full details of the process see Chapter 22.

2.13 Letter evidencing previous receipt of Housing Benefit (HB)/Local Housing Allowance (LHA)

If a landlord is considering renting their property to a tenant in receipt of or who will be claiming HB (called LHA for private rented sector tenants), they should read Chapter 22. If a tenant has been in receipt of LHA at their previous address, the landlord should obtain a copy of the letter awarding LHA. This letter may indicate the amount of LHA the tenant will receive and therefore provide some confirmation of whether they can afford the rent. This will only be accurate if there have not been any changes in the tenant's circumstances that affects their LHA entitlement since the decision letter.

The letter will also provide details of the tenant's housing benefit office, reference number and their national insurance number. The address for the tenant in the letter should be the same as the address on their bank statement, letters confirming other benefits and from which a landlord's reference (if any) is sought.

This chapter demonstrates that there is a considerable amount of information that a landlord can and should get about a tenant. A landlord that obtains this information has a responsibility to keep the information safe, secure and not to make unauthorised use of it or divulge it to third parties without authorisation. The information should only be used in circumstances related to the tenancy.

Once a landlord has received the documentation from and satisfactory references about a prospective tenant the next stage is the tenancy agreement.

3   THE TENANCY AGREEMENT

Once a landlord has decided upon a tenant, following consideration of the matters mentioned in Chapter 2, attention needs to be given to the most important document of the tenancy, a written tenancy agreement.

A tenancy agreement is a contract between a landlord and tenant for the occupation of a property at a rent. Like most contracts a tenancy can be agreed orally, by conduct or in writing. It is preferable for it to be in writing to provide a record of the matters which were agreed and the parties who agreed it.

The tenancy agreement will impose certain rights and obligations on both the landlord and tenant through its terms. In addition there are rules about how the tenancy agreement operates. These rights, obligations and rules can come from several sources. They are:-

- what a landlord and tenant agree to called 'express terms';
- what court rulings or Parliament states that a landlord or tenant should do or are entitled to, called 'implied terms'; and

rules that Parliament or the court applies to a tenancy. Some implied terms and rules can be excluded by express terms of the tenancy agreement and some will override any express terms to the contrary in the tenancy agreement.

A landlord should ensure that they understand and abide by their obligations in the tenancy agreement even if the tenant is not doing so. This protects a landlord from legal action for breach of the terms of the tenancy. It will not be a defence to legal action for a landlord to state that the tenant has also breached the tenancy agreement. Two wrongs don't make a right.

Standard express terms between a landlord and tenant should include the following:-

- parties to the contract;
- rent and rent review term (can be express or rules apply);
- break clause;
- serving of notices (can be express or rules apply);
- property to be let (address, inventory, schedule of condition, description);
- length of the tenancy (fixed term or periodic);
- date the tenancy begins;
- the deposit (express plus rules apply);
- payment of utilities;
- assignment (can be express or implied);
- sub-letting (can be express or implied);
- furniture and goods;
- landlord's right of entry (can be an express or implied term);
- end of tenancy provisions;

- ways to end the tenancy agreement (can be express but rules will apply);
- use of the property; and
- guarantor.

A landlord should ensure that the express terms of the tenancy agreement cover all aspects of the property and all eventualities of the tenancy. If an obligation is not expressed between the parties and is not covered by an implied term or rule it could mean that neither the landlord nor the tenant is obligated to do it.

The implied terms of the tenancy agreement will usually cover the following matters:

- quiet enjoyment of the property;
- landlord not to derogate from the grant of the tenancy;
- landlord's obligation to repair (see Chapter 7);
- landlord's right of entry (see Chapter 7);
- furniture to be fit for their intended purpose (see Chapter 7);
- tenant to treat the property in a tenant-like manner; and
- tenant not to commit waste.

There are also rules which are not terms of the tenancy agreement but affect the way the agreement operates. They usually include the following matters:

- details of the landlord's address where notices can be served;
- Section 13 Notices (see paragraph 3.3.2);
- unfair terms in Consumer Contract Regulations;
- joint tenancies (see Chapter 12);
- succession following the death of a tenant (see Chapter 6);
- safety regulations (see Chapter 7);
- providing written terms of the tenancy (see paragraph 1.8);
- energy performance certificates;
- provision of a rent book where rent is paid weekly;
- licensing of properties (see Chapter 11); and
- condition of the property (see Chapter 10).

3.1   Express terms

3.1.1   Parties to the contract

The parties to the tenancy agreement are usually the landlord(s) and the tenant(s) but, may also include an agent and a guarantor(s). All parties to the contract should be clearly identified and their agreement to the terms evidenced by their signatures.

A person or an organisation putting itself forward as, or recording their name on a tenancy agreement as the landlord does not, in the eyes of the law, make them a landlord. A landlord is the person or organisation who will immediately and lawfully be entitled to possession (use and control) of the property once the current tenancy lawfully comes to an end.

The landlord is the person or organisation that owns the superior legal interest or legal right in the property, usually out of which the tenancy was directly granted. This means someone with a superior tenancy who may sub-let the property, a leaseholder or a freeholder. If a person or organisation does not fit that description they should not portray themselves as the landlord. To do so can create complications at a later date when possession is sought and legal proceedings are imminent. For example, when agents record their details on the tenancy agreement as if they are the landlord.

3.1.2   Rent and rent review terms

Strictly speaking, rent is the sum of money paid by a tenant to a landlord for the occupation of the property. Rent terms have, however, been drafted over time to include other charges that are incidental to renting the property. This allows a landlord to pursue a range of other charges as rent and have the full range of legal remedies, including possession proceedings, available to deal with them as rent arrears.

A rent term should state the amount, frequency, date and manner of payment. The rent term may also specify that there should be no deductions from the rent for whatever reason and that there should be no set off. A set off is where a tenant claims that the landlord should give them monetary compensation for a breach of the terms of the tenancy and withholds an equivalent sum in rent. The rent term may also specify that no rent is payable in part or whole if the property is uninhabitable in part or whole through no fault of the tenant such as fire, flood or storm.

If a tenancy of a property is for a period longer than 12 months a landlord should consider having a rent review term. Such a term will normally provide for an increase in rent upon the passing of time or the happening of a specific event and may require one or both parties to the tenancy to do something (such as serve notices upon each other) before the increase takes effect. With such a term the timing of the notices can be crucial so as to provide each party with certainty about the rent or give either party ample opportunity to end the tenancy.

If a tenancy agreement does not have a rent review term, a landlord can seek to use the Section 13 Notice procedure to increase the rent. For full details of this procedure see paragraph 3.3.2.

3.1.3   Break clause

A break clause is a term in the tenancy agreement that usually allows either party to end the fixed term before it runs its full course. A landlord should give consideration to having a break clause in the tenancy agreement, especially if the length of the fixed term is longer than twelve months. If a landlord finds himself wanting to recover possession during the fixed term, a break clause may be the only term that allows him to do so. Likewise, a break clause should also benefit a tenant who may need to terminate the tenancy before the fixed term expires.

During a fixed term if a landlord cannot prove a ground for possession under the Housing Act 1988 Schedule 2 (whether or not based on the tenant being in breach of the tenancy), a landlord wishing to obtain vacant possession will need to exercise the break clause to bring the fixed term to an end. Once the fixed term has ended a statutory periodic tenancy will arise. As the tenancy is now periodic a landlord can use the Section 21 Notice procedure to recover possession. Full details of the procedure are set out in Chapter 21.

A break clause should state precisely how, when and by whom it can be operated. A landlord or tenant should follow the provisions of the clause exactly. If there is no break clause in a tenancy the landlord and tenant will be contractually bound for the duration of the fixed term. If a landlord wishes to regain possession in the fixed term they will need to establish a ground for possession and be successful in court proceedings based on it. If a tenant wishes to end the tenancy during the fixed term they will need to offer an early surrender which a landlord has the option of accepting or not.

3.1.4   Serving of notices

There are a number of notices that a landlord might need to serve on a tenant and vice versa during a tenancy. Some of the notices are:
* Section 13 Notice to increase the rent (by landlord);
* Section 8, 21(1)(b) and 21(4)(a) Notices to get possession (by landlord);
* Notice to Quit (by landlord or tenant);
* Notice related to a break cause (by landlord or tenant); and
* Notice in relation to rent review term (by landlord or tenant).

These notices have to give a minimum time period to the party on whom it is served. The time period does not begin to run until the notice is actually or legally assumed to have been received by the party. It is therefore important to know when a party has or is legally assumed to have received the notice and therefore when the time period begins to run. It should be clear as to how, where and when notices should be served and this should be set out in the tenancy agreement.

If the tenancy agreement does not include a term stating how notices should be served, a landlord will need to ensure that the notice is received by the tenant. This can be achieved by giving the notice to the tenant directly, or to their spouse or servant (servant is usually irrelevant nowadays). The best method is to hand the notice to the tenant, with a witness present, and to ask the tenant to sign and date a copy of the notice as being received. If the tenant refuses to acknowledge receipt, having a witness is helpful. If the tenant is avoiding the landlord this method of service can be problematic. If it is posted, or left at the property, a landlord will not be entirely sure that proper service of the notice occurred until the tenant acknowledges receipt or the court rules to that effect.

A good express term on the serving of notices that can be incorporated into a tenancy agreement is set out in the Law of Property Act 1925 Section 196. Under sub-sections 3 and 4 of Section 196 service will occur:

- where a notice is sent by registered post to the tenant, by name, at their place of residence, business or office and that letter is not returned undelivered in which case service shall be deemed to have occurred at the time at which the registered letter would in the ordinary course be delivered; and
- where a notice is left at the last known place of residence or business in the UK of the tenant and is affixed or left for him on the land or any house or building.

Sending a notice by post (recorded or special delivery) can be problematic. A tenant may not sign for the item in which case there is no confirmation of receipt. If the tenant does not answer for the post, the post office will hold the item at their depot and leave a calling card. Eventually, if the tenant does not collect the item the post office will return it to the sender. This process may take a few weeks before the landlord realises that service has failed. If there was a tight deadline for the notice to be served that deadline may be missed and the process will need to start again with a new notice and expiry date.

If a term provides for the notice to be served by being left at the property a landlord should take the following steps in doing so:-

- on the day of service purchase a newspaper and obtain a receipt for it. It is best to purchase the newspaper near to the property to prove that the landlord was in the area of the property on the day of service;
- bring a camera or a phone with a camera;
- carry adhesive tape or drawing pins to attach the notice and newspaper to the property;
- attend the property with the notice, newspaper, attaching device and camera;
- attach the notice and newspaper to the direct front door of the property (not the communal door);
- take several pictures and include the door number or any distinct features of the door and/or property in the photograph;
- place the notice through the letter box and take a picture when doing so. If there is no letter box leave it attached to the door;

- retain the newspaper, the receipt and the pictures for the court hearing; and
- download the pictures to a laptop, PC or device where it is accessible if the phone or camera were to be lost.

It is not uncommon when the relationship of landlord and tenant has broken down for tenants to refuse access to the property, not answer the door, ignore or refuse recorded delivery and for it to be difficult to communicate with them. It is at this point that a term in the tenancy agreement regarding serving of notices will become valuable. A landlord will need to be able to demonstrate that notice was served in accordance with the term in the tenancy agreement.

3.1.5   Deposit

There should be a term in the tenancy agreement about the deposit. This term should specify what can be claimed against the deposit such as rent arrears, damage to the property, legal costs, interest, cost to re-let the property, removal of possessions left in the property, cleaning and any other costs arising as a result of a breach of the tenancy agreement by the tenant. This will ensure that the deposit can be used in multiple situations. Chapter 4 deals with Deposits and the Deposit Protection Schemes.

3.1.6   Use of the property

If a tenancy agreement does not have an express term dealing with how the property may be used, it is possible that a tenant could use the property for whatever lawful purpose they choose. This could include a business use resulting in a landlord finding that they have a business tenancy rather than an AST.

A tenancy agreement should therefore specify the use to which the landlord agrees the tenant can put the property. Most residential tenancy agreements will exclude use of the property for a trade, profession or business.

3.1.7   Payment of utilities

In some cases the payment of utilities can be straightforward where a tenant rents a self-contained property and the relevant suppliers are informed of their tenancy or there are prepaid meters for the gas and electricity. In houses in multiple occupation (HMOs) and other sharing arrangements it is important that the tenancy agreement sets out who is responsible for paying what, when and how. If utilities are included in the rent a landlord may want to ensure there is a fair usage term in the tenancy agreement to deal with any excessive use or waste of the inclusive utilities.

If the property is self-contained and the tenant is responsible for paying the utilities a landlord ought to take meter readings at the beginning and end of the tenancy as part of the inventory.

3.1.8 Description of the property (inventory and schedule of condition)

The tenancy agreement should clearly identify the property to be rented. This is usually straightforward for a self-contained property but may need clarification for properties where there are sharing arrangements. The description should include address and if there are sharing arrangements (e.g. HMOs, resident landlords) the parts of the property that are shared and the extent to which it is shared.

Once the extent of the property subject to the tenancy has been established it is important for a landlord to have a detailed and accurate inventory of the property and its contents. An inventory is basically a detailed list of the features and contents of the property with a description of their condition at the time the property is being let. It is worthwhile paying for a professional inventory of the property.

An inventory will provide vital evidence if a landlord seeks deductions from the deposit for damage beyond fair wear and tear at the end of the tenancy and it is disputed. The inventory should be accompanied by photographs or video of the property to support its contents.

3.1.9 Length of the tenancy

It is expected that both a landlord and tenant will know the period for which a tenancy has been agreed (6/12/24/36 months). This period is known as the fixed term and a tenancy agreement should clearly set this out. A term of the tenancy agreement may allow for the fixed term to be ended earlier and/or renewed. At the end of a fixed term several things can happen:-

- a tenant can leave the property and the tenancy comes to an end;
- a tenant can continue living in the property with no further agreement with the landlord in which case a statutory periodic tenancy will come into existence;
- the fixed term can be renewed automatically or by the landlord and tenant; or
- the landlord and tenant can agree to a contractual periodic tenancy.

The parties to a tenancy can agree whatever length of tenancy they wish. However, certain rules will apply depending on the length of the tenancy. If the initial fixed term of a tenancy is more than three years it will need to be created by a deed. A deed is a legal document written in a certain form that usually transfers or creates rights and is signed by the parties as well as witnesses who evidenced them signing the deed. An AST can be created without a fixed term i.e. it can be a contractual periodic tenancy from the outset. However, under the rules relating to ASTs a landlord will not be able to obtain an order for possession based on the Section 21 Notice procedure in the first six months of the tenancy.

3.1.10 Assignment

An assignment occurs where a tenant to whom a landlord rents a property transfer their rights and obligations under the tenancy agreement to another person/organisation who then becomes the new tenant of the landlord. This can occur without the landlord knowing. An assignment must be effected by a deed (for definition of a deed see above paragraph).

3.1.10.1 *Assignment of fixed term ASTs*
If an AST is in its fixed term, whether or not a tenant can assign it depends upon the terms of the tenancy. If there is no term dealing with assignment the tenant can assign the tenancy freely. A term prohibiting assignment can be absolute in that no assignment whatsoever is allowed. It can also be qualified in that the consent of the landlord is required. Where the landlord's consent is required it is implied into the tenancy that such consent will not be unreasonably withheld.

3.1.10.2 *Assignment of contractual periodic or statutory periodic ASTs*
ASTs which are periodic tenancies (contractual or statutory – see paragraph 1.8) have an implied term that the tenant cannot assign the tenancy without the consent of the landlord. Because consent of the landlord is required, a lawful assignment cannot occur without their knowledge. In this instance a landlord does not have to act reasonably when deciding whether or not to withhold consent. If the tenancy has been periodic from the outset any term dealing with assignment will apply and this implied term will be of no effect.

A landlord should have a term in the tenancy agreement that prohibits or, if not, restricts a tenant's ability to assign the tenancy.

3.1.11 Subletting

This occurs where the original landlord enters into a tenancy with a tenant (called the "first tenant") for a property and the first tenant enters into a further tenancy (called a "sub-tenancy") with someone (called the "sub tenant") for a part or the whole of the same property therefore becoming their landlord. If the criteria for an AST as mentioned in Chapter 1 are satisfied the sub-tenancy can be an AST. The first tenant remains responsible to the original landlord for compliance with the terms of the tenancy. The sub tenant is responsible to the first tenant for compliance with the terms of the tenancy they created.

3.1.11.1 *Sub-letting of fixed term ASTs*
If a tenancy is in its fixed term a landlord will need to have a term in the tenancy agreement prohibiting or restricting sub-letting otherwise the tenant will be free to sub-let. A term dealing with sub-letting can be absolute in that no

sub-letting whatsoever is allowed. It can also be qualified in that the consent of the landlord is required. Where the landlord's consent is required it is implied into a fixed term tenancy that such consent will not be unreasonably withheld.

3.1.11.2   Sub-letting of contractual periodic or statutory periodic ASTs

ASTs which are periodic tenancies (contractual or statutory – see paragraph 1.8) have an implied term that the tenant cannot sub-let the property without the consent of the landlord. In some instances the law requires that a landlord should act reasonably when deciding whether to give or withhold consent. However, this is not a requirement of this implied term and so the landlord can withhold consent for any reason.

If the tenancy has been periodic from the outset any term dealing with sub-letting will apply and this implied term will be of no effect.

3.1.11.3   Effect of unlawful sub-letting

Where a first tenant sub-lets a property in breach of a term (express or implied) prohibiting sub-letting the sub-tenancy will be valid between the first tenant and the sub-tenant.

The original landlord cannot end the sub-tenancy until he has ended the first tenancy. While the first tenancy exists the original landlord has no direct legal relation with the sub-tenant. The original landlord is not therefore directly entitled to possession against the sub-tenant. If the original landlord seeks to end the sub-tenancy without ending the first tenancy, the sub-tenant can defend the proceedings on the basis that the first tenancy exists and only their landlord (the first tenant) can recover possession against them.

If the first tenancy is in the fixed term a landlord can make a claim for possession based on the Housing Act 1988 Schedule 2 ground 12. This ground states that *"any obligation of the tenancy (other than one related to the payment of rent) has been broken or not performed"*. This is a discretionary ground for possession so that even if a landlord proves the ground to the court a possession order may not be made.

If the first tenancy is periodic and the tenant has sub-let the whole of the property they will no longer be occupying the property as their only or principal home. This is one of the conditions for the existence of an AST. The tenancy will therefore cease to be an AST and become a common law tenancy. The landlord can therefore serve a Notice to Quit on the first tenant and seek possession based on the fact that the Notice to Quit has ended the tenancy and the landlord is entitled to possession (see paragraph 5.3).

When the landlord obtains a possession order against the first tenant it can also be enforced against the sub-tenant. A landlord can therefore apply for a bailiffs' warrant (see paragraph 5.7) to evict whoever is in occupation of the property without starting separate proceedings against the sub-tenant.

Whether or not the first tenant can obtain a possession order against the sub-tenant will depend upon whether or not they can satisfy a ground or a procedure for lawfully recovering possession. The fact that the sub-tenancy was granted in breach of the first tenancy is not a ground for possession.

If the first tenant surrenders their tenancy and the landlord accepts the surrender, the sub-tenancy will become effective against the landlord as if it was a first tenancy. The same rules apply where the first tenancy has been forfeited.

If a sub-letting is lawful (i.e. not in breach of the tenancy), the sub-tenancy becomes the first tenancy when the original first tenancy has ended.

A landlord should have a term in the tenancy agreement prohibiting or restricting a tenant's ability to sub-let the property.

3.1.12 Furniture and white goods

If furniture and white goods (i.e. fridge, freezer, cooker, washing machine) are provided with the property there should be a term in the tenancy agreement specifying who will be responsible for repairs, replacement and maintenance. There is an implied term that the items provided will be fit for their intended purpose. There are also rules to be complied with in the form of electrical and gas safety regulations. It is therefore more suitable for a landlord to carry out repairs to ensure they comply with the above regulations. A landlord cannot pass the obligation of complying with these regulations to a tenant by a term to that effect in the tenancy agreement.

3.1.13 Landlord's right of entry

A tenancy agreement should have a term that expressly provides for a landlord to enter the property for inspection, emergency, to carry out repairs, viewings for sale or re-let and any other eventualities under the tenancy that may require a landlord's access to the property.

The term should specify that access may be for the landlord, their agent and any authorised third party such as a surveyor or plumber.

The term should state the length of notice to be given to a tenant for the landlord to enter the property and the hours in which access may be exercised.

It is common for landlords not to carry out inspections of their properties and to discover serious breaches of the tenancy only when the tenant is about to or has left the property. A prudent landlord should inspect their property about three months after it is let as this should be sufficient time for a tenant to settle in.

Following what a landlord finds on the first inspection, a landlord may have cause to carry out more or less frequent inspections during the course of the tenancy. Too many inspections by a landlord which cannot be justified could be a breach of the implied term of the tenancy to allow the tenant quiet enjoyment (see paragraph 3.2.1).

3.1.14 End of tenancy provisions

There are issues that may arise when a tenancy ends and even after a tenant has vacated the property. These include possessions being left in the property, finalisation of bills, transfer of utilities and forwarding address.

There should be an express term that allows for a reasonable period of time to expire (14 days) after the tenancy has ended and the property vacated, following which, a landlord can dispose of possessions left behind in the property by a tenant. A landlord should be able to seek the costs of doing so from the deposit, additionally, if the disposal results in proceeds of sale the term should specify how those proceeds will be dealt with.

Terms in the tenancy agreement should provide for:-
- the tenant or landlord to give notice to the utility company of the tenant's departure (if the bill is in their name);
- details of whose name the utilities should be transferred to;
- meter readings to be taken;
- forwarding address to be provided;
- property to be cleaned; and
- items in the property to be returned to their original positions to assist the checkout process.

3.1.15 Ways to end the tenancy agreement

There are some grounds for possession under the Housing Act 1988 Schedule 2 that will only be available to a landlord (in certain instances such as the fixed term) if the landlord has given notice to the tenant that possession may be required based on the ground(s) before or at the commencement of the tenancy. A term in the tenancy agreement is one method of complying with this.

Other grounds for possession will only be available to a landlord during the fixed term of the tenancy if the tenancy agreement expressly states this.

The table at paragraph 21.3.1sets out the various grounds for possession under the Housing Act 1988 Schedule 2 and states whether a landlord needs to bring it to the attention of the tenant before the tenancy or incorporate the ground into the tenancy agreement for it to be available to a landlord.

3.1.16 Guarantor

A guarantor is a person or organisation who puts themselves forward as being responsible for the tenant's obligations under the tenancy in the event of the tenant's non-compliance. This means that they will be responsible (if the tenant defaults) for paying the rent and compensating for damage to the property amongst other things. There may be several reasons why a tenant will require a guarantor. Some of them are:

- tenant fails a credit check;
- tenant is a student and not in employment;
- tenant has resided in the UK for a short time and cannot provide sufficient referencing information;
- tenant income is low;
- tenant fails affordability scoring.

The guarantor should provide the same documentation and be subject to the same checks as the tenant as set out in Chapter 2. There is no point in having a guarantor whose referencing is as bad as or worse than the tenant, who cannot afford to pay the rent or is a person about whom a landlord has such little information that no successful enforcement action can be taken against them for the tenant's liabilities.

If a tenant provides a suitable guarantor a landlord should ensure that they sign the tenancy agreement as the guarantor. If this step is not taken a landlord might find a guarantor successfully arguing that they are not bound by the terms of the tenancy.

3.2   Implied terms

3.2.1   Landlord to allow their tenant quiet enjoyment of the property

Despite the words used in this term it does not mean that a tenant must necessarily live in a very quiet and peaceful environment. What it means is that a tenant should be able to use the property in a manner expected of tenants and a landlord should not unnecessarily interrupt a tenant's ability to do so.

This term has been breached by landlords:

- cutting off utilities;
- restricting or stopping a tenant's access to the property;
- harassment of a tenant;
- creating or being responsible for a nuisance (such as infestation); and
- unlawfully evicting the tenant.

Any unreasonable interference by a landlord with a tenant's right to use the property for the purposes of a tenancy will potentially breach this term. If a landlord is exercising a legal right there will be no breach of this term, such as a legal right to enter and inspect premises.

3.2.2   Landlord not to derogate from the grant of the tenancy

This basically means that a landlord should not grant a tenancy and then either act, or omit to act, in a way which makes it impossible for the tenancy to exist. A landlord will be in breach of this term where they grant a tenancy of a flat above shops and then carry on activity in the shop which makes it impossible for the tenant to live in the property. The tenant effectively does not have a tenancy under these circumstances.

3.2.3   Landlord's right of entry/access for repairs

It is an implied term of ASTs (Housing Act 1988 Section 16) that the tenant will allow the landlord access to the property and all reasonable facilities for carrying out repairs for which the landlord is responsible. However, this clause does not cover access for a landlord to inspect the property and therefore an express term covering access is preferable.

3.2.4   Furniture is fit for their intended purpose

When a landlord lets a furnished property it is an implied term of the tenancy that the premises are fit for human habitation. It is also an implied term that the furniture is fit for its intended purpose. This does not apply if the property is unfurnished.

3.2.5   Tenant to treat the property in a tenant-like manner

It is an implied term of a tenancy that a tenant should treat the property in a tenant-like manner. This means that their behaviour and the way they treat the property should be what is expected of a reasonable tenant.

A reasonable tenant should report disrepair to the landlord promptly, ensure that neither they nor their guests damage the property and its contents, do chores such as replacing light bulbs and small do-it-yourself repairs. They should keep the property aired to minimise condensation and warm so that pipes do not freeze. The property should be kept clean, secure and free from rubbish. This list is not exhaustive.

3.2.6   Tenant not to commit waste

Waste occurs when a tenant does or fails to do something which results in a deterioration of the state of the property. There is an implied term that a tenant should not commit waste.

3.3   Rules relating to tenancies

3.3.1   Details of a landlord's address where notices can be served

Under the Landlord and Tenant Act 1987 Section 48 rent is not lawfully due from a tenant unless and until the landlord provides the tenant with an address in England or Wales where the tenant can serve legal notices upon the landlord.

This rule can be complied with at any time, by the landlord providing the required details and immediately thereafter rent will lawfully become due.

3.3.2   Rent increase

It is not uncommon for a landlord to write to a tenant informing them that the rent will be increased to a specified sum from a certain date. It is also not uncommon for tenants to believe that the rent increase is valid and start to pay the increased rent, thereby agreeing to it.

However, at a later date the tenant may be able to claim that the rent increase was unlawful and either seek the return of the money or stop paying rent to set off the increased payments.

There are several lawful ways to increase the rent:
*   a landlord and tenant can agree a new rent. This is different from the landlord simply telling the tenant what the new rent will be;
*   there can be a term in the tenancy agreement that allows a landlord to increase the rent. By the tenant signing the agreement they have agreed to the rent being increased in this way;
*   if there is no term in the tenancy agreement dealing with rent increase and a landlord and tenant fail to agree an increase, a landlord can use the procedure set out in Housing Act 1988 Section 13. This procedure does not apply to tenancies in the fixed term.

3.3.2.1   Completing a Section 13 Notice where the procedure is being used for the first time

A proper Section 13 Notice will normally have a title with the words "Housing Act 1988 Section 13(2) as amended by the Regulatory Reform (Assured Periodic Tenancies) (Rent Increases) Order 2003".

The form will refer to guidance notes for both the landlord and tenant, and usually include the notes towards the end of the notice.

In the tenant's section the tenant's name(s) should be completed.

In the following section the full address of the rented property for which a rent increase is sought should be completed.

In the subsequent section starting with the word "from" the landlord's or their agent's name, address and phone number should be completed and indicated whether they are the landlord or agent.

At the paragraph numbered 2 insert in the first part the new rent proposed and indicate if it is to be paid weekly, monthly or by another period. In the second part of paragraph 2 insert the current rent and indicate if it is being paid weekly, monthly or by another period.

The paragraph numbered 3 does NOT have to be completed if:-

- the tenancy is a new one (i.e. it is not more than 12 months old). However, if the tenancy is older the landlord should write the date the proposed new rent increase is going to take effect which will be the same as the date in paragraph 4; or

- the tenancy is a statutory periodic AST that came about at the end of a fixed term or when a Rent Act tenant died and the successor to the tenancy obtains an Assured Tenancy.

If any of these exceptions apply a landlord should write in the space below where the date should have been written, the exception so that it is clear why the paragraph has not been completed.

At the paragraph numbered 4 a landlord should write the date the new rent is to take effect. This date must comply with all of the following requirements:-

- A minimum period of notice must be given to the tenant. That minimum period does not begin to run until the notice is actually served or is legally deemed to have been served on the tenant (i.e. not the date it is posted but the date it actually is, or is legally deemed to have been received by the tenant). Tenancies are usually for a period which is weekly, fortnightly, monthly, quarterly, six monthly or yearly. The notice period will be one month if the tenancy is monthly or for a shorter period; six months if the tenancy is yearly; and three months if the tenancy is quarterly.

- The date the new rent is to take effect must not be less than 52 weeks from the date the last rent increase took effect or, if the tenancy is new, the date when the tenancy began. This does not apply if the tenancy is a statutory periodic AST following on from the end of a fixed term or it is a statutory periodic tenancy following on from the death of a Rent Act tenancy. If this exception applies a landlord can increase the rent as soon as they comply with the minimum notice period described above.

- The proposed new rent must start at the beginning of a period of the tenancy.

At paragraph 5 if charges are included in the rent there is a table to complete indicating the existing charge and the proposed new charge, if any. If there is no charges in the rent nil should be entered in all the boxes. No variable charges should be stated i.e. charges that fluctuate at different rental periods.

The notice should be signed and dated by the landlord or agent and they should be identified as such by deleting the description that doesn't apply to them.

A landlord or agent should ensure that the notice is served in accordance with any term in the tenancy agreement about the service of notices and that it is served in time for the tenant to receive the minimum notice period before the date the rent increase is to take effect.

3.3.2.2   *Completing a Section 13 Notice where the procedure has been used before to increase the rent*

All sections/paragraphs from the beginning of the form up to but not including the paragraph numbered 3 should be completed as set out in paragraph 3.3.2.1 above.

The paragraph numbered 3 requires the date the "first" rent increase took effect after 11 February 2003. If the last rent increase was before 11 February 2003 this paragraph does not need to be completed.

At the paragraph numbered 4 the landlord should put the date the new rent is to take effect. This date must comply with the following requirements:-

- A minimum period of notice must be given to the tenant as set out in paragraph 3.3.2.1 above plus the date the new rent is to take effect must not be less than 52 weeks from the date the last rent increase took effect using this Section 13 procedure.
- However, if the above date will result in the rent increase taking effect one week or more before the anniversary of the date given in paragraph 3 (i.e. the date when the first rent increase took effect after 11 February 2003) the starting date for the new rent must not be less than 53 weeks from the date on which the rent was last increased.
- The proposed new rent must start at the beginning of a period of the tenancy.

The remainder of the notice i.e. paragraph 5 onwards should be completed as described in paragraph 3.3.2.1 above.

Within the notice period a tenant can take no action in which case the rent increase will take effect on the date given in the notice. Alternatively, the tenant can refer the notice to the Rent Assessment Committee to decide on a market rent for the property.

A landlord should attach a copy of the Section 13 Notice to the tenancy agreement and monitor rent payments to ensure the increased rent is being paid.

A Section 13 Notice cannot be served in respect of a house which should be, but is not, licensed.

3.3.3   Weekly tenancies and rent book

If a tenant is occupying a property for residential purposes and the rent is paid weekly a landlord is required to provide the tenant with a rent book. A landlord commits a criminal offence if he fails to do so and if convicted will be subject to a fine.

3.3.4   Energy Performance Certificate (EPC)

A landlord is required to have an EPC before their property is put on the market to be rented. It should also be provided to a prospective tenant upon request. An EPC will last for 10 years and will show the following information about a property:-

- the current energy efficiency rating and energy costs;
- recommendation on saving energy, increasing energy efficiency and reducing costs; and
- indication of what the energy efficiency rating of the property can be improved to.

It was probably hoped that market forces would pressure a landlord into making their home more energy efficient i.e. those with a low rating would take longer to rent and at a lower price. However, there is such a demand for rental properties that this effect does not seem to have taken place.

It is anticipated that in the near future a landlord will be penalised for having a home that is not energy efficient. Whilst it is not compulsory and therefore the prices have not been hiked up, landlords should aim to get their properties more energy efficient and the EPC normally gives an indication of how much more energy efficient a property can be.

Some landlords who have tenants in receipt of benefits may be able to get a qualifying tenant to apply for a grant to improve the energy efficiency of the rented property. As this sum is a grant and does not have to be repaid by either the landlord or the tenant, both parties stand to gain from making an application. A landlord should encourage this.

3.3.5   The Unfair Terms in Consumer Contract Regulations 1999

The Unfair Terms in Consumer Contract Regulations apply to terms in a contract between a supplier and a consumer which have not been individually negotiated. In the context of a tenancy the supplier is the landlord, and the consumer is the tenant. If the tenant has been provided with a pre-prepared tenancy agreement, there will be terms of the tenancy that have not been individually negotiated.

The regulations require that the terms should be fair and clear to the consumer. A term which is found to be unfair will not be binding on the consumer. It is open to a tenant to challenge terms they believe are unfair. A tenant can challenge such a term by referring it to the Office of Fair Trading (OFT). The OFT has a duty to consider any complaint about unfair terms.

THE TENANCY AGREEMENT

If the OFT considers that a term is unfair it has the power to take action on behalf of the consumer to stop the use of the term. It can apply to the court for an injunction.

With regard to a tenancy agreement the following terms would be agreed between the parties and therefore not be subject to the regulations: -
- the amount of rent to be paid; and
- the length of the tenancy.

The regulations state that a term is unfair if it goes against the requirement of good faith and causes a significant imbalance in the parties' rights and obligations arising under the contract to the detriment of the tenant. Terms in the tenancy agreement should be expressed fully, clearly and legibly and if it disadvantages the tenant it should be more prominent. The landlord should not take advantage of the tenant's weaker bargaining position. The tenant should have the chance of reading the tenancy agreement before signing it.

Examples of unfair terms are: -
- A rent increase clause that does not stipulate when and how the rent will be increased can be deemed unfair as it allows the landlord too much discretion and gives the tenant too much uncertainty.
- An absolute ban on subletting and assignment of fixed term tenancies may be decided to be unfair as it will keep tenants paying for a tenancy they no longer want and one which they could have passed to someone else.
- Charging other expenses as rent is potentially unfair. This includes interest, administration charges, service charges and cleaning charges as a tenant could face eviction for their failure or inability to pay.
- A clause that imposes a financial penalty on the tenant for their failure to pay rent such as £20 per day until the rent is paid in full.

4 DEPOSITS

The deposit protection legislation only applies to ASTs. It does not apply to resident landlord tenancies and company lets. From 6 April 2007 whenever a new AST is created or whenever an existing AST is renewed for a further fixed term the deposit must be protected in one of the deposit protection schemes. If a fixed term tenancy is granted before 6 April 2007 and became and remains periodic after that date the deposit does not need to be protected.

New rules came into effect from 6 April 2012 in relation to tenancy deposit as a result of the Localism Act 2011. These new rules have significant impact and the consequences are explained in the text below.

4.1 Definition of deposit

Under the legislation a deposit is defined as money held by the landlord as security for the performance of obligations and settlement of any liability of the tenant as a result of the tenancy.

A landlord or agent cannot avoid protecting the deposit by requiring as a term of the tenancy that the deposit be dealt with in a way that is contrary to the legislation.

A landlord or agent cannot require a deposit which is not money.

4.2 Protecting a deposit

There are three main requirements in relation to protecting a deposit:
1. the deposit must be protected in one of the deposit protection schemes;
2. the landlord should comply with the initial requirements of a scheme; and
3. prescribed information must be given to the tenant and relevant person.

A relevant person is someone or an organisation (such as local authority, parent, guarantor or employer) who paid the deposit on behalf of the tenant in agreement with the tenant.

There are three authorised deposit protection schemes. They are:-
* Deposit Protection Service (DPS)
* My Deposits
* Tenancy Deposit Scheme (TDS)

With the Deposit Protection Service (DPS) a landlord or agent pays the deposit in its entirety into the scheme. The deposit is kept in a bank account and at the end of the tenancy the deposit will be paid in accordance with what is agreed between the landlord and tenant and communicated to the scheme.

If no agreement can be reached between the landlord and the tenant, there are provisions under the scheme to resolve any dispute. There is no charge for this service. A landlord based overseas must use the custodial scheme unless the property is managed by a UK-based agent.

My Deposits and the Tenancy Deposit Scheme (TDS) operate an insurance-based scheme. Under these two schemes the landlord or agent holds the deposit during the tenancy. An insurance premium is paid against the landlord or agent keeping the deposit unlawfully. At the end of the tenancy the deposit is dealt with in accordance with the tenancy agreement. Should the landlord or agent not deal with the deposit appropriately the scheme will pay the deposit or outstanding amount to the tenant and seek to recover this from the landlord or agent.

It is uncommon for a regular landlord to use the Tenancy Deposit Scheme as landlords using this scheme are required to be a member of an approved professional body where client money protection insurance is required.

From 6 April 2012 a landlord or agent has 30 days in which to protect the deposit in one of the relevant schemes. Prior to this date a landlord or agent had 14 days in which to protect the deposit.

4.2.1   Providing the prescribed information

From 6 April 2012 a landlord or agent is required to provide the tenant and relevant person with the prescribed information about the scheme where the deposit is protected within 30 days of receipt of the deposit. Prior to this date a landlord or agent was required to provide the prescribed information to the tenant and relevant person within 14 days of receipt of the deposit.

The prescribed information to be provided is set out in The Housing (Tenancy Deposits) (Prescribed Information) Order 2007. It includes the following:-

1. the name, address, telephone number, e-mail address and any fax number of the scheme administrator where the deposit is protected;
2. any information contained in a leaflet supplied by the scheme administrator to the landlord which explains the operation of the scheme;
3. the procedures that apply under the scheme by which an amount in respect of a deposit may be paid or repaid to the tenant at the end of the tenancy;
4. the procedures that apply under the scheme where either the landlord or the tenant is not contactable at the end of the tenancy;
5. the procedures that apply under the scheme where the landlord and the tenant dispute the amount to be paid or repaid to the tenant in respect of the deposit;
6. the facilities available under the scheme for enabling a dispute relating to the deposit to be resolved without recourse to litigation;
7. the amount of the deposit paid;
8. the address of the property to which the deposit relates;

9. the name, address, telephone number, and any e-mail address or fax number of the landlord;

10. the name, address, telephone number, and any e-mail address or fax number of the tenant, including such details that should be used by the landlord or scheme administrator for the purpose of contacting the tenant at the end of the tenancy;

11. the name, address, telephone number and any e-mail address or fax number of any relevant person;

12. the circumstances when all or part of the deposit may be retained by the landlord, by reference to the terms of the tenancy; and

13. confirmation (in the form of a certificate signed by the landlord) that—

    (a) the information he provides is accurate to the best of his knowledge and belief; and

    (b) the tenant has been given the opportunity to sign any document containing the information provided by the landlord.

4.2.2 What happened under the old legislation if a landlord failed to comply?

The Housing Act 2004 provided that where a deposit has been paid and:-

*   the initial requirements of an authorised scheme has not been complied with (i.e. the requirements imposed by the scheme that a landlord ought to comply with on receiving a deposit or the prescribed information that should be provided to the tenant or relevant person has not been provided within the period of 14 days); or

*   the tenant or relevant person has been notified by a landlord that a particular scheme applies but has not been able to get confirmation from the scheme that the deposit is being held in accordance with the scheme;

the tenant or relevant person may make an application to the court.

If the court is satisfied of the above matters the court must either:-

*   order the deposit to be repaid to the applicant; or

*   order that the deposit be paid into a custodial scheme within 14 days of the order; and

*   must order that the landlord pays to the applicant three times the deposit within 14 days of the order.

Early court cases on the above matters saw landlords being ordered to repay the deposit, plus pay a penalty of three times the deposit and court costs. However, cases in the more senior courts decided on the issues in such a way as to make the penalties for non-compliance ineffective.

The rulings of the courts were to the following effect:-

*   a landlord had until the date of a court hearing about the deposit to protect the deposit;

- a landlord had up until the date of the court hearing about the prescribed information to provide the prescribed information;
- a tenant or relevant person could not seek a penalty equal to three times the deposit after the tenancy had ended.

Therefore during the tenancy a landlord need only protect the deposit when a court hearing was imminent on the matter and if the tenancy has ended a landlord need not protect the deposit at all.

In addition a landlord would not be able to serve a valid Section 21 Notice if a deposit has been taken and:-
- it is not held in accordance with an authorised scheme;
- the initial requirements of a scheme have not been complied with;
- the prescribed information has not been given in relation to the deposit. However, if it is subsequently given a valid Section 21 Notice may be served on the tenant. If the deposit given is not money. However, upon its return a valid Section 21 Notice may be served on the tenant.

The only real sanction for a landlord not protecting a deposit was that they could not use the Section 21 Notice procedure to recover possession.

4.2.3   What is intended under the new legislation?

Under the amendments to the Housing Act 2004 a tenant or relevant person may make an application to the court where a landlord receives a deposit and:-
- the initial requirements of an authorised scheme has not been complied with within the period of 30 days; and/or
- the information below has not been given to the tenant or relevant person in the prescribed form or a form substantially to the same effect within the period of 30 days following receipt of the deposit: the authorised scheme applying to the deposit; compliance by the landlord with the initial requirements of the scheme; the operation of sections of the Housing Act 2004 in relation to the deposit as may be prescribed; and/or
- the tenant or relevant person has been notified by the landlord that a particular authorised scheme applies to the deposit but has not been able to obtain confirmation from the scheme administrator that the deposit is held in accordance with the scheme.

A tenant or relevant person can bring an action for any of the above breaches of the legislation by a landlord even after the tenancy has ended.

If the tenancy has *not* ended and an application is made to the court for the above breaches the court must either:-
- order that the deposit be repaid to the applicant; or
- order that the deposit be paid into a custodial scheme; and

- order the landlord to pay to the applicant a sum not less than the deposit and not more than three times the deposit.

If the tenancy has ended before or after the making of an application for the breaches noted above the court:-
- may order the person holding the deposit to repay part or all of it to the applicant; and
- must order the landlord to pay to the applicant a sum not less than the deposit and not more than three times the deposit.

In addition a landlord will not be able to serve a valid Section 21 Notice if a deposit has been taken and:-
- it is not held in accordance with an authorised scheme;
- the initial requirements of a scheme have not been complied with; and
- the prescribed information has not been given in relation to the deposit. However, if subsequently given, a valid Section 21 Notice may be served on the tenant. If the deposit given is not money. However, upon the return of the property a valid Section 21 Notice may be served on the tenant.

A landlord or agent can serve a valid Section 21 Notice if the deposit has been returned to the tenant in full or with agreed deductions or an application has been made before the court by the tenant or relevant person which has been judged on, withdrawn or settled between the parties.

As seen above, under the earlier legislation, a landlord did not have to protect the deposit and/or provide the prescribed information until the date of a court hearing on the matter. This could have encouraged some landlords not to bother to protect the deposit at all. However, from 6 April 2012 if a tenancy continues and the landlord ought to have protected the deposit but did not do so they will have 30 days to protect the deposit.

The new legislation makes it clear that if a landlord fails to protect the deposit and/or provide the prescribed information within 30 days, on day 31 the tenant or relevant person can take action against them. If a landlord protects the deposit and/or provide the prescribed information after 30 days but before the date of the court hearing the court case can proceed against them.

The new rules in relation to tenancy deposit will not apply to tenancies that ended before 6 April 2012. Those tenancies will be dealt with under the earlier legislation.

In a recent Court of Appeal case[1] under the new rules a landlord had protected the deposit but failed to give the tenant the prescribed information. The Court of Appeal decided that providing the prescribed information was not a minor

---

[1] *Ayannuga v Swindells* (2012) CA (Civ), 6 November 2012

procedural matter as argued by the landlord. It was of real importance due to the information it gave to the tenant. The landlord was ordered to return the deposit plus pay a penalty of three times the deposit. The landlord must provide the prescribed information and not rely on it been given to some degree by the deposit protection scheme. The tenant's counterclaim came about because the landlord brought an action for possession based on rent arrears.

5 RESIDENT LANDLORDS

The law gives tenants who live in close proximity to their landlord less protection from eviction than tenants who do not. Some examples of close proximity are where a tenant and a landlord:-

- live in separate flats in the same building, but the building is not a purpose-built block of flats, the most common scenario being a converted house **(Non-excluded tenancy); or**

- live in the same property where the tenant has exclusive use of a room and shares facilities i.e. bathroom and/or kitchen with the landlord or with a member of the landlord's family with the landlord living in a different property in the same building **(Excluded tenancy).**

- If the landlord and tenant live in separate flats in a purpose-built block of flats the tenant will have an AST with the full protection against eviction that goes with that type of tenancy.

5.1   Matters common to resident landlord tenancies

5.1.1   Residence of the landlord

The property that a landlord occupies in close proximity to or shares with a tenant must be the landlord's only or main home and this residence must exist at the time the tenancy is created and throughout the duration of the tenancy.

5.1.2   Documents to obtain before the tenancy

A landlord should get sufficient documents/information from and carry out relevant checks on their tenant as detailed in Chapter 2. This will enable a landlord to identify the tenant, know where they work and/or from where they receive benefits. Having their bank statement and other relevant documents can facilitate the full range of enforcement actions, for a money judgment, as set out in Chapters 15 to 20.

5.1.3   Tenancy agreement

A landlord should have a written tenancy agreement that sets out what both parties expect from each other at the commencement, during and at the end of the tenancy. A landlord should not use an AST agreement for these tenancies as they are not AST. It is common for arrangements where the landlord shares accommodation with the tenant not to be in writing.

5.1.4   Deposit

A landlord should take a deposit and the tenancy agreement ought to specify the circumstances in which a landlord might make deductions from the deposit. As this is not an AST, there is no requirement for the deposit to be protected in a tenancy deposit scheme.

5.1.5 Inventory/schedule of condition

An inventory and schedule of condition is vital to provide a snapshot of the condition and contents of the property at the commencement of the tenancy. Its purpose is to determine whether any damage to the property at the end of the tenancy is beyond fair wear and tear and therefore justifies deductions from the deposit. An inventory and schedule of condition will protect the interests of both the landlord and tenant at the end of the tenancy. An inventory should be accompanied by photographic and/or video evidence.

5.1.6 Repairs

The Landlord and Tenant Act 1985 Section 11 imposes repairing obligations on a landlord whenever there is a tenancy of residential property for a duration of no more than seven years. As pointed out in Chapter 7, in addition to the repairing obligations under the Landlord and Tenant Act 1985 there are other ways in which a landlord can be liable for harm caused to the possessions of or the person of a tenant, other occupier or visitor to the property. It is therefore essential that a landlord keeps their property in good repair.

5.2 Recovering possession of an excluded tenancy

If an excluded tenancy is in the fixed term with no break clause a landlord will generally have to wait until the fixed term has expired to recover possession, unless the landlord and tenant come to an agreement to end the tenancy early (i.e. a surrender).

Given the proximity of the living arrangements (i.e. sharing of facilities) it is not advisable for a landlord to agree a fixed term excluded tenancy. Should it be necessary for there to be a fixed term, it should be for a period of around three months. If the landlord and tenant relationship irretrievably breaks down both parties could find themselves in an awkward living situation whilst waiting for the fixed term to expire.

If a fixed term excluded tenancy was agreed, the tenancy will come to an end at the expiration of the fixed term. If a landlord wants the tenant to leave, when the fixed term expiry date is approaching the landlord should have a discussion with the tenant about the following matters:-

- when they are expected to leave;
- what the check-out procedure is;
- forwarding address; and
- how the deposit will be dealt with.

In anticipation of the tenant leaving a landlord should read Chapter 24 and apply the matters that relate to their particular tenancy.

If there is no fixed term, i.e. a periodic tenancy, a landlord is required to give notice to the tenant. As it is an excluded tenancy there is no need for the notice to be formally in writing. However, a written notice provides evidence of the notice itself, when it was served, the period of time given to the tenant and when they are expected to leave.

The notice should give a reasonable amount of time for the tenancy to come to an end. What is reasonable depends on the reason why the tenant is required to leave, what is fair under the circumstances, the period of the tenancy and any other relevant matters.

Under normal circumstances a reasonable period will be a period of the tenancy. If the tenancy is weekly a week's notice would be sufficient. Additionally, the notice should end on the date when rent is next due under the tenancy. If there is a written agreement that stipulates the length of the notice, the landlord will be contractually bound to that period.

Once a valid notice expires the tenancy comes to an end and a landlord does not need a court order for possession. The landlord can arrange the check-out with the tenant.

If the tenant refuses to leave, a landlord cannot use force to remove them. To do so can incur criminal and civil penalties. A landlord should simply wait until the tenant is out and change the locks. Once this has been done the tenant should be contacted to let them know that the notice ended the tenancy, the locks have been changed and no access will be given to them except to collect their belongings by an appointment.

The tenant's belonging should be stored and the tenant given a reasonable period of time to collect them. To avoid uncertainty, there should be a term in the tenancy agreement dealing with the disposal of the tenant's possession (if left at the property for a certain period of time) following the end of the tenancy. If a landlord finds himself holding a tenant's possession for an unreasonable period of time without the tenant making arrangements to collect them, the possessions can be disposed of under the procedure set out in paragraph 13.1.

If a landlord anticipates that there could be trouble when the tenant returns to collect their possession or upon the tenant being notified that the lock has been changed the landlord should contact the local police and have someone who is a credible witness present at the property at the time the tenant returns. Tenant's belongings should not be kept to cover any monetary claim against them under the tenancy. If a landlord wants to recover outstanding money from the tenant they should read Chapters 15 to 20.

5.3 Recovering possession of a non-excluded tenancy

Under a non-excluded tenancy the landlord and the tenant do not share facilities such as kitchen, bathroom and/or lounge. They are likely to share a communal entrance to their individual properties. Where there is a non-excluded tenancy the law requires a more formal procedure to recover vacant possession.

If the tenancy is in the fixed term it is unlikely that a landlord will be able to recover possession of the property. There are no grounds for possession as in the case of an AST during the fixed term. Any breach of the tenancy will have to be dealt with under the terms of the contract and common (judge made) law. At the end of the tenancy the Protection from Eviction Act 1977provides that a landlord will need a court order to obtain vacant possession if the tenant is unwilling to leave.

Following the end of a fixed term tenancy a landlord can simply start court proceedings on the basis that the fixed term has ended and no new fixed term or periodic tenancy has come into being. There is no formal notice for a landlord to serve at the end of a fixed term. To prevent a further tenancy coming into being at the end of the fixed term a landlord should ensure the following:-

- Any payment by the tenant for their continued occupation of the property is accepted as a charge for use and occupation and is not referred to as rent.
- If a landlord complies with any repairing or other obligation under the previous tenancy they should let the former tenant know that this is done to protect their investment and not as an obligation under a tenancy.
- No reference should be made to tenancy provisions in any communication with the tenant.
- It should be confirmed in communication with the tenant that the tenancy has ended.

If the tenancy is periodic, either from the beginning or by an express or implied agreement between the parties after the fixed term has ended, a landlord will have to serve a Notice to Quit on the tenant. A Notice to Quit is not a Section 21 Notice (which is used for ASTs).

5.3.1 Completing a Notice to Quit

A proper Notice to Quit will contain the heading "Notice to Quit"

It will usually have words to the following effect *"This Notice is the first step towards requiring you to give up possession of your home, you should read it carefully"*.

The form should have a section requiring the tenant(s) name(s) and address and a section requiring the landlord/licensor's name and address with wording to specify the capacity in which they act (landlord/licensor).

The form should have a section for the address of the rented property to be entered, usually after the words "*… deliver or give up possession of …*"

A section of the form will require the date the notice is to expire to be completed. The length of notice to end a non-excluded tenancy may be stipulated in the tenancy agreement. This will be valid as long as it is not shorter than the minimum notice period specified below. It can be for a longer period. If there is a term in the tenancy agreement dealing with the notice such as the length, (subject to the minimum period) when, where and how to be served it should be strictly followed. If there is no provision about length of notice in the tenancy agreement the landlord must give the following minimum periods of notice:-

- if rent is payable weekly, four weeks' notice;
- if rent is payable monthly, one month's notice;
- if rent is payable quarterly, three months' notice.

Additionally, the expiration date in the notice must either be the *last day* or the *first day* of a period of the tenancy. If the tenancy agreement specifies which one should be used this should be followed. If there is nothing in the tenancy agreement dealing with this matter a landlord can serve a valid notice using either of these dates as long as the tenant receives the minimum notice period.

Examples of Notice periods:-

June 2011

M	T	W	T	F	S	S
		1	2	3	4	5
6	7	8	9	10	11	12
13	14	15	16	17	18	19
20	21	22	23	24	25	26
27	28	29	30			

M	T	W	T	F	S	S
1	2	3	4	5	6	7
8	9	10	11	12	13	14
15	16	17	18	19	20	21
22	23	24	25	26	27	28
29	30	31				

July 2011

M	T	W	T	F	S	S
				1	2	3
4	5	6	7	8	9	10
11	12	13	14	15	16	17
18	19	20	21	22	23	24
25	26	27	28	29	30	31

August 2011

5.3.1.1 Example using the **beginning of a period** of the tenancy as the expiration date

Weekly tenancy – a tenancy begun on Saturday 5 February 2011 and is a weekly tenancy. The end of a period of the tenancy is every Friday and the beginning of a period of the tenancy is every Saturday. Rent is due at the beginning of each period of the tenancy i.e. every Saturday. Using the calendar above if notice is served on Tuesday 21 June 2011, then the minimum four weeks' notice period ends on Monday 18 July 2011. However, that date is not the beginning of a period of the tenancy. The next beginning of a period of the tenancy after the minimum four weeks' notice period is Saturday 23 July 2011.

Monthly tenancy – a tenancy begun on Saturday 5 February 2011 and is a monthly tenancy. The end of a period of the tenancy is the 4th of each month and the beginning of a period of the tenancy is the 5th of each month. Rent is due at the beginning of a period of the tenancy which is the 5th of each month. If notice is served on Tuesday 21 June 2011, then the minimum one month's notice period ends on 20 July 2011. However, that date is not the beginning of a period of the tenancy. The next beginning of a period of the tenancy after the minimum one month's notice period is 5 August 2011.

*5.3.1.2   Example using the **end of a period** of the tenancy as the expiration date*
Weekly tenancy – a tenancy begun on Saturday 5 February 2011 and is a weekly tenancy. The end of a period of the tenancy is every Friday and the beginning of a period of the tenancy is every Saturday. Rent is due at the beginning of each period of the tenancy i.e. every Saturday. If notice is served on Tuesday 21 June 2011, then the four weeks' minimum notice period ends on Monday 18 July 2011. However, that date is not the end of a period of the tenancy. The next end of a period of the tenancy is Friday 22 July 2011.

Monthly tenancy – a tenancy begun on Saturday 5 February 2011 and is a monthly tenancy. The end of a period of the tenancy is the 4th of each month and the beginning of a period of the tenancy is the 5th of each month. Rent is due at the beginning of a period of the tenancy which is the 5th of each month. If notice is served on Tuesday 21 June 2011, then the minimum one month's notice period ends on Wednesday 20 July 2011. However, that is not the end of a period of the tenancy. The next end of a period of the tenancy is Thursday 4 August 2011.

If the date in the notice for when it is to expire is wrong (i.e. the tenant does not receive the minimum notice period or it does not end at the beginning or ending of a period of the tenancy) the tenancy will not have been ended by the Notice to Quit and the court will not grant a possession order in proceedings based on the notice.

The Notice to Quit can have an expiry date clause stipulating when it will expire rather than having a specific date or it can have both. The clause will normally read to the following effect *"This Notice will expire at the next beginning of a period of the tenancy after the expiration of four weeks; one month; three months;* (delete as appropriate) *following the service of the Notice"* or in the alternative *"This Notice will expire at the next end of a period of the tenancy after the expiration of four weeks; one month; three months;* (delete as appropriate) *following the service of this Notice"*.

This means that if a landlord cannot remember the exact period of the tenancy and therefore the date to be used in the notice this clause can cover that situation. However, a landlord must be careful not to start court proceedings too early.

A Notice to Quit should contain the following prescribed information:-

The minimum length of notice is 28 days or longer if the period of tenancy is longer, (e.g. a quarter's notice if rent is paid quarterly, up to a maximum of six months' notice for a yearly tenancy).

Notice must expire on the last or first day of the period of the tenancy.

After the date shown in the notice, Court proceedings may be begun at once but no later than 12 months from the date this notice is served. After this time the notice will lapse and a new notice must be served before possession can be sought.

INFORMATION FOR TENANTS

1. *If the tenant or licensee does not leave the dwelling, the landlord or licensor must get an order for possession from the court before the tenant or licensee can lawfully be evicted. The landlord or licensor cannot apply for such an order before the notice to quit or notice to determine has expired.*

2. *A tenant or licensee who does not know if he has any right to remain in possession after a notice to quit or determine expires can obtain advice from a solicitor. Help with all or part of the cost of legal advice and assistance may be available under the Legal Aid Scheme. He should also be able to obtain information from a Citizen's Advice Bureau, a Housing Aid Centre or a rent officer.*

If the notice does not contain the prescribed information it will not be valid. The Notice to Quit must be signed and dated by the landlord or their agent or representative and the capacity in which the person who signed the form acts must be indicated i.e. landlord, agent or representative.

5.3.1.3   Serving the notice on the tenant

This is the process by which the Notice to Quit actually comes or is legally deemed to have come to the attention of the tenant. The period of time given in the notice does not begin to run until the notice has been served or legally deemed to have been served on the tenant.

If a landlord prepares a Notice to Quit dated 18 June 2011 for a monthly tenancy and gives a minimum one month's notice which ends on 17 July 2011 (which is also the last day of a period of the tenancy), the notice will have to be actually served or legally deemed to have been served no later than 18 June 2011 for the tenant to get the minimum time period of one month. If the landlord posted the notice on 18 June 2011 even by first class it would arrive after 18 June 2011 and the tenant would not have received the minimum notice period.

The first thing a landlord should do when preparing to serve a notice is to check whether there are any terms in the tenancy agreement dealing with notices. A landlord should comply with any terms that stipulate how, when and where notices are to be served on the tenant. If there is no term in the tenancy agreement dealing with how notice is to be served a landlord should ensure that the notice comes to the attention of the tenant.

Due to the close proximity of the living arrangements between the landlord and the tenant of a non-excluded tenancy, there should be ample opportunities for notice to be served. The most likely form of service will be giving the notice directly to the tenant or leaving it in, or attached to, the property.

A landlord may need to provide the court with evidence of service of the notice. This can take several forms:-
1. an acknowledgement by the tenant that they have received the notice (such as signing and dating a spare copy of the notice or providing a letter of acknowledgement);
2. a witness statement together with pictures of the notice being left in or attached to the property; or
3. a witness statement confirming the notice was given to the tenant.

When the Notice to Quit expires the tenancy comes to an end. A landlord should not do anything that can result in a new tenancy occurring between them and the tenant.

If money is collected for occupation of the property it should be referred to as a charge for use and occupation and not rent. If works are done in the property it should not be referred to as performing an obligation under the tenancy but a protection of the landlord's investment.

5.4 Starting court proceedings for possession

Once the fixed term or the Notice to Quit has expired a landlord can commence court proceedings for possession. If a landlord starts court proceedings before the fixed term or the Notice to Quit has expired, a tenant can use that fact as a complete defence to the proceedings. A landlord can start court proceedings again based on the same notice after it has expired, provided the notice is not otherwise invalid.

There can potentially be problems for a landlord who did not specify the expiry date in the notice but used an expiry date clause instead. The procedure to use to avoid starting court proceedings before the notice period has expired under the expiry date clause depends upon whether the tenancy is weekly, monthly or for another period.

If the tenancy is weekly a landlord should:-
- wait for the minimum four weeks' notice period to expire; plus
- wait for at least a further week (seven days) after the end of the four weeks' period so that the expiry date clause can take effect.

If the tenancy is weekly the last day or first day of a period of a weekly tenancy will occur in every seven days period. Therefore as long as the landlord gives the minimum four weeks' notice and waits at least seven days after it expires, the expiry date will have occurred under the clause.

If the tenancy is monthly a landlord should:-
- wait for the minimum one month's notice to expire; plus
- wait a further month (up to 31 days) after the end of the one month's notice period so that the expiry date clause can take effect.

If the tenancy is monthly the last day or first day of a period of the tenancy will occur every month. Therefore as long as the landlord gives the minimum one month's notice and waits at least a month after it expires, the expiry date will have occurred under the clause.

The same principle applies for quarterly and yearly periodic tenancies. As mentioned earlier if it is a fixed term tenancy, the tenancy will end at the expiration of the fixed term and no notice needs to be served before starting court proceedings.

To commence court proceedings a landlord must complete the following forms:-
- Claim Form for Possession of Property (Form N5);
- Particulars of Claim for Possession (rented residential premises) (Form N119);

and provide:-
- a copy of the notice;
- evidence of service of the notice (see above);
- tenancy agreement (if any);

plus pay a court fee.

5.4.1 Completing Claim Form for Possession of Property (Form N5)

In court proceedings for possession a landlord is referred to as the claimant because they are bringing the proceedings. A tenant is referred to as the defendant (whether or not they provide a defence) because the proceedings have been brought against them. A landlord should complete the form as follows.

In the box at the top right of the form with the words "In the" the name of the local county court for the area where the property is located should be inserted. This can be found online at http://hmctscourtfinder.justice.gov.uk/HMCTS/.

RESIDENT LANDLORDS

The landlord(s) full name(s) and address(s) should be completed in the claimant section.

The tenant(s) full name(s) and address(s) (which is usually the address of the rented property) should be completed in the defendant section. A landlord cannot proceed against one of several joint tenants even if the landlord only wants one of them to vacate the property. A landlord who wants to keep some of the joint tenants has to take and enforce proceedings against all of the joint tenants, following which a new tenancy can be granted to the joint tenants the landlord wants to remain in the property.

The full address of the rented property should be completed in the section that reads "The claimant is claiming possession of:"

In the following sentence the words in brackets (does not include) should be crossed out so that it reads "which (includes) residential property". As the claim for possession is not based on rent arrears the words in brackets (the claimant is also making a claim for money) should be crossed out.

In the box at the bottom left of the first page titled "defendant's name and address for service" the name and address of only one tenant should be inserted. If there is more than one tenant an additional form should be completed with the same information mentioned above and the name and address for service of the individual tenant written in this box. This should be repeated so that there is a separate form for each tenant.

In the court fee section the relevant court fee should be inserted. A check online at the court service website (www.justice.gov.uk/courts/fees) or enquiries with the local county court office can confirm the fees to be paid.

On page two of the form in the section titled "Grounds for possession" "other" should be marked and in the space provided the following words should be inserted "Possession is sought of a Non-Excluded tenancy that has been terminated by a Notice to Quit". If no Notice to Quit was served, as in the case where the fixed term has expired, the following words should be inserted "Possession is sought of a Non-Excluded tenancy that ended when the fixed term expired, no new fixed term or periodic tenancy has been agreed".

The questions that follow below about demotion of tenancy, suspending the right to buy, and the Human Rights Act 1988 should all be answered "No".

In the section at the top right side of page two titled "Anti-social behaviour" the boxes should be left blank.

In the section of the form titled "Statement of Truth" a landlord should cross out the words in brackets (the claimant believes) so that it reads (I Believe). All of the second line worded "I am duly authorised by the claimant to sign this statement" should be crossed out. The landlord should then sign and date the form. In the line below the signature the landlord should cross out the words in brackets (Litigation friend) and (Claimant's solicitor) so that it reads (Claimant). An agent cannot complete the statement of truth. The landlord should then write their full name in the line below which starts with the words "Full name".

A landlord should note that signing a Statement of Truth without believing the information given in the form can lead to court proceedings for contempt.

In the last section of the form titled "Claimant's or claimant solicitor's address to which documents or payments should be sent if different from overleaf" the landlord should insert the address to which documents should be sent, if different from the landlord address at the beginning of the form.

5.4.2 Particulars of Claim for Possession (rented residential premises) (Form N119)

As with Form N5 above in Form N119 the landlord is the claimant and the tenant is the defendant. The Particulars of Claim for Possession (rented residential premises) Form N119 should be completed as follows by the landlord.

In the boxes at the top right corner of page one insert the name of the county court in whose locality the property is situated. This can be found on line at the court service website (http://hmctscourtfinder.justice.gov.uk/HMCTS/). Insert the landlord(s') name(s) in the claimant section and the tenant(s') name(s) in the defendant section.

At paragraph 1 the full address (including postcode) of the property for which a possession order is sought should be inserted.

At paragraph 2 the names of the people living in the property should be inserted. If it is not the tenant(s) living in the property and the landlord does not know the occupiers name(s) a description of the persons e.g. "woman and two children" can be inserted. However, given the close living arrangements it is expected that a landlord would know who is living in their property.

At paragraph 3(a) insert the type of tenancy i.e. "Non-excluded tenancy" and the date when the tenancy began. If the date the tenancy began is not known, the month and year can be inserted such as "June 2011".

At paragraph 3(b) insert the amount of rent and the frequency at which it is paid (e.g. weekly, fortnightly or monthly).

At paragraph 3(c) insert the daily rent rate. This is calculated by taking the monthly rent multiply it by 12 months and divide by 365 days or the weekly rent multiplied by 52 weeks and divided by 365 days.

Paragraph 4(a) is not to be completed as the claim for possession is not based on rent arrears. If a landlord chooses to recover rent arrears they can do so in a separate action (see Chapter 15 to 20).

Paragraph 4(b) is not to be used as the landlord is not claiming breach of the terms of the tenancy.

At paragraph 4(c) insert "the tenant was granted a Non-excluded tenancy which has now been terminated by a Notice to Quit" or if the landlord is seeking possession after the fixed term has ended insert "the tenant was granted a Non-excluded fixed term tenancy and the fixed term has now ended with no further fixed term or periodic tenancy being agreed".

At paragraph 5 insert "N/A" as possession is not been sought on the basis of rent arrears.

Paragraph 6 requires details about the notice. The words in brackets (notice of breach of lease), (notice seeking possession) and (notice seeking a demotion order) should be crossed out so that it reads "the appropriate (notice to quit)..." and insert the date it was served on the tenant.

In the space below, although it is not necessary, details can be provided on how the notice was served on the tenant. If there is a term in the tenancy agreement dealing with service it should be referred to and demonstrate that it has been complied with. Reference should be made to any evidence of service and attach the evidence to the Particulars of Claim.

An example of this could be "the Notice to Quit was served on the tenant by being left at the property in accordance with term [xx] of the tenancy agreement. Attached is a picture of the notice being left at the property along with a copy of the day's newspaper".

Paragraph 7 requests details about the tenant's circumstances. Something about the tenant can be inserted, if known, such as they are working, they are on benefits, they have somewhere else to go, but it is not necessary to do so.

Paragraph 8 requests details about the landlord's circumstances, such as does the landlord have a mortgage. However, it is not necessary to complete this for the possession claim.

Paragraph 9 is to be ignored in its entirety.

Paragraph 10 is to be left as it is, so that the landlord is requesting everything in it from the court.

Paragraph 11 should be marked "no".

Paragraph 12, 13, 14 and 15 do not apply.

In the final section of the form titled "Statement of Truth" the landlord should cross out "The claimant believes" so that it reads "I believe that the facts stated in these particulars of claim are true". The entire sentence beginning with the words "I am duly authorised..." should be crossed out. The statement of truth should be signed and dated by the landlord where indicated. In the line below the landlord's signature the words "Litigation friend" and "Claimant's solicitor" should be crossed out so that it reads "Claimant". The landlord should insert their full name below.

A landlord should note that signing a Statement of Truth without believing the information given in the form can lead to court proceedings for contempt.

5.5   Issuing court proceedings

A landlord should take/send three copies of the:-
* Claim Form for each tenant;
* Particulars of Claim accompanying each copy of the Claim Form; and
* supporting document to each copy of the Claim Form (i.e. pictures of the notice being served),

to the county court for the area (district) in which the property is located along with the relevant court fee (the court fee can be found by contacting the court or online at www.justice.gov.uk/courts/fees).

The court staff will review the documents and if they are in order collect the fee and issue the proceedings (stamp documents with court seal, give a court reference number, a Notice of Issue and notification of a hearing date). The hearing date will not be less than 28 days and not more than eight weeks from the date the proceedings are issued.

The court will normally serve the tenant with a copy of the court documents which will include a set of the papers filed by the landlord as well as a defence form, guidance notes and details of a hearing date.

The tenant usually has 14 days after been served with the court proceedings to provide a defence. However, if the tenant fails to provide a defence at that time it does not mean that the landlord has won their case as the tenant can provide a defence at the hearing.

5.6   The court hearing

On the date of the court hearing the landlord should attend court before the appointed time. Upon entering the court house and passing through the security procedure a landlord should check the court list to see which court will be hearing their case. There is usually a list of the courts and the names of the cases they will be hearing in the court foyer. On identifying the court the landlord should go to the specific court and wait outside until they see the court usher.

RESIDENT LANDLORDS

On seeing the court usher the landlord should let them know their identity and what case they are attending. The landlord may be able to confirm whether or not the tenant is in attendance if they have seen them since arriving at court.

If the tenant is not in attendance the hearing may be delayed until they arrive or until it is clear that they will not be attending the hearing.

It is usual for a court, on a first hearing, to have several cases listed at the same time and to hear them according to whatever circumstances present itself on the day. When the court is ready to hear the case the parties will be called into court by the usher and directed to where they should be seated.

If the hearing is in a judge's chambers (i.e. judge's office) it is usual that the judge will already be seated at the table and the parties will be shown where they should sit.

If the hearing is in open court the parties will be shown where they should go by the court usher and may initially be seated. The judge may not be present in court when the parties enter. If the judge is not present in court when the parties enter the court usher will let the parties know when the judge will be coming into court and direct them to stand whilst the judge enters the court. The parties will be told when they can be seated.

The judge will normally start proceedings by confirming the names and identities of the parties to the case, the type of action being heard, who should give evidence and when. The parties should refer to the judge as "Sir/Madam". If in doubt a landlord can always ask the court usher how the judge should be addressed.

A landlord should be prepared with the relevant documents to prove the following matters:-
1. the tenancy is a Non-Excluded tenancy;
2. the Notice to Quit has been prepared correctly;
3. the Notice to Quit has been served on the tenant correctly; and
4. court proceedings were issued after the notice expired.

If court proceedings were issued following expiration of the fixed term the landlord should be prepared to prove the following:-
*   the tenancy is a non-excluded tenancy;
*   the fixed term has expired;
*   court proceedings were issued after the fixed term expired; and
*   no new fixed term or periodic tenancy has been granted.

If the above requirements have been proven to the court's satisfaction an order for possession will be made. The only defence a tenant can have is that one or more of the above requirements have not been satisfied.

The tenant can provide a defence before the hearing in which case a copy will be sent to the landlord or the tenant can provide their defence at the hearing. If substantial issues are raised by either party that cannot be resolved at the hearing, the judge may adjourn the hearing to a future date and give directions (instructions) to either party so that the claim can be decided at the future hearing date.

At the hearing a landlord will need to satisfy the court of the following matters:-

- The tenancy is a non-excluded tenancy. This can be proved by showing the court the tenancy agreement and provide evidence of the proximity to which the landlord lives to the rented property. Evidence should also be provided to show the court that the landlord has lived at the relevant property at the date the tenancy was granted and throughout the tenancy.
- The Notice to Quit has been prepared correctly. The judge will usually examine the notice to ensure that it is correct, or in the case of a fixed term tenancy, information that the term has expired.
- The Notice to Quit has been correctly served. The landlord may be able to do this via a witness who accompanied the landlord when the notice was been served, pictures of the notice been served, confirmation from the tenant that they received the notice on a particular date and any term in the tenancy agreement dealing with service of notice.
- Court proceedings were issued after the notice expired, or in the case of a fixed term tenancy, the period expired. This will normally be evident to the court from the documentation available.

On making a possession order the court will usually give the tenant two to four weeks to vacate the property. If the tenant can show that the time period would cause exceptional hardship the court can extend it to six weeks.

If the tenant fails to vacate the property on the date given in the possession order a landlord cannot remove the tenant from the property. To do so could amount to a criminal offence. A landlord will need to get a bailiffs' warrant for eviction. This is made by an application to the court on form N325 with the appropriate fee.

5.7   Completing Form N325

In completing this form the landlord is referred to as the claimant and the tenant is referred to as the defendant, as in the earlier proceedings.

At section 1 the landlord name(s) and address(es) should be completed.

At section 2 the landlord's correspondence address should be completed if it is different from the address given in section 1 for the landlord, otherwise leave blank.

RESIDENT LANDLORDS

At section 3 the tenant's name(s) and address(es) should be completed.

Section 4 should be left blank.

At section 5 in the first box the date of the court order requiring the tenant to give up possession of the property should be entered. In the second box of section 5 the date the court order required the tenant to give up possession (i.e. vacate the property) should be entered. In the third box of section 5 a description of the property should be entered. This should be the full address of the property including the postcode and whether it is a flat, house, and on what floor.

In the top right box the name of the county court to which the application is being made should be entered. This will usually be the county court in which the possession order was made.

In the second box in the top right of the form headed "Claim No", the Claim number for the proceedings resulting in the possession order should be entered. This should be on the court order for possession.

In the box on the right of the form that starts with the words "I certify that" in the first paragraph cross out the two sentences that are in brackets so that it reads "the defendant has not vacated the land as ordered" All of the second sentence should be crossed out. The landlord should then sign and date the form and delete the words in brackets (Claimant Solicitor) so that it reads "Claimant".

The box which asks "if there is more than one defendant and you are not proceeding against all of them..." should be left blank.

In the penultimate section of the form the contact number of the landlord and the tenant if available should be entered.

In the final section any matters known about the tenant or occupants of the property that may be relevant to the bailiffs should be entered. This may include the number of persons likely to be in the property, whether the tenant has a history of violence, whether they might be disabled, mentally ill, have dogs or any relevant matters. A landlord cannot apply for a bailiffs' warrant for possession before the date given in the possession order for the tenant to vacate the property has expired.

On completing the form the landlord should present it to the court with the relevant fee. Information on fees can be found at the court service website www.justice.gov.uk/courts/fees or by making enquiries at the local county court.

The court will process the application and write to the landlord and the tenant notifying the parties of the date when the bailiffs will attend the property and secure vacant possession.

In anticipation of the date the bailiffs' warrant will be executed a landlord should have a locksmith on standby to change the locks after the tenant has left and any other resources required to secure the property to ensure that the tenant cannot re-enter after the bailiffs have left.

6 DEATH OF A TENANT

The death of a tenant does not terminate an AST. The legal position of an AST upon the death of a tenant depends upon whether:-

- it is a joint or sole tenancy;
- it is a fixed term or periodic tenancy;
- the deceased tenant had a will or died intestate (i.e. without a will);
- the deceased tenant had a spouse/partner who lived with them.

6.1   Death of a joint Assured Shorthold Tenant

In a joint tenancy, upon the death of one of the joint tenants the tenancy will pass to the other joint tenant(s) automatically. No written agreement is needed with the landlord to give effect to this as it comes about by the operation of the law.

6.2   Death of a sole Assured Shorthold Tenant

6.2.1   Fixed term tenancy

If a sole assured shorthold tenant dies and they have a fixed term tenancy, it will pass under their will or the rules of intestacy.

6.2.2   Periodic tenancy

If a sole assured shorthold tenant (who themselves did not succeed to the tenancy) dies and they have a contractual or statutory periodic tenancy (see paragraph 1.8), the tenancy will pass to their married partner or the person who lived with them as if they were their married partner. The married partner or person who lived with them as their married partner must have lived with the deceased tenant immediately before their death and must have occupied the property as their only or principal home. This is a statutory succession and will override any provision in a will or the rules of intestacy. Transfer of the tenancy happens automatically and does not require any documentation to take effect.

If a sole assured shorthold tenant of a contractual or statutory periodic tenancy with no partner (married or unmarried) to succeed to the tenancy (statutory succession) dies, the tenancy will pass under their will or rules of intestacy.

6.3   Who deals with a deceased tenant's estate (including their tenancy)

When a person dies the property they owned is referred to as their estate. If a deceased person leaves a will the person who deals with their estate is called their "executor" and is appointed under the will. If a deceased person does not leave a will someone can be appointed by the court to deal with their estate and is called an Administrator. If a deceased person does not leave a will and there is no one to be appointed as an administrator the person who deals with their estate will be the office of the Public Trustee.

If a landlord needs to serve a notice with regard to a tenancy, following the death of the tenant, it should be served on the successor to the tenancy, or the administrator, executor or Public Trustee as the case may be as well as being left at the property.

If the estate of a deceased tenant (including the tenancy) is being dealt with by the Public Trustee and there is no successor or no one to inherit the tenancy, the tenancy will remain an AST.

6.4 Can a landlord end an AST when a tenant dies?

6.4.1 Fixed term AST being inherited

If a fixed term AST has been inherited under a will or the rules of intestacy, whether or not the landlord can terminate the tenancy is subject to the normal rules that apply to any other fixed term AST.

If there is a break clause and the criteria is satisfied for it to be used the landlord can exercise the break clause to end the fixed term and use the Section 21 Notice procedure to recover possession (see Chapter 21).

If there is no break clause a landlord will usually have to wait until the fixed term has expired then use the Section 21 Notice procedure to recover possession.

If there is a ground for possession arising under the Housing Act 1988, Schedule 2, during the fixed term the landlord can use the ground under a Section 8 Notice to recover possession such as rent arrears (see Chapter 21).

6.4.2 Contractual periodic or statutory periodic AST being inherited

If the deceased tenant had a married or unmarried partner who was living in the property as their only or principal home immediately before their death they will have succeeded to the periodic tenancy. If there is no spouse/partner it passes under the tenant's will or intestacy.

If a contractual periodic or statutory periodic AST is inherited under a will or the rules of intestacy, a landlord can recover possession from the person who inherited the tenancy using the Housing Act 1988, Schedule 2, ground 7. Ground 7 reads as follows:

> *The tenancy is a periodic tenancy (including a statutory periodic tenancy) which has devolved under the will or intestacy of the former tenant and the proceedings for the recovery of possession are begun not later than twelve months after the death of the former tenant or, if the court so directs, after*

the date on which, in the opinion of the court, the landlord or, in the case of joint landlords, any one of them became aware of the former tenant's death.

For the purposes of this ground, the acceptance by the landlord of rent from a new tenant after the death of the former tenant shall not be regarded as creating a new periodic tenancy, unless the landlord agrees in writing to a change (as compared with the tenancy before the death) in the amount of the rent, the period of the tenancy, the premises which are let or any other term of the tenancy.

A landlord may, however, choose to use the Section 21 Notice procedure to recover possession of the periodic tenancy regardless of whether it is succeeded to by a married or unmarried partner or inherited under a will or the rules of intestacy. The tenancy rules for possession that apply to a contractual periodic or a statutory periodic AST apply to such a tenancy that has been inherited.

6.5 Other rules that apply upon the death of a tenant

Fixed term tenancy: the deceased tenant's estate will remain liable for the rent for the duration of the fixed term. It is likely that the office of the Public Trustee would seek to surrender the tenancy and avoid further rent liability if there is no one to succeed to or inherit the tenancy.

Periodic tenancy: if there is no one to inherit the tenancy the Public Trustee Office may serve a Notice to Quit on the landlord.

If a tenant dies and was in rent arrears, the arrears become a debt that is dealt with in the deceased tenant's estate. Whether or not a landlord can recover the arrears of rent depends upon the solvency of the estate. A landlord might be able to recover the arrears to the extent of any deposit that has been taken in respect of a tenancy provided the deposit has been protected in a deposit protection scheme and any clause of the tenancy dealing with deposits covers rent arrears.

If someone succeeds to the tenancy under statutory rules or inherits the tenancy under a will or rules of intestacy they do not take on the arrears of rent of the deceased tenant. They will therefore commence their period of the tenancy with a clean slate.

If a tenant is in receipt of Housing Benefit to assist them with paying their rent, upon their death the Housing Benefit payment will cease regardless of the deceased tenant's continuing liability under the tenancy. If a landlord is aware of the death of a tenant and continues to receive Housing Benefit after that event, the landlord could be asked to repay those sums under the over-payment provisions.

6.6   What should a landlord do upon a tenant's death?

If a tenant dies a landlord needs to act quickly to ensure that the property does not stand empty for a lengthy period, with no rent being paid. Obviously a landlord will be expected to act sensitively to what will be a difficult situation for those concerned. A landlord should make enquiries applying the above-mentioned rules to see whether the tenancy passed to someone else by succession, will or intestacy.

It is possible for someone to succeed to the tenancy and be unaware of this fact. Ignorance does not stop a succession from happening as it occurs by the operation of the law. If someone has succeeded to the tenancy or inherited it and wish to continue with the tenancy the landlord should make arrangements for them to pay the rent. They should also be provided with a copy of the tenancy agreement so that they are aware of the rental liability as well as their other rights and responsibilities under the tenancy. They should have the landlord's contact details and an address upon which notices can be served on the landlord.

It is advisable that the landlord updates the inventory and gets the new tenant to sign and date it as representing the condition of the property at the date they assumed occupation of the property.

A tenant who has succeeded to a tenancy or inherited it under a will or intestacy is not responsible for any rent arrears, other liability or damage to the property by the deceased tenant. If a landlord wishes to recover these monies they should seek to recover it from the deposit and/or the deceased tenant's estate.

A landlord should also seek to get as much documentation as they possibly can from the new tenant (as mentioned in Chapter 2) so that, should it become necessary, enforcement action can be taken against the new tenant for a money judgment. If the new tenant needs to make a claim for Housing Benefit (Local Housing Allowance) a landlord should read Chapter 22. The landlord should also seek to obtain the documents required of a tenant in receipt of LHA as set out in Chapter 2.

If it is established that the tenancy has passed to someone who does not wish to continue with it the landlord should provide them with and get them to complete a deed of surrender. If this is done a landlord can lawfully resume possession of the property. One joint tenant cannot surrender a tenancy. If surrender is to be done by joint tenants all the joint tenants must act together in the surrender (see Chapter 14).

If a landlord establishes that there is no one who has succeeded to the tenancy and no will, the estate of the deceased will vest in the office of the Public

Trustee. If it cannot be established that someone has inherited the tenancy the procedure a landlord should use to recover possession depends upon whether the tenancy is a periodic or fixed term tenancy.

If the tenancy is periodic a landlord can use the Section 21 Notice procedure.

If the tenancy is in the fixed term a landlord should seek to agree a surrender of the tenancy with the office of the Public Trustee. If not the deceased person's estate will remain liable for the rent for the full fixed term. It would be prudent for the office of the Public Trustee to avoid such liability to the estate of the deceased tenant. If the tenant was in arrears of rent at the time of death or arrears occur following their passing the landlord can always use the Section 8 Notice procedure stipulating ground 8 to recover possession if the criteria can be satisfied as set out in Chapter 21.

If a landlord needs to serve a notice in respect of a deceased tenant they should serve the notice on the Personal Representative (administrator or executor) of and at the last known address of the deceased tenant.

A copy of the notice should also be served on the Public Trustee office (www.justice.gov.uk/about/ospt).

A landlord should bear in mind that a notice does not end an AST, a court order is required to end it.

7 REPAIRS

A landlord's obligations under the tenancy to carry out repairs and maintain the property comes from several sources: the tenancy agreement, statute law, case law (judge made law) and regulations. There are books solely dedicated to this subject and this chapter cannot cover the topic in great detail. Below is a summary of the main repairing obligations of a landlord and how a landlord can be held liable for defects in their rented property. There are separate chapters dealing with damp and mould growth, infestation, Housing Health and Safety Rating System (HHSRS) and Houses in Multiple Occupation (HMO) regulations.

7.1   Landlord and Tenant Act (LTA) 1985 Section 11

LTA 1985 Section 11 applies to tenancies of residential properties granted for less than seven years and arises because of the contract. It does not apply to tenancies granted to a local authority, social landlord or similar body although the obligations can be contractually imposed (via the tenancy agreement) on a landlord in these tenancies. A landlord cannot include a term in the tenancy agreement limiting, excluding or modifying the operation of Section 11.

In tenancies to which Section 11 apply landlords are under an obligation to put and keep in repair: -

- the structure and exterior of the property (including walls, windows, steps, external doors, roof, paved gardens, fences, gates, gutters, drains, external pipes, chimney, steps and pathways. It does not include fittings, decorations, internal plaster finish, light bulbs, door handles, kitchen cupboard doors and handles);
- installations for the supply of water and sanitation (including water pipes, taps (but not washers), stop cock, water storage tanks, basins, sinks, baths, splash backs, tiling, flooring, piping, WCs, drains, extractors and showers);
- installations for the supply of gas (including gas piping, valves, outlets and flues);
- installations for the supply of electricity (including electric wiring, sockets, switches, fuse box, light pendants (but not bulbs) and mains switch);
- installations for the supply of heating and hot water i.e. radiators, radiator valves, boilers, pipes for heating and hot water, thermostats, water tanks, storage heaters, under floor heating and similar equipment; and
- common areas under the control of the landlord.

The list above is not exhaustive, but is intended to give guidance to a landlord.

If disrepair causes damage to the décor of the property the landlord will be responsible for fixing the décor as well i.e. paint finish, wall paper, plaster, coves, carpets, tiling, floor boards, lino and curtains, as well as carrying out the repairs.

Any tenancy to which Section 11 applies has an implied term that the tenant will allow the landlord or any person authorised by the landlord in writing, at reasonable times of the day and upon giving 24 hours written notice, access to the premises for the purpose of viewing its condition and state of repair.

A landlord is not liable under Section 11 to carry out repairs or to compensate the tenant for disrepair unless the landlord receives notification of the disrepair. As a landlord does not live in the property the landlord has limited opportunities of finding out what is wrong with the property unless a tenant tells them. A landlord will, however, bring notification upon themselves if they, their agent or representative visited the property and the disrepair came or ought to have come to their attention. A landlord has a reasonable period of time to carry out repairs after receiving notice. What is a reasonable period of time depends upon the circumstances of the disrepair and whether it is an emergency.

A landlord is not required to carry out repairs if the disrepair came about as a result of the tenant's failure to look after the property as a reasonable tenant would (i.e. in a tenant-like manner), or if the tenant has damaged the item constituting the disrepair. A landlord is not required to rebuild or reinstate the property in the event of damage or destruction by fire, flood, or other uncontrollable events or to repair or maintain anything the tenant is entitled to remove from the property.

The courts recognise that there is a difference between disrepair and a design defect. The landlord is not usually required to repair the latter unless it is causing a disrepair for which the landlord is responsible.

The court also recognises that there is a difference between a repair and an improvement. Whilst a landlord is responsible for repairing the property there is no obligation to improve. Repair is replacing or fixing what is there, improvement is providing something that was not there to begin with. Indeed, when a court is looking at the degree of repair to be carried out to a property consideration is given to the age, character and expectant life of the property. However, in some instances the only way to reasonably carry out a repair is to carry out an improvement to the property.

If a landlord fails to comply with Section 11 obligations the tenant can commence court proceedings and may be entitled to the following:-
- an order requiring the repairs to be carried out;
- compensation for the disrepair; and
- legal costs.

A tenant is usually responsible for repairing: internal plaster, door handles, kitchen drawers, kitchen cupboard handles and doors, tap washers, replacing bulbs, keeping drains and gutters free from obstruction, accidental damage by tenant and infestation caused by the tenant, their guests or visitors.

7.2 Landlord obligations under the Defective Premises Act 1972

As seen above, all ASTs of seven years or less are subject to repairing obligations imposed on the landlord under LTA 1985 Section 11. Where a tenancy is subject to the above repairing obligation or an express term requiring the landlord to carry out repairs, the landlord owes to all persons who might reasonably be affected by a defect in the property (contractors, work men, guest of tenant, tenant's household, tenant or council employees) a duty to take reasonable care to see that they are reasonably safe from personal injury and/or damage to property caused by the relevant defect. This extends the duty to carry out repairs beyond the contractual tenant and to any person reasonably expected to be on the premises.

The duty is owed if the landlord knows whether by notification from the tenant or other means or if the landlord ought to have known of the defect, given the circumstances. This means that the landlord does not necessarily need to have received notice if they ought to have known about the defect such as carrying out a recent inspection of the property or repairing something that is related to the defect which is deemed to have brought the defect to their attention.

If an AST gives the landlord the express or implied right to enter the property to carry out any maintenance or repair of the property (and it is almost certain that they all do) then from the time the landlord is and continues to be able to exercise that right he shall be treated as being under an obligation to the tenant and any person reasonably expected to be in the property, for the relevant disrepair.

Additionally a landlord who has designed, built and/or managed the building of a property will be liable for failure to build the property properly, to every person who acquires a lawful interest in the residential property. Failure to build it properly includes failing to work in a workmanlike or professional manner or use proper materials.

7.3 Furnished property to be fit for human habitation

There is an implied obligation on landlords who let furnished property that the property must be fit for human habitation at the beginning of the tenancy, but not beyond that time. Matters that can make a property unfit for human habitation includes infestation, water leak, no or lack of some utilities and dangerous premises. A property may be in disrepair but remain fit for human habitation or may not be in disrepair but is unfit for human habitation in the case of infestation.

7.4 Common law negligence

If a landlord designed, built or oversaw the building of the property they owe a duty of care, similar to all builders, to take reasonable care to ensure that the dwelling does not contain any latent defects which can cause damage to property or personal injury. They can be liable for any negligence in discharging their role in the design, build and construction of the property.

If a landlord carries out work or repairs whether obligated to do so or not they will be liable to injured parties if those works are carried out negligently. A landlord may also be negligent in discharging their duty as landlord if they knew of repairs and failed to carry them out.

7.5 Environmental Protection Act 1990

This statute comes into effect when there is a property in such a state (whether by one major item of disrepair or multiple smaller items of disrepair) so as to be prejudicial to health (physical or mental). Prejudicial to health means a healthy person becoming sick or a sick person deteriorating further or is a public or private nuisance. This covers conditions such as: condensation, damp, draughty and ill-fitting doors and windows. Any person suffering from the statutory nuisance i.e. tenant, household member, guest, visitors can give a landlord 21 days' notice to get rid of the statutory nuisance. Following this the person suffering from the statutory nuisance can make a complaint to the magistrates' court if the statutory nuisance exists or is likely to occur.

A person (tenant or other) affected by a defect in the property that satisfies this legislation can bring a private prosecution against the landlord in the magistrates' court. The magistrates' court can fine the landlord, order works to be done, compensation to be paid and costs. A landlord's failure to comply with the magistrates' court order can lead to contempt of court proceedings and imprisonment. Proceedings must be brought against the person responsible for the statutory nuisance. The court can direct the local authority for the area in which the property is located to carry out the works where the responsible person and the owner or occupier of the property responsible cannot be found.

Alternatively, a person aggrieved by a statutory nuisance may inform the local authority for the area where the property is located. The local authority must take steps to investigate and if satisfied that a statutory nuisance exists, or is likely to occur or recur serve an abatement notice on the person responsible for it. The notice will require the person responsible to take steps to get rid of the statutory nuisance. Failure to comply with the notice is an offence and a fine can be imposed. If the responsible person does not comply with the notice the local authority can carry out the works themselves and recover their reasonable expenses from the person responsible. A responsible person can appeal against the abatement notice to the magistrates' court.

7.6 Liability under the Occupiers Liability Act 1957

Where there is a resident landlord or a landlord retains control of common parts (as in Houses in Multiple Occupation) a duty is owed to all visitors (not just the tenants) to ensure in all reasonable circumstances that the visitor will be safe to use the premises for the purpose of their visit. This goes beyond the matters the landlord is obligated to repair under the tenancy and no notice is required of any defect.

If a visitor willingly assumes a risk or a landlord utilises an independent contractor and has taken reasonable steps to ensure they are competent and the work is done properly no liability will incur to the landlord.

7.7 Gas Safety (Installation and Use) Regulations 1998 (as amended)

The body responsible for enforcing this regulation is the Health and Safety Executive (HSE). This regulation applies to all residential tenancies and licences of less than seven years. A landlord is responsible for ensuring that all gas appliances, gas fittings, flues and pipe works to such appliances are maintained in good working order and an annual safety check is carried out on them by a Gas Safe (no longer Corgi) registered engineer. The tenant is to be provided with a copy of the reports or gas safety certificate within 28 days of the check and the records kept for two years. The landlord is not responsible for gas appliances installed and removable by the tenant.

Breach of the regulation can result in a fine and civil liability to anyone injured as a result of non-compliance.

7.8 Term implied as to common parts

Where a letting includes common parts, such as Houses in Multiple Occupation, over which a landlord retains control and which a tenant is entitled to use there is an implied term that the landlord will take reasonable care to ensure that those common parts is not in a state that will cause damage to the tenant or their property. Reasonable care must be taken to maintain the common parts which the tenant is entitled to use. A landlord will be liable for disrepair to the common parts without having received notice of the disrepair, because it is under the landlord's control.

7.9 Electrical safety

Defective electrical wiring, installations and/or appliances in a property can cause injury and/or death through fires and electrocutions.

A landlord's obligations to ensure electrical safety in the property are set out in:-

- Landlord and Tenant Act 1985 section 11 (see 7.1 above);
- Housing Act 2004 under the Housing Health & Safety Rating System (see Chapter 10);
- Management of Houses in Multiple Occupation (England) Regulations 2006 (see Chapter 11);
- Building Regulations Part P; and
- the Electrical Equipment (Safety) Regulations 1994; and other regulations.

This list is not exhaustive. Landlords have legal requirements in respect of: electrical works in the design, building, conversion, extension of their property; for the supply and maintenance of appliances; for wiring and installations in the property. A landlord should ensure that these matters are carried out to a safe standard.

Whilst there is no requirement for a landlord to have an electrical safety certificate the best way for a landlord to achieve the above is by getting a competent registered electrical engineer to carry out an inspection of the property and appliances and provide a satisfactory certificate which should be renewed when it has expired. Any works recommended following an electrical safety inspection should be carried out by a competent professional and a satisfactory certificate issued after.

Landlords should ensure that any electrical appliances provided with the tenancy are safe. This means that they should not pose a risk of injury or death to humans and animals, or damage to property. To ensure that they are safe may require the landlord to repair and/or replace electrical appliances as well as provide user instructions.

7.10 General Product Safety Regulations 1994

Any product supplied to a consumer must be safe. If there is any risk involved with the use of a product it should be made known to the user if it is not obvious. The property and its fixtures and fittings ought to be safe.

7.11 Furniture and Furnishings (Fire) (Safety) Regulations 1988

A landlord must ensure that furniture and furnishings supplied with the property meet fire resistance requirements.

7.12 Smoke alarms

A landlord is not usually required to provide a smoke alarm except in the case of Houses in Multiple Occupation, but it would be sensible to do so for every property they own.

A smoke alarm can prevent injury to person and/or damage to property where a landlord might be responsible for the same under one of the various repairing obligations mentioned above. It may also save a landlord's investment from being burnt down and an insurance claim becoming a necessity. Landlords are not guaranteed to recover their full loss from an insurance claim.

Building regulations require all properties built after 1992 to have a mains wired smoke alarm fitted on every level in the property. If a smoke alarm is fitted a landlord will be responsible for maintaining them as an electrical installation. However, if it is battery operated it will usually be the tenant's responsibility to replace batteries. This should be clearly stated in the tenancy agreement.

7.13 Nuisance

If a landlord owns adjoining property such as another dwelling in a converted building, common parts in a block of flats or neighbouring property they can be liable in nuisance for anything which is kept upon that adjoining or neighbouring land that affects a tenant's property such as water leaks and infestation.

7.14 Building regulations

If a landlord proposes to carry out certain qualifying work on a property they will need to get building approval from the local authority for the area in which the property is located, under the Building Regulations. Qualifying work includes:-

- structural changes to a building;
- converting a house to flats;
- new, extension or replacement drainage;
- kitchen extension or loft conversion;
- replacement windows;
- electrical installation work unless done by a member of a recognised Competent Person Self-Certification Scheme.

Landlords should check with the local authority who can advise on:-

- whether the work needs building regulation approval;
- what the criteria is for approval;
- how to apply; and
- what fee is payable.

7.15 Summary

A landlord should ensure that their property, fittings, fixtures, furnishing and appliances are in good repair at the commencement and during the tenancy. A property will always need maintenance and a landlord should therefore make sure they have a budget and system for reminding or requiring them to carry out regular maintenance and repair. A landlord should also ensure that the tenancy agreement allows them to and that they actually carry out regular inspections of their property.

A claim for disrepair by a tenant can amount to substantial compensation being paid, works being done and legal costs incurred that will always be more expensive than carrying out the work in the first place. Compensation for disrepair can set off a claim for rent arrears and defeat a claim for possession based on rent arrears. In some instances a landlord may find themselves guilty of a criminal offence and be subjected to a fine.

A property is also a landlord's investment and anyone would be expected to look after their investment. A disrepair dealt with at an early stage will usually stop the defect becoming more widespread, prevent or limit secondary damage and limit the expense of rectifying the problem.

A tenant can carry out repairs that a landlord has failed to do under their repairing obligations and deduct the costs of those repairs from the rent. However, if a tenant decides on this course of action they must follow very strict guidelines to be able to defend any claim for rent arrears resulting from their deduction from the rent.

8   INFESTATION

8.1   Causes of Infestation

A property can be infested as a result of infestation:-
1.   that was always there and the origins are unknown;
2.   brought into the property by the tenant;
3.   brought into the property by the landlord;
4.   brought into the property by a third party; or
5.   originating from a neighbouring property.

A tenant can cause infestation in several ways. They may bring it into the property when moving in their possessions, through food sources, pets, guests, visitors or the way they take care of or fail to take care of the property.

Workmen may cause infestation by poor workmanship thus allowing access points for infestation or bringing it on to the property with their tools or work materials.

A landlord may have let the property with infestation therefore causing it from the outset, brought it on to the property at a later date, allowed infestation through disrepair or be liable as the owner of neighbouring property from which the infestation originates.

Neighbours, whether their property is in residential or commercial use, will be responsible for infestation that originates from their property.

8.2   Effects of Infestation

Infestation can cause:-
- damage to the rented property (such as wood termites or cockroaches damaging the electrics);
- Injury to health (diseases, infections, bites, stings, even entering a person's orifices);
- damage to personal possessions (clothes, furniture and effects);
- breach of covenant of quiet enjoyment;
- nuisance and annoyance (including a statutory nuisance); and
- derogation from the grant of a tenancy.

Common infestations include:-
- mice;
- ants;
- cockroaches;
- bed bugs; and
- fleas.

INFESTATION

Under case law a landlord is required to ensure that a furnished property is fit for human habitation at the commencement of the tenancy. This means that a landlord must ensure at the commencement of the tenancy that the property is free from infestation. If a landlord fails to tackle the infestation properly at that stage and it re-emerges or is discovered at a later date the landlord will be responsible for dealing with it.

If a property is rented to a tenant free of infestation and becomes infested at a later date, whether the landlord is responsible or not will depend on the cause of the infestation.

8.3   Who is responsible?

If the infestation is caused by the tenant, the landlord will not be responsible and the tenant will be liable to eradicate the infestation and pay for any damage to the property.

If the infestation is caused by a third party they will be responsible for eradicating the infestation and pay for any damage to the property and the tenant.

The landlord will be in the same position as a third party if they caused the infestation. They will have to eradicate it, repair any damage and compensate the tenant.

If the property is a single dwelling house and is rented as such with the garden, pathway and exterior up to a neighbouring property and the neighbour is the source of the infestation the owner or person responsible for the neighbouring property will be liable.

If the rented property is a flat conversion in a house and the landlord owns the house, the landlord will have retained ownership of the common parts. Infestation coming from the retained common parts will make the landlord responsible despite the original source being another flat or a property on neighbouring land. The same applies to a purpose-built block of flats rented by a landlord who owns the entire block.

A tenant's claim for compensation (damages) for infestation can be substantial. At the first sign of infestation a landlord should get a competent pest control expert at the property to assess the infestation, identify the source, provide a report and take remedial action.

If a landlord can identify the source and someone else is responsible for the infestation the landlord can have a cause of action against them. A prudent landlord should keep a record of the infestation and what treatment has taken place. This may act as a defence or mitigating circumstances should a claim be made against the landlord.

9 DAMP AND MOULD GROWTH

Damp and mould growth can be brought about by several factors; the most common being disrepair, design defect of the property and lifestyle of the tenant.

9.1 Design of the property – condensation

Condensation occurs when warm moisture-filled air in a property (moisture comes from breathing, cooking, bathing, laundry (especially where clothes are dried indoors)) comes into contact with a cold surface, cools and the moisture becomes water. The wet surfaces created by condensation provide the setting for mould growth to occur.

There does not have to be disrepair for condensation to occur although disrepair can contribute to it by adding moisture (in the case of a leak) or producing colder surfaces (if the heating is not working). The most obvious cold surfaces in a property are the windows and external walls. The most obvious rooms with a lot of moisture are the kitchen and bathroom. Buildings designed with poor insulation and poor ventilation will have colder surfaces and inadequate air circulation, therefore increasing condensation.

A tenant cannot bring an action for disrepair against a landlord for damp and mould growth caused by the design of the property. A defect in the design is not disrepair. For an action for disrepair to succeed the tenant will need to show that something in the property has stopped working or deteriorated and as a result it is in disrepair. As stated a property can have nothing wrong with it but suffers from condensation due to its design.

A tenant may be able to take action against a landlord for failing to abate a statutory nuisance under the Environmental Protection Act 1990, or prove liability under the Occupiers Liability Act 1972. A landlord may face action under the Housing Health and Safety Rating System (see Chapters 7 and 10).

9.2 Life-style of the tenant – condensation

If a tenant has a lot of furniture or possessions in a room against a cold wall it will contribute to condensation and mould growth as it will stop warm air circulating and provide colder surfaces upon which air cools and forms water.

Additionally, if a tenant fails to use the heating system adequately, does activities beyond what is expected of a reasonable tenant so that a lot of moisture is generated, overcrowds the property, blocks ventilation channels or fail to open the windows, the likelihood of condensation will increase.

A landlord will not be responsible for condensation brought about by the tenant's conduct. In this instance a landlord may be able to bring court proceedings against the tenant or seek deductions from the deposit for the tenant failing to treat the property in a tenant-like manner or allowing voluntary waste.

9.3   Disrepair – damp and mould growth

There are items of disrepair that can lead to condensation, damp and mould growth because of cold surfaces, excessive moisture, damp surfaces and/or reduced air circulation. They include:-

- defective damp proof membrane;
- defective heating system;
- draughty and ill-fitting windows;
- water leak through faulty plumbing and installations;
- leaking gutter;
- blocked drains; and
- faulty extractor fans.

Landlords can face several actions when there is damp and black mould growth in the property brought about by a disrepair.

A landlord can be found guilty of failing to abate a statutory nuisance under the Environmental Protection Act 1990. This is not a prosecution that results in a prison term but it can result in a fine, compensation to the tenant, an order for works and costs. If the landlord fails to comply with the order they can eventually be imprisoned through contempt of court proceedings.

A tenant can also make a complaint to the local authority's Environmental Health department that deals with private tenancy issues. These departments may have various names at different councils. The local authority should carry out an inspection of the property and may be able to take action against the landlord and/or carry out the remedial work and recover the costs from the landlord. Chapter 7 sets out other ways in which a landlord can be held responsible for the disrepair.

9.4   Effects of damp and mould growth

Damp and mould growth can cause damage to the property and its contents as well as serious health effects on a tenant, especially those that are vulnerable, i.e. old, young or sick. Some effects of damp and mould are:-

- damage to walls, plaster, woodwork, décor;
- damage to furniture, clothing, appliances
- respiratory problems;
- eye infections;
- asthma; and
- eye and skin irritation.

10 HOUSING HEALTH & SAFETY RATING SYSTEM (HHSRS)

In addition to all the legislation, regulations and case law that affect the state in which a landlord keeps their property there is also the HHSRS.

This is a system that is enforced by the local authority for the area in which a property is located. Different local authorities will enforce this system to various degrees depending on their priorities and resources. The local authority will first have some information that makes it appropriate for them to inspect the property to determine whether a category 1 or 2 hazard exists. Hazards are rated as category 1 or 2 based on their severity.

A hazard is any risk of harm to the health or safety of an actual or potential occupier of the property. Under the HHSRS there are 29 prescribed hazards which include damp and mould growth; excess cold; security of the dwelling against unauthorized entry; lack of adequate lighting; exposure to noise; falls associated with baths, showers or level surfaces; harm from electricity, fire hazards, design and layout. When a local authority decides on the type and severity of hazard (category 1 or 2) that exists there are several actions they can take:-

- serve an improvement notice (category 1 & 2 hazard);
- make a prohibition order (category 1 & 2 hazard);
- serve a hazard awareness notice (category 1 & 2 hazard);
- take emergency remedial action (category 1 hazard);
- make an emergency prohibition order (category 1 hazard);
- make a demolition order (category 1 & 2 hazard);
- declare a clearance order (category 1 hazard); or
- make a slum clearance declaration (category 2 hazard).

10.1 Improvement notice

This is a notice requiring the person on whom it is served to take remedial action on the property with regard to the hazard(s) that have been identified. An improvement notice will set out:-

- whether the notice is served in respect of a category 1 or 2 hazard;
- the property on which it exists;
- the type of hazard;
- the cause of the hazard;
- the action to be taken and on which premises to take it;
- the time for remedial action to start and end (at least 28 days from the date of the notice); and
- details of the right of appeal and time period to appeal.

An improvement notice may specify that it is suspended until a certain date or on the occurrence of a specified event. The notice usually takes effect 21 days from the date it is served or the date when any suspension comes to an end.

An improvement notice and any variation or revocation is required to be served where relevant on the licence holder of an HMO, person having control of a property, person managing a property, the owner of a flat who should take action under the notice, owner of common parts or specified premises. Copies of the notice are to be served on all persons with a relevant interest (freeholder, leaseholder or mortgagee) in and occupiers of the specified property.

10.1.1 Revocation of an improvement notice

An improvement notice will be revoked if the requirement of the notice has been satisfied, or may be revoked if the local authority considers that as an appropriate course of action. If the improvement notice was served in relation to more than one hazard it can be revoked for some and continue in force for the other hazards. The revocation can come about from the authority's own initiative or by an application from the person on whom the notice was served.

10.1.2 Variation of an improvement notice

A local authority may vary an improvement notice with the agreement of the person on whom it has been served in which case the variation will take effect immediately. The variation can come about from the authority's own initiative or by an application from the person on whom the notice was served. When this occurs the varied notice takes effect after any period for appeal against the variation has expired or when it is confirmed on an appeal.

If the authority decides to vary or revoke the improvement notice or refuse to vary or revoke, a notice to that effect must be served within seven days of the decision and contain the:-
* decision;
* reasons;
* right of appeal; and
* period in which to appeal.

10.1.3 Appeals against the original or a variation or refusal to vary or revoke an improvement notice

The recipient of an improvement notice (not the recipient of copies of the notice) may appeal to the Residential Property Tribunal (RPT) against the making of the notice, the variation of or refusal to vary and refusal to revoke the notice.

The appeal may be based on other persons being responsible for complying with the notice or that another course of action is the best course for the local authority to take where an original notice is concerned.

10.1.3.1   Time limit to appeal

An appeal against an original notice must be made within 21 days of the date it was served. An appeal against a variation or decision refusing to vary or revoke the notice must be made within 28 days of the date of the decision. An appeal may be made out of time if there is a good reason for the original delay and in any delay in applying for permission.

10.1.3.2   Decision on appeal

The appeal is treated as a re-hearing which usually means no new facts are considered. However, matters of which the local authority was unaware may be considered. The RPT may confirm, quash or vary the improvement notice or in the case of a decision on the variation or revocation of an improvement notice confirm, reverse, vary the decision or revoke the notice.

10.1.4   Enforcement of an improvement notice

A local authority may, with the agreement of the person on whom the notice has been served, take the action that that person ought to have taken under the notice. The local authority will assume the rights that the person on whom the notice was served had in relation to occupiers and anyone with an interest in the property. Any expense incurred by the local authority will be borne by the person on whom the notice was served.

Alternatively, the local authority can take action without the agreement of the person on whom the notice was served if the notice was not complied with or if reasonable progress is not being made for the notice to be complied with by a set deadline. The action taken will be at the expense of the person on whom the notice has been served. The local authority will be required to serve a notice before taking action without agreement.

Failure to comply (beginning and completing remedial action) with an improvement notice is an offence unless the offender had a reasonable excuse for not complying. If convicted, the offender can be subject to a fine.

10.2   Prohibition order

A prohibition order is an order imposing restrictions on the use of a property. It can restrict:-
- the use of the property;
- the purpose(s) for which the property is used; number of or type of people occupying the property; and
- can also specify the part or all of the property to be occupied.

The prohibition order must state:-

- whether it is made in respect of a category 1 or 2 hazard;
- the details of the hazard;
- where it exists;
- the cause;
- the remedy to be taken and when;
- the property on which the prohibition applies;
- the right of appeal, period of appeal; and
- date the decision is made.

The prohibition order may be suspended for a period of time or until an event occurs. It ought to be served on all owners and occupiers of the whole or part of the relevant property, the person managing or having control of the property, the landlord's agent and mortgagee of the property (in the case of an order affecting the common parts of flats all flat owners and occupiers in the building) within seven days of the date the order is made.

A person subject to a prohibition order may seek approval from the local authority to use specified parts of the property or for it to be subjected to a specified use. If the authority refuse the approval that decision is subject to an appeal to the RPT within 28 days of the date of the decision.

A prohibition order starts to operate 28 days after the date in the notice on which it was made. It may be varied or revoked on the application of any person on whom a copy of the order has been served or the local authority's own initiative. Where the local authority makes a decision on variation or revocation of the order the notice must be served on everyone who should have been served with the original order within seven days of the date the decision was made.

10.2.1 Revocation of a prohibition order

A prohibition order must be revoked if the hazard to which it relates no longer exists on the specified property. The authority may revoke a prohibition order if there are special circumstances for doing so or it is the appropriate thing to do. The order may also be part revoked where it relates to more than one hazard. A revocation comes into force when it is made.

10.2.2 Variation of a prohibition order

A prohibition order may be varied with the agreement of everyone on whom the order was served in which case it takes effect immediately. Where variation has not occurred with the agreement of everyone served with the order it comes into effect when the period for an appeal has expired without an appeal being made or when an appeal has been made and determined. Where the order has been suspended, the terms of the suspension (i.e. time period or event) may be the subject of a variation.

A decision on a variation, revocation or refusal to vary or revoke a prohibition order must set out the:-

- decision;
- reason;
- date;
- right of appeal; and
- period in which to make an appeal.

10.2.3 Appeals against the original or a variation or refusal to vary or revoke a prohibition order

An appeal may be made to the RPT in respect of the affected property by:-

- an owner or occupier of part or the whole;
- a person managing or in control of the property;
- a mortgagee of the whole or part of the property; or
- every owner or mortgagee of the premises which contain the common parts.

An appeal may be on the grounds that another type of enforcement is more suitable. An appeal may be made against a decision to vary or to refuse to vary or revoke the order.

10.2.3.1   *Time limit to appeal*

An appeal against the original order or a decision of the local authority to vary or to refuse to vary or revoke the order must be made within 28 days of the date the order/decision was made. An appeal may be made out of time if there is good reason for missing the deadline as well as any subsequent delay in making a late application.

10.2.3.2   *Decision on appeal*

The appeal is by way of a re-hearing although matters of which the local authority was unaware at the time of their decision can be considered. The RPT may confirm, quash or vary the prohibition order. In relation to a decision to vary or refuse to vary or revoke a prohibition order the RPT may confirm, reverse or vary the decision or revoke the order.

10.2.4 Enforcement of a prohibition order

An offence is committed if a person, knowing of the prohibition order, uses the property in contravention of the order or allows someone to do so. The person who commits the offence can be subject to a fine plus a penalty of not more than £20 for every day or part day that the contravention occurs after the conviction. It is a defence if the offender has a reasonable excuse for not complying.

If possession of the property is necessary to comply with the Prohibition Order the person on whom the notice is served will not have to comply with the relevant security of tenure protections in obtaining possession.

The RPT also has the power to end or vary a lease of a property that has become the subject of a Prohibition Order.

10.3 Hazard awareness notice

This is a notice informing the person on whom it is served of the existence of a hazard arising as a result of a defect with the property in relation to which it is served. The notice informs the recipient of the:-

- nature of the hazard (category 1 or 2);
- property on which it exists;
- cause of the hazard;
- premises on which the cause of the hazard exists (if different);
- reason for serving the notice;
- reason why it is the most appropriate form of action; and
- remedial action to be taken.

The service of a hazard awareness notice and copies of the notices is the same as set out for improvement notices mentioned above at paragraph 10.1.

10.4 Emergency remedial action

A local authority can take emergency remedial action (action that the authority considers immediately necessary to remove the imminent risk of serious harm associated with the hazard) in respect of a relevant property under the following circumstances:-

- a category 1 hazard or hazards is deemed to exist;
- the hazard involves an immediate risk of serious harm to the health or safety of the occupants of a property; and
- no management order is in force for the property.

The remedial action may involve the local authority entering upon the premises themselves and doing the remedial work at the expense of the person upon whom the notice was served.

Within seven days of starting to take remedial action the local authority must serve a notice stating the:-

- hazard;
- property on which it exists;
- cause of the hazard;
- the premises on which the remedial action is or will be taken;
- nature of the remedial action;
- authority or power for taking that action;
- when it has or will be taken;

- right of appeal; and
- timescale to appeal.

The notice must be served on the same persons on whom an improvement notice would have been served under paragraph 10.1. A warrant can be issued for the local authority to gain entry to the premises for the purposes of emergency remedial action. A local authority will be entitled to recover their expenses reasonably incurred in taking action.

10.5 Emergency prohibition orders

A local authority can make an emergency prohibition order (an order which immediately prohibits the use of any premises) under the following circumstances:-

- a category 1 hazard(s) is deemed to exist;
- there is an immediate risk of serious harm to the health or safety of the occupants of a relevant property; and
- there is no management order in force.

The order must identify the:-

- property;
- hazard;
- cause;
- which property the prohibition is to be applied to;
- what the prohibition is;
- remedial action that would revoke it;
- date on which it is made;
- right of appeal; and
- timescale in which to appeal.

An emergency prohibition order is subject to the same rules as a prohibition order in respect of notices, revocation, variation, enforcement and appeals as set out in paragraph 10.2 above.

10.5.1 Appealing against an emergency remedial action or an emergency prohibition order

An appeal may be made to the RPT by a person on whom an emergency remedial notice has been served, or by a relevant person in connection with an emergency prohibition order.

There are 28 days in which to appeal from the date in the emergency remedial notice when the remedial action was or is to be started or the date in the emergency prohibition order when the order was made.

An appeal may be made out of time if there is good reason for the delay. The appeal will be on the material before the local authority at the time the decision is made although matters which were unknown to the authority may be considered.

The tribunal may confirm, reverse or vary an emergency remedial order or may confirm, vary or revoke an emergency prohibition order from a particular date.

10.6 Demolition orders

If a local authority is satisfied that a category 1 or 2 hazard exist making a demolition order may be a course of action that they can take. This order may not be made in relation to a building subject to a management order or in respect of a listed building.

A demolition order will require the building to be vacated within a specified period of at least 28 days from the date the order becomes effective and be demolished within a further six weeks, or after the date it is vacated if longer than the six weeks period or such other period specified by the local authority.

The demolition notice must be served on an owner or occupier of the premises affected in part or whole, on anyone authorized to let the premises and any mortgagee within seven days of the date the order is made. The notice can be deemed to have been served if left at a visible/prominent part of the premises.

In the event of no appeal the demolition order comes into effect 28 days from the date the order is made. A person wishing to appeal the order must do so within 28 days, of the date the order was made, to the RPT. An occupier with an unexpired term of three years or less cannot appeal. A decision on an appeal may confirm, quash or vary the demolition order. The appeal decision does not become effective until any further appeal time limit has expired without an appeal.

Where a demolition order has become effective the local authority may serve a notice on the occupants of the property stating the effect of the order, the date they are required to leave the premises and requiring them to leave before that date or within 28 days following the service of the notice. If they remain in the property beyond this time the local authority or owner can obtain a possession order without needing to comply with the statutory protection offered to their type of tenancy. The court must require the occupant to leave within two to four weeks of any order. An offence will be committed where a person either takes up occupation or let the premises to someone knowing that a demolition order has become effective.

10.7 Clearance areas

If a local authority is satisfied that all the residential buildings in an area contain a category 1 hazard and any other buildings are dangerous to the health and safety of people living in the area, the area may be declared as a clearance area i.e. an area to be cleared of all buildings.

A clearance area can also be declared if the area is dangerous or harmful to the health or safety of people living in the area due to the properties bad arrangement i.e. narrow or badly arranged streets.

A clearance area may be declared if a category 2 hazard exists in the circumstances above and the circumstances of the case are specified by an order of the Secretary of State.

Before making a declaration of a clearance area a notice must be served of this intention on everyone with an interest in a building (owner, mortgagee, freeholder and occupiers), to be included in the clearance area as well as publish it in at least two local newspaper for the affected area and invite representations within a reasonable period.

The authority must take steps to secure suitable accommodation for all persons to be displaced because of the declaration of a clearance area.

11 HOUSES IN MULTIPLE OCCUPATION (HMOs)

There are several definitions that if satisfied can classify a property as an HMO. However, the definition that most people will be familiar with is the one that, if satisfied, subjects the HMO to mandatory licensing: **where there is a property which is three storeys or more occupied by five or more people who are living in two or more households.** If a property satisfies that definition it will require a mandatory licence.

However, there are wider definitions of HMOs and although they are not required to be licensed they are subject to some rules and regulations governing HMOs.

No HMO will exist if the building is occupied only by two persons who form two separate households. Neither will an HMO exist where a resident landlord and his household occupies a property with no more than two other persons who are not part of their household.

11.1 Classification tests

There are five tests that can lead to a building being classified as an HMO.

11.1.1 The 'standard' test

The standard test is met where there are two or more households renting separate living accommodation in the same property or part of a property where they share facilities and the sole purpose of the accommodation is for living.

11.1.2 The self-contained flat test

The self-contained flat test is met where there are two or more households renting separate living accommodation in a self-contained flat where they share facilities and the sole purpose of the accommodation is for living.

11.1.3 The converted building test

The converted building test is met where the property or part of the property originally consisted of living accommodation with more living accommodation being added and there are two or more households renting separate living accommodation where they share facilities and the sole purpose of the accommodation is for living.

11.1.4 The converted block of flats test (section 257 HA 2004)

Under this HMO definition a property or part of a property has been converted into self-contained flats. However, the conversion work did not comply with building standards and less than two thirds of the flats are owner-occupied.

11.1.5 The HMO declaration test

This is where a local authority serves a notice declaring a property to be an HMO where it would have satisfied the standard, self-contained or converted building HMO test but failed to do so because the sole purpose of the property is not for living.

They are rules that apply to all HMOs and there are additional rules that apply to HMOs that are required to be licensed.

11.2 Rules applying to all HMOs except converted block of flats HMO

The rules applying to all HMOs can be found in the Management of HMO (England) Regulations 2006. Below is a summary of those rules.

Rules applying to a person managing (i.e. owner or lessee receiving rent directly or indirectly)

11.2.1 The requirements of a manager of an HMO

The requirements are:-
- provide each household with their name, address and telephone number as well as displaying it somewhere prominent in the HMO;
- keep all fire exits clear from obstruction and in repair;
- maintain all fire-fighting equipment and fire alarms;
- ensure fire notices are displayed in positions clearly visible if there are more than four occupiers;
- take all reasonable measures to protect the occupants of the HMO from injury relating to its design, structural condition and number of occupants;
- if a roof or balcony is unsafe, make it safe or prevent access as long as it is unsafe;
- if a window sill is at or near floor level to fit bars or take steps to ensure it is safe for the occupants;
- keep in good, clean, working condition the water supply and drainage and not unreasonably cause the water supply and drainage to be interrupted;
- produce the latest gas appliance test certificate to the local authority within seven days of request;
- not unreasonably cause the gas or electricity supply to the HMO to be interrupted;
- obtain, keep and provide on request a valid electrical safety certificate of fixed electrical installations;
- ensure all common parts are in a safe state, good working condition, free from obstruction, clean and in good decorative repair;
- ensure fixtures, fittings and appliances used by two or more households are good, safe and clean;

- ensure the external of the property i.e. outbuildings, boundary fences, garden, forecourt used by two or more households are safe, clean, in good repair, tidy and does not constitute a danger to occupiers; and
- if any part of the HMO is not in use ensure that part and access to it is kept clean and free from rubbish.

With regard to the living accommodations of the HMO a landlord/manager must:-
- ensure that it and the furniture supplied in it are in clean condition at the beginning of a letting;
- maintain internal structure in good repair;
- keep fixtures, fittings, appliances, internal structure, windows and means of ventilation in good repair and clean working order.

With regard to waste disposal the manager must ensure that:-
- there are suitable and adequate facilities for each household for the storage of refuse for disposal; and
- ensure that there are suitable arrangements for waste disposal from the HMO.

11.2.2 Requirements of occupiers of HMOs

The requirements are:-
- not to prevent the manager from performing their duty;
- allow reasonable access to their living accommodation to carry out obligations with regard to the HMO;
- provide the manager with reasonably requested information to carry out obligations in respect of the HMO;
- reasonably avoid damage to the HMO, its fixtures, fittings and appliances;
- store and disposal of waste in accordance with arrangements;
- comply with reasonable fire safety instructions.

As noted above not every HMO is required to be licensed. There are three licensing schemes that can apply to a private sector landlord's property.

Mandatory licensing: This is the licensing that most landlords with a HMO are aware of. A license will be required for an HMO that is three or more storeys, is occupied by five or more persons who are not part of the same household.

Additional licensing: This occurs where a local authority take steps that require a description of HMOs not fitting the criteria for mandatory nevertheless to be licensed as an HMO because they are in a designated area. The area is usually designated because the description of HMOs in it are poorly managed leading to problems of empty properties and anti-social behaviour.

Selective licensing: This occurs where a local authority takes steps to designate an area as subject to selective licensing because it fits a set of criteria. The criteria can either be:-

- the area is suffering anti-social behaviour and private sector landlords are failing to take action they should take to combat it. The local authority believes this course of action along with other measures will reduce or end the problem; or
- the area has or is likely to have low housing demand and this course of action along with other measures will improve the social or economic standing of the area.

This licensing applies to any tenanted property in the selected area except properties subject to a management order or are licensed as HMOs. This is currently been enforced within the London Borough of Newham.

If a landlord is not sure whether their property is subject to licensing they should:-

- ascertain whether or not their property is an HMO using the five tests above;
- if the property qualifies as a HMO check if it is subject to mandatory licensing; and
- if the HMO is not subject to mandatory licensing make enquiries with the local authority for the area in which the property is located to see if they operate an additional or selective licensing scheme.

If the local authority does not operate an additional or selective licensing scheme, the property does not need to be licensed. If the local authority does operate an additional or selective licensing scheme the landlord should check their property against the criteria for additional or selective licensing to see if it should be licensed.

If a landlord is in doubt an application can always be made for a licence. If the property does not require a licence the application fee should be returned in full.

11.3 Applying for a mandatory HMO licence

A local authority is required to take reasonable steps to ensure that all those required to apply for a licence do so. It is usually the person with control of the HMO that is required to apply for the licence. This may be the landlord or a managing agent. A local authority can grant a licence to the applicant or someone else more appropriate if they and the applicant agrees. A licence fee will usually accompany the application and will be determined by the local authority. Newham Council's fees are based on the number of bedrooms in the property and in January 2013 were:-

- Up to 5 rooms - £950
- 6 to 9 rooms - £1,100
- 10 to 14 rooms - £1,250
- 15 to 19 rooms - £1,400
- Renewal fees start from £550 up to £750.

If a landlord has an HMO that is required to be licensed and wishes not to proceed with licensing they can be granted a temporary exemption licence which can be for three months and extended for a further three months. This is to allow the landlord time to take steps to exempt the property from the licensing requirements, such as reducing the number of occupants or converting the property to a building that does not need licensing.

If a local authority refuses to extend the initial three months of the temporary exemption from licensing, a decision to that effect must be issued which also notifies the applicant of their right to appeal the decision.

An HMO licence will only relate to the property for which it has been granted and will not last longer than five years from its grant. The licence is personal to the licence holder and cannot be transferred in life or death.

11.3.1 Persons to inform about the application

The applicant of an HMO licence is required to inform the following persons of their application or provide them with a copy of it:-
- mortgagee;
- owner of the property to which the application relates if the applicant is not the owner;
- any tenant or leaseholder of the property or a part of it (does not include statutory tenants or tenants whose tenancy is less than three years);
- the proposed licence holder if that is not the applicant;
- the proposed management agent if that is not the applicant; and
- person(s) who have agreed to be bound by the licence conditions.

The above mentioned persons must be provided with:-
- the applicant's and any proposed licence holder's name and full contact details including email, phone and/or fax;
- what part of the Housing Act 2004 the application is being made i.e. Part 2 (mandatory) or Part 3 (additional) licensing; and
- the address of the HMO property, the name and address of the local authority to which the application will be made and when it will be submitted.

11.3.2 Considerations for the granting of a licence

In deciding whether or not to grant an HMO licence the local authority will consider the following matters:-

1. suitability of the property for the maximum number of occupants;
2. appropriate person available to be the licence holder;
3. whether the proposed licence holder is a fit and proper person;
4. whether the proposed manager is either the person having control of the house or such a person's agent/employee and whether they are a fit and proper person;
5. suitability of the licence holder and manager (if they are separate persons); and
6. that the management arrangements are satisfactory.

11.3.3 Prescribed property standards for an HMO licence

In order for a property to obtain an HMO licence it will need to meet the following standards:-

- the rooms/bedsits, bathroom and kitchen must have adequate heating and ventilation;
- if being shared there must be at least one bathroom (bath/shower & toilet) for up to four sharers;
- a separate toilet with sink for every five sharers in addition to the bathroom;
- if there are five or more occupiers every room/bedsit must contain a wash basin unless it has a sink;
- all wash basins, sinks, shower and bath must have a constant supply of cold and hot water;
- all bathrooms and toilets must be suitably located, be fit for purpose and of adequate size and layout;
- if all or some of the rooms/bedsits do not have kitchen facilities there must be a suitably located and adequate sized, layout and equipped kitchen to store, prepare and cook food;
- if the rooms/bedsits contain the only cooking facilities these facilities should be adequate in terms of appliances, equipment, worktop area, water supply, storage cupboard and refrigeration;
- if there is no adequate shared washing facilities for a room/bedsit a suitable enclosed and laid out toilet and bath/shower must be available for the exclusive use of the occupiers within the living accommodation or in close proximity; and
- the HMO must have adequate fire precaution facilities.

11.3.4 Fit and proper person test

One of the tests that a local authority will employ in determining whether or not to grant an HMO licence to a proposed licence holder or manager is whether they are a fit and proper person. In determining this, a local authority will look at the following factors:-

- offences involving fraud, dishonesty, violence, drugs and sexual offences;
- practice of unlawful discrimination in the carrying or connection of any business;
- breaches of any housing or landlord and tenant law, or actions contrary to codes of practice applied by the local authority for the management of HMOs; and
- association with anyone whose is involved with the above matters and the local authority considers the association relevant to the test of a fit and proper person.

The local authority will assume that the person having control of the HMO is the person to be the licence holder unless the contrary is shown. This may mean that the manager of an HMO (if the manger is not the landlord) is more appropriate to be considered as the licence holder than the landlord.

11.3.5 Management arrangements

The local authority will also consider the management arrangements for the property. In doing so the following factors will be considered:-
- whether the persons involved in management are competent for the job;
- whether other persons involved in management (other than the manager) are fit and proper;
- whether the management structure and funding arrangements are suitable.

11.3.6 Licence conditions

If a local authority decides to grant a licence, the licence can impose conditions relating to the following matters:-
- the management, use and occupation of the HMO;
- the contents and condition of the HMO;
- the conduct of the occupants and their guests;
- the prescribed standards;
- training for manager; and
- gas, electrical appliances, fire and furniture safety.

11.4 Written terms of the tenancy

A licence conditions may not change the terms of the tenancy or licence under which the HMO is occupied (although a change can come about as a result of the licence conditions) neither may it bind someone other than the licence holder unless that person consents.

The fact that a licence may impose conditions covering something that is enforceable under the HHSRS procedure does not stop that procedure being used subsequently.

11.5 Variation of licences

A local authority can vary a licence if the licence-holder agrees or if there has been a change of circumstances since the original licence was granted. A change of circumstances can include the discovery of new information.

If the variation relates to the maximum number of households/persons or the standards applicable for the number of households/persons the authority must apply the same standards that were applicable at the time the licence was granted unless these have been changed by regulations.

11.6 Revocation of licences

A local authority may revoke a licence with the agreement of the licence holder or on matters concerning the licence holder, the HMO or the regulations.

If the revocation relates to the maximum number of households/persons or the standards applicable for the number of households/persons the authority must apply the same standards that were applicable at the time the licence was granted unless it relates to regulations that have changed.

11.7 Procedure for the grant, refusal, variation or revocation of a licence

Before granting, refusing to grant, varying or revoking or refusing to vary or revoke a licence the local authority must serve a notice (with a copy of the proposed licence where a grant is being considered) on the applicant and all relevant persons (i.e. persons mentioned in paragraph 11.3.1). Those served will be given 14 days to respond to the notice. If following responses the local authority decides to grant a modified licence to that originally proposed the local authority must serve a notice on the applicant and relevant persons and give seven days for a response. The notice must set out the proposed modifications.

If the local authority decides to grant, refuse to grant, vary, refuse to vary, revoke or refuse to revoke a licence it must serve a notice setting out the reason(s) (with a copy of the licence if a decision has been made to grant it), how to appeal and the period to do so on the applicant, (proposed or actual) licence holder and relevant persons.

The applicant or any relevant person may appeal within 28 days of the date of the decision to the Residential Property Tribunal. Appeals can be made out of the time limit if there is good reason to do so.

An appeal normally considers the matters that existed at the time the decision was made (re-hearing) but may consider matters that the authority did not know about. The Tribunal may confirm, reverse or vary the decision being appealed.

11.8 Occupation of an HMO

The occupants of an HMO are usually assured shorthold tenants of the room they have exclusive possession of, together with the right to the share the common areas and facilities in the terms set out for occupation of the HMO. As such all the rules relating to ASTs apply to the tenants of an HMO. Alternatively, the occupants of an HMO may be licensees. This is where the occupant does not have exclusive possession and use of a room and may have to share its use and/or allow unrestricted access. The rules relating to licences will therefore apply.

11.9 Future of HMO

Recent changes in housing benefit (HB) regulations means that there will be a growing demand for HMO accommodation.

From January 2012 generally, a single person between the ages of 25 and 35 years old will no longer be entitled to HB to cover the costs of renting a one bedroom self-contained property. Their HB entitlement will be reduced to a room in a shared house rate.

Single persons affected by this change in the HB regulations will need to rent a room in a shared property and give up their one bedroom self-contained property. This will increase the demand for HMOs by single persons in receipt of HB. Single persons who are in receipt of HB and rent a room in an HMO who would leave at the age of 25 years old will now have to remain in similar accommodation for another 10 years therefore reducing the supply. Prior to this change only single people under the age of 25 were subject to the room in a shared property rate.

11.10 Additional licensing

A local authority may decide that its entire district or a particular area of its district should be subject to additional licensing for a particular description of HMOs. Before an order for additional licensing is made the local authority must consider that the description of HMOs in the order are being managed inadequately leading to problems for the occupants or members of the public. These problems are usually anti-social behaviour. The local authority must consider other courses of action along with additional licensing.

Additional licensing will not come into force unless it is confirmed or already generally approved by the local authority.

Once additional licensing has been confirmed or approved the local authority must publish it stating whether it was confirmed or approved, the date it comes into force and any other relevant information.

Additional licensing applies for a maximum period of five years. The licensing should be regularly reviewed and a consequence of such review may be revocation. The procedures for the application, grant, variation and revocation of additional licensing or refusal of any of the above are the same as set out in paragraph 11.3 for a mandatory licence.

11.11 Selective licensing

For an area to be subject to selective licensing it must meet one of the criteria mentioned below:-

- it is or is likely to become an area of low housing demand; or
- the area suffers from significant anti-social behaviour and private sector landlords are failing to take the action they should to deal with the problem arising from their tenancies.

In both cases the local authority is of the view that selective licensing measures amongst other actions will lead to resolving the problem.

11.11.1 Designating an area to be subject to selective licensing

Before designating an area the local authority will need to consult persons likely to be affected and consider their representations. Local authorities must consider if there are other options to selective licensing to achieve their housing objectives and whether selective licensing amongst other measures will achieve it.

After a designation of selective licensing has been made the local authority must publish a notice setting out the date the designation was made, how it was made, when it takes effect and any other relevant matters. A designation has a maximum duration of five years and the notice will set out the duration.

All the rented properties in the designated area will need to be licensed. The exceptions to this is an HMO being licensed under the relevant provisions, or an HMO for which there is an exemption notice in place, or a property subject to a management order.

11.11.2 Exemption notice from selective licensing

A landlord or person having control of a property which has become subject to selective licensing may notify the local authority of their intention to ensure that the property is exempt from licensing and request a temporary exemption notice.

The authority will decide the application and, if granted, the property will be exempt from licensing for a period of three months while the landlord or person having control take steps to ensure it is exempt from licensing. In exceptional circumstances a further three months exemption notice can be granted.

If the local authority refuses to serve a temporary exemption notice the applicant must be informed of the decision, the date, the reasons, the right to appeal and the period in which to appeal. An appeal may be made to the Residential Property Tribunal within 28 days of the date of the notice. The appeal is by a re-hearing but may consider matters of which the local authority was not aware. The Tribunal may confirm or reverse the decision.

11.11.3 Application for a selective licence

An application for a licence is made to the local authority for the area that has been designated and a fee may be payable. Newham Council's fees as at 28 January 2013 are:-

- Discounted fee (for a limited period) £150;
- Full fee £500;
- Renewal fee £500.

The application process is similar to that of mandatory licensing of an HMO. The local authority may require that particular persons are given information about the application and specify the information/documentation to accompany an application. The local authority may grant a licence to the applicant or another person if they and the applicant agree. The local authority must be satisfied that the proposed licence holder is a fit and proper person and the most appropriate to be the licence holder and the proposed manager is a person having control of the house or an agent or employee of such a person. The proposed manager must be a fit and proper person and the proposed management arrangements must be satisfactory.

In determining who is a fit and proper person the local authority will consider whether the person has committed offences involving fraud, dishonesty, violence, drugs or a sexual offence. The authority will also consider whether the person has practised unlawful discrimination in connection with a business or breached housing, landlord or tenant law. The authority will consider whether the applicant has associated with anyone who fails the requirements above and whether that association is relevant to whether the person is fit and proper.

The local authority will consider whether the management arrangements for the house are satisfactory. In doing so, the local authority will assume that the person having control of the house is the most appropriate person to be a licence holder and give consideration to whether the persons involved in the management of the house has sufficient competence for the role, whether they are a fit and proper person and whether the management and funding arrangements are satisfactory.

11.11.4 The licence

A licence is intended to ensure a minimum standard. A licence will be for a maximum of five years and may contain requirements with regard to:-

- the management, use and occupation of the house;
- the contents and condition of the house;
- the conduct of the occupants and their guests;
- the prescribed standards;
- training for manager;
- gas, electrical appliances, smoke alarm, fire and furniture safety; and
- referencing for potential occupiers.

11.11.5 Written terms of the tenancy

A licence should not seek to impose on or alter the terms and conditions under which someone occupies the house. The licence is personal to the licence holder and cannot be transferred. If the licence holder dies the licence comes to an end.

11.11.6 Variation of licences

A local authority can vary a licence off its own initiative or by an application by the licence holder or relevant person. The variation may happen if there has been a change of circumstances since the licence was granted or if new information has been discovered. Variation may be by agreement or by the notice procedure. If variation is through agreement it is effective at the time it is made. If not with agreement the variation is effective at the time when an appeal that can be made about the decision has expired (28 days).

11.11.7 Revocation of licence

A local authority may revoke a licence with the agreement of the licence holder or on its own initiative as a result of circumstances relating to the licence holder or the property. This may include:-

- serious or repeated breaches of the licence;
- a licence holder or manager no longer being a fit and proper person; or
- the person involved in management no longer being competent to do so.

In relation to the house, a licence may be revoked because:-

- the house is no longer subject to licensing;
- licence has been granted as an HMO; or
- if the structure of the property would lead to the authority not granting a licence on similar terms if it was applied for at the time of the revocation.

If the licence was revoked with agreement it is effective at the time of the revocation, if not, the revocation is effective at the time when the period in which to appeal has expired without an appeal (28 days).

11.11.8 Procedural requirements and appeals against licence decisions

Before granting a licence the local housing authority must serve a notice and copy of the proposed licence on the applicant and relevant persons and consider any representations made. The notice must set out the reason for granting the licence, the main terms and the consultation period. If as a result of representations the local authority proposes to grant a modified licence it must issue a similar notice as was followed with the originally proposed licence. The notice must set out proposed modifications, the reason(s) for them and the consultation period.

If the local authority decides to refuse to grant a licence it must serve a notice to that effect on the applicant and any relevant person and consider any representations. The notice must set out the reason(s) for the refusal and the consultation period.

On granting the licence, the local authority must provide the applicant and any relevant person with a copy of the licence and a notice setting out the reason for the grant, the date, the right of appeal and period in which to appeal. This must be done within seven days of the decision.

If the local authority refuses to grant a licence it must serve on the applicant and relevant persons a notice setting out the decision, the reason, the right of appeal and the period in which to do so. This notice must be served within seven days of the decision.

11.11.9 Procedure relating to variation or revocation of licences

Before varying, refusing to vary, revoking or refusing to revoke a licence the local authority must serve a notice on the licence holder and any relevant person and consider representations made. The notice must set out the effect and reason for the variation, revocation or refusal to do either, as well as the consultation period.

If following the consultation period the local authority proceeds to vary, revoke, refuse to vary or refuse to revoke the licence they must serve the licence holder and any relevant person with a notice containing the decision, reason, date, right of appeal and period to appeal within seven days of the decision.

11.11.9.1 Appeals against licence decisions

The applicant or any relevant person may appeal to a Residential Property Tribunal against a decision to refuse or grant a licence or the terms of the licence. A licence holder or relevant person may appeal against a decision to vary or revoke or to refuse to vary or refuse to revoke a licence.

The time limit to appeal is 28 days from the date the decision was made. An appeal may be made out of time if there is good reason for missing the deadline.

An appeal is a re-hearing of the original decision but may consider matters of which the local authority was unaware. The decision being appealed may be confirmed, reversed or varied. The tribunal may direct the local authority to grant a licence and dictate the terms of the licence.

11.12 Sanctions in relation to licensing of houses

An offence is committed in the following situations:-
* a person having control of or managing a house which is required to be licensed, but it is not licensed; or
* a person subject to a licence fails to comply with any condition of the licence.

A person who fails to have a licence is liable to a fine not exceeding £20,000 and a person who fails to comply with a condition of the licence is liable to a fine.

A local authority or an occupier may make an application to the Residential Property Tribunal for a rent repayment order where a property is not licensed. This order only applies to occupiers whose rent is paid with the assistance of HB.

A Section 13 Notice to increase the rent cannot be served in relation to a house which should be but is not licensed.

11.13 Interim and final management orders

Interim and final management orders can be made in respect of an HMO or a house subject to selective licensing.

An interim management order has a maximum duration of 12 months. It allows a local authority to take immediate steps to protect the health, safety or welfare of persons occupying the house and/or owning or occupying nearby premises. It allows other steps to be taken with regard to the proper management of the house pending a licence being granted, the order being revoked or a final management order.

A final management order is an order with a maximum duration of five years which is aimed to secure the proper management of the house via a management scheme.

11.13.1 Interim management orders

A local authority *must* make an interim management order in the following circumstances:-

- the property is an unlicensed HMO or house subject to selective licensing; and
  - (a) it is unlikely to be licensed in the near future; or
  - (b) the health and safety condition is satisfied;
- the property is a licensed HMO or house subject to selective licensing and the licence has been revoked but the revocation is not yet in force; and
  - (a) when the revocation is effective it is unlikely that the house will be licensed in the near future; or
  - (b) when revocation comes into force the health and safety condition will be satisfied.

A local authority *may* make an interim management order where:-
- it is an HMO that is not required to be licensed; and
- on an application to the Residential Property Tribunal the local authority is authorized to make an such an order (despite any pending appeal); and
- the tribunal considers that the health and safety condition is satisfied; and
- has had regard to previous compliance or non-compliance with HMO regulations.
- Or, it is a house to which special management order applies, and on an application to the Residential Property Tribunal the local authority is authorized to make such an order (despite any pending appeal).

The health and safety condition is:-
- an order is necessary to protect the health, safety or welfare of occupants in the house or occupants or person having an estate in premises near to the house; and
- the health and safety condition will not be satisfied if the matter could suitably be resolved under the HHSRS hazard process.

11.13.1.1 Local housing authority's duties once interim management order is in force
Once the order comes into the force the local authority must:
- take immediate action necessary to protect the health, safety or welfare of direct or nearby occupants of premises or those with an estate in nearby premises;
- ensure the house is insured against destruction or damage; and
- take steps considered appropriate for the management of the house;
  In due course the local authority will need to consider:
- for an unlicensed house grant a licence or make a final management order; or revoke the interim management order and take no further action.

When an interim management order is in force the authority has the right to:-
- possession subject to preserved occupants;
- do whatever a person having an estate or interest could do in relation to the house;

- create a leasehold or licence to occupy part of the house if written consent is given by the person who but for the order would have that right; and
- register the interim management order as a local land charge.

The immediate landlord is not entitled to receive any rents and cannot exercise management powers or create any interest in the property. The local authority may:

- use the rent to meet relevant expenditure and pay remainder to the landlord(s); as well as
- keep and allow inspection of full accounts of income and expenditure in relation to the house.

11.13.1.2 *Variation of interim management orders*

The local authority may decide to vary an interim management order on its own initiative or on the application of a relevant person. The order may be varied if the local authority considers it appropriate to do so. Any variation will take effect after the time limit for making an appeal has expired without an appeal being made.

11.13.1.3 *Revocation of interim management orders*

A local authority may on its own initiative or on the application of a relevant person revoke an interim management order. A revocation may take place under the following circumstances:-

- the property is no longer an HMO or a house subject to selective licensing;
- a licence has been granted by the local authority and will come into force upon the revocation;
- a final management order is to replace the interim management order; or
- it is appropriate to revoke the order.

A revocation does not take effect until the time in which to appeal has expired without an appeal being made.

11.13.2 Final management orders

Where an interim management order is in effect a local authority has a **DUTY** to make a final management order if the interim management order expires and on that day the house is required to be licensed but the authority is unable to grant a licence.

Where an interim management order is in effect a local authority has a **POWER** to make a final management order if the interim management order has expired and although the house is not required to be licensed the authority requires the final management order to protect the health, safety and welfare of occupants or neighbouring occupants and owners on a long term basis.

A final management order comes into effect on the expiration of the period to appeal such an order without an appeal being lodged (28 days) or on the decision of an appeal on the matter. The order has a duration of five years, unless it stipulates that it will end before that date.

Once a final management order is in force the local authority must:-
- properly manage the house in accordance with the management scheme;
- review the operation of the order and management scheme periodically;
- if appropriate vary or revoke the current order;
- if appropriate grant an HMO or selective licensing order; and
- ensure suitable insurance protection is maintained.

While a final management order is in force the local authority:-
- has the right to possession subject to the rights of preserved existing occupiers;
- has the right to do anything which a person having an estate or interest in the house would be able to do;
- may create a lease or licence. However, it cannot have a fixed term expiring after the order ceases to have effect or is terminable by a notice to quit or a notice of more than four weeks duration unless consent is received from the landlord. This does not apply to ASTs created when there is more than six months for the final management order to expire;
- can act in the landlord's capacity of a lessee;
- can register the final management order as a local land charge;
- is entitled to rent payments;
- will exclusively apply management powers in respect of the property; and
- does not prevent anyone disposing of their interest in the property.

A final management order must contain a management scheme, i.e. a scheme setting out how the local authority is to manage the property. The scheme will cover matters such as work and expenditure to be done on the house to distribution of rent proceeds.

The authority must keep full accounts of income and expenditure and afford inspection of them.

A local authority may vary a final management order, either of its own volition or on the application of a relevant person. A local authority may revoke a final management order if:-
- the house cease to be required to be licensed as an HMO or selective licensing property; or
- a licence has been granted in respect of the above;
- a further final management order has been made which will replace the existing order; or
- in any other appropriate circumstance.

Revocation will come into force when the time period for making an appeal has expired without one being made.

11.13.2.1 Requirements before making final management order

When a local authority seeks to make a management order it must:-

- serve a copy of the proposed order with a notice on each relevant person;
- state in the notice that a final management order is proposed, the reason, the main terms (including management scheme) and the consultation period; and
- consider representations made to the notice.

If following representations the order is to be made but with modifications the local authority must serve a notice on each relevant person about the proposed modifications, the reasons, the consultation period and consider any representations. This process is not required if the modifications are not deemed material.

After the order is made the local authority must serve a copy of the order and a notice stating the reasons for the order, the date it is made, the effect and end date on all occupiers of the property and each relevant person. On final management orders the local authority must set out how the house is to be managed.

The relevant persons will also be informed about the right to appeal and the period in which to bring an appeal. This notice must be served within seven days of it being made.

11.13.2.2 Variation and revocation of management orders

In order to vary an interim or final management order the local authority must serve a notice stating that a variation is being proposed, the effect, the reasons and period of consultation on each relevant person and consider the representations made.

If following the above process the local authority proceeds with the variation they must serve a copy of their decision and a notice setting out the reasons, the date, the right of appeal and period of appeal on all relevant persons within seven days of the decision being made. None of this is required if the variation is not considered material.

If the local authority decides to refuse to vary an interim or final management order the authority must serve a notice stating that a refusal is proposed, the reason and the period of consultation. The notice must be served on all relevant persons and representations considered.

If the local authority decides to proceed with its refusal the authority must serve a notice setting out the decision, the reasons, the right of appeal and period to appeal, within seven days of the decision being made.

If the local authority seeks to revoke a management order the authority must serve a notice setting out the reasons and the period of consultation on all relevant persons and consider representations received.

If the local authority then decides to go ahead with the revocation it should serve a notice setting out the decision, the date, reasons, right of appeal and period to appeal on all relevant persons within seven days of the decision being made.

If the authority refuses to revoke an order it should follow the same procedure set out for revoking the order.

11.13.2.3 *Right to appeal against making of order etc.*

A relevant person can appeal to a Residential Property Tribunal against the authority's decision to:

- make or refuse to make an interim or final management order;
- the terms of the order or management scheme;
- a decision to vary or revoke; or
- refusal to vary or revoke an interim or final management order.

If no appeal is made the order becomes final on the points that could have been appealed. An appeal should be made within 28 days but can be accepted later with good reason for the delay.

An appeal to the Residential Property Tribunal is by a re-hearing although information can be considered of which the local authority was unaware. The decision being appealed can be confirmed, varied or revoked.

12 JOINT TENANTS

A joint AST is a common tenancy in today's rental market. With rental prices at a high, many young working professionals will rent a property with their peers as joint tenants to share rent and expenses therefore making their arrangement affordable. The same format is employed by students and low paid workers.

For a joint AST to exist the following must occur:-

- all the tenants must get joint possession of the entire property under the one agreement;
- as far as the landlord is concerned the property is rented as a single unit to all of the tenants. The landlord has not allocated rooms or determined the living arrangements of or apportioned the rent due amongst individual tenants;
- the interest of each joint tenant must be the same (i.e. they have equal use of the entire property), granted at the same time (the tenancy began at the same time) and be for the same duration (they have the same fixed or periodic term); and
- the tenants must all sign the same written agreement (if there is one) or conclude the same verbal agreement or act jointly by conduct to create a joint tenancy.

A joint tenancy will *not* exist where:-

- separate agreements are signed;
- separate tenancies are created;
- tenancies start at different times;
- different parts of the property are rented to different people; or
- the tenants are charged different rents.

The characteristics of a joint tenancy are set out below.

12.1 Maximum number of tenants

The maximum number of joint tenants permitted to hold a legal interest in a property is four. If more than four persons are noted on a tenancy agreement as tenants only the first four names will be joint tenants. The remaining persons noted as tenants will have a beneficial interest in the property.

12.2 Liability

The nature of a joint tenancy is that all the tenants as a group, and each tenant as an individual, are responsible for the performance of all the tenants' obligations under the tenancy. A landlord can choose to take court action against one, more than one or all joint tenants for breach of the tenancy regardless of which individual tenant was at fault. A landlord can take court action against one or any number of joint tenants for all the rent arrears regardless of how the tenants may have divided the rent amongst themselves.

12.3 Succession

Joint tenants have a single tenancy amongst them. When one joint tenant dies the single tenancy continues with the remaining joint tenants. As each joint tenant already has the right to occupy the entire property that right is not diminished when one of them becomes deceased (this is known as the right of survivorship). The deceased tenant's interest does not pass under their will or under the rules of intestacy.

12.4 Surrender/abandon

One joint tenant cannot surrender a tenancy. As the joint tenants own a property interest that cannot be divided they cannot give up a share of it. All joint tenants will need to act together to surrender a tenancy.

Likewise, one joint tenant cannot abandon a property. There is no separate share of the property interest that a joint tenant can leave behind for the landlord to resume and rent to someone else. All joint tenants will need to abandon the property simultaneously.

If a joint tenant seeks to surrender or abandon the property without the other joint tenants doing the same act, the tenancy will continue and the joint tenant who has left will remain contractually liable to the landlord as long as the tenancy exists. This is the case even if they have rented another property.

12.5 Service of notice

A landlord is required to serve a notice on each and every joint tenant for the notice to be valid. This does not mean that there should be separate notices but that the details of all the joint tenants must be on any notice. A landlord cannot seek to serve a notice on one of the joint tenant's interest in the property and leave the remaining joint tenants' interest untouched. The interest is not separated amongst them. For notice to be effective all tenants' names should be included on the notice and it must be served on all of them.

If one joint tenant serves a Notice to Quit individually without including the other joint tenants in the act, that notice, if valid, will bring the tenancy for all joint tenants to an end when it expires. There is no share of the tenancy that the individual joint tenant can separately terminate. The landlord can thereafter recover possession by simply proving to the court that one of the joint tenants has ended the contractual tenancy by the notice and the landlord is therefore entitled to possession.

A notice exercising a break clause needs to be served by all the joint tenants to be valid.

12.6 Guarantor(s) of a joint tenant

If one of the joint tenants has a guarantor under the tenancy agreement, the guarantor will be liable for all of the obligations and breaches under the tenancy by one or all of the joint tenants as this is the extent of the individual tenant's liability for whom they are being a guarantor.

A landlord can take court action against the guarantor for a breach of any of the joint tenants' obligation under the tenancy, even if they purport to be the guarantor of an individual joint tenant. However, a guarantor of a joint tenant may contractually limit the extent to which they may become liable to a specific sum.

12.7 Replacing a joint tenant

A common issue that arises with joint tenancies is where a joint tenant leaves and another person purports to take their place in the property. This will usually be with the agreement of all the joint tenants and sometimes the landlord.

12.7.1 The position if it is a fixed term tenancy

The first point to note is that there is an existing tenancy amongst the joint tenants that needs to be formally brought to an end for a joint tenant to leave. If a joint tenant simply leaves they will remain jointly and individually responsible for any breaches of the tenancy until it is formally brought to an end.

If it is a fixed term tenancy with a break clause that can now be exercised, all the joint tenants must exercise the clause together. Doing so will bring the fixed term to an end. However, as not all the joint tenants are vacating the property a periodic tenancy will come into being. This periodic tenancy will need to be terminated by a joint tenant(s) serving on the landlord a Notice to Quit. When the Notice to Quit expires a joint tenant can leave the tenancy. They will be liable for any rent and breach(es) of the tenancy up to that date.

The joint tenants remaining in the property can find a replacement tenant and come to a new arrangement with the landlord. If no new arrangement is made with the landlord, the remaining joint tenants and any new replacement tenant are trespassers. However, if the landlord wishes to evict them, the landlord will need to get a possession order and a bailiffs' warrant. This will be a simpler possession order to obtain as set out in paragraph 5.3.

If there is no break clause a joint tenant will be unable to end the tenancy and will remain liable under its terms until it has ended by the expiration of the fixed term. The only way to terminate it during the fixed term will be to surrender the tenancy to the landlord. All joint tenants will need to act together in the surrender and the landlord can choose whether or not to accept it. If a surrender is accepted a new tenancy can then be made with any joint tenants that wish to remain in the property along with any replacement for the leaving joint tenant.

12.7.2 The position if it is a periodic tenancy

Likewise with a fixed term tenancy, there is an existing tenancy that needs to be formally brought to an end. This process is easier as the tenancy is periodic. The joint tenant wishing to leave does not need to act with the other joint tenants.

The joint tenant wishing to leave can individually serve a Notice to Quit on the landlord. When the Notice to Quit expires the tenancy comes to an end and they can leave. Any joint tenants remaining in the property are trespassers. However, a landlord who wishes to secure vacant possession of the property will need to get a possession order and a bailiffs' warrant.

If the landlord wishes to continue occupation of the property with the remaining joint tenants and the replacement joint tenant they can agree a new tenancy. A new tenancy can be inferred if the landlord collects rent from the existing and replacement tenant and otherwise act as if a tenancy exists.

12.8 Serving Section 8, Section 21, Notice to activate a break clause and Notice to Quit on joint tenants

A landlord should always comply with any terms in the tenancy agreement about how, when and where notices should be served.

In completing any of the notices mentioned above a landlord should include the name of each and all joint tenants. Any documents prepared for court proceedings, such as claim form and particulars of claim, should have the names of each and all joint tenants. Apart from that the notices and documents are completed in the same way detailed in other parts of this book for sole tenants.

13 TENANT ABANDONS PROPERTY

When a tenant abandons a property it can lead to several problems for the landlord including: -

- loss of rent;
- previous rent no longer attainable in the market;
- possible invalidation of insurance cover as property is empty; or
- lengthy void period due to uncertainty.

The questions a landlord is faced with include:-

- Should and when can they re-enter the property and take possession?
- What should they do with possessions a tenant has left behind?
- What should they do about occupants a tenant has left in the property?

Before taking any action a landlord has got to be absolutely certain and beyond any doubt that a tenant has abandoned the property. If a landlord acts too hastily (and a tenant who they thought had abandoned the property returns) they could face one or all of the following actions listed below: -

- trespass for entering the property;
- breach of the covenant of quiet enjoyment;
- be liable for the tort of interference with goods (if they interfered with the tenant's possessions);
- be subject to an action for unlawful eviction (civil and criminal penalties).

It used to be the perceived wisdom that a landlord was under a duty to mitigate their loss if a tenant abandons the property. In doing so a landlord was expected to take reasonable steps to re-let the property at a reasonable rent. This meant that the tenant's liability to the landlord became limited.

However, in a recent case the court held that a landlord could elect not to seek to repossess the property but instead sue the tenant for rent arrears. This may be especially so if the landlord could not have achieved the same contractual rent because the market rent had declined. However, a landlord will need to take an objective view as to whether the tenant would be able to pay the outstanding rent if they were successful in obtaining a money judgment. There are also the problems and costs of locating the tenant.

A landlord may need to notify their insurance company of the non-occupation of the property so as not to invalidate their insurance cover. It is possible that a property in a state of abandonment is more likely to be subject to burglary and vandalism.

A landlord should be absolutely sure that a tenant has abandoned the property. Some investigative work should be undertaken. If a landlord has obtained the information from the tenant that is recommended in Chapter 2 of this book the following action can be taken:-

- seek to contact the tenant by phone, text, letter and email;
- write to the tenant at the address of the property asking them to make contact;
- if the tenant is working, make enquiries at their work place or with their employer;
- if the landlord has details of a friend, family or next of kin of the tenant they should be contacted;
- any guarantor should be contacted immediately and notified of the circumstances (it would be in a guarantor's interest to get the tenant to contact the landlord);
- if the tenant is or was in receipt of housing benefit, enquiries can be made with the Housing Benefit Office to see if they are in receipt of housing benefit at another address or for the landlord's property;
- if the tenant has children that attend a local school, enquiries can be made at the school, or the landlord can visit the school at opening or closing time to find the tenant;
- enquiries can be made of the neighbours who may have seen the tenant moving or not as the case may be;
- a tracing agent can be instructed to search for the tenant (this will be at a cost); and/or
- look the tenant up on Facebook, Twitter or other social network sites.

The results of the above enquiries, as well as checking the property as set out below, over a period of time may confirm to a landlord whether or not a tenant has abandoned the property.

If the tenancy agreement allows a landlord to give notice and enter the property for the purposes of an inspection a landlord should give notice in accordance with term of the tenancy (such as notice in writing, giving a period of 48 hours' notice and only entering the property in a specified time frame).

Should a landlord choose to enter the property they should give the required notice, serve it correctly and leave contact details with the notice. If no contact is received from the tenant the landlord should proceed to inspect the property at the time set out in the notice.

The landlord should take a witness (where possible) and a camera to the property. They should seek to enter the property with the keys they should have retained. If the landlord does not have keys to enter the property they should consider contacting a locksmith beforehand. The landlord should also have two letters prepared for the tenant; one letter for the event that they entered the property and the tenant was not there, and the other for the event that they had to break into the property and the locks were changed. The letter should state that after seeking contact with the tenant over a period of time and by a number of methods, in accordance with the tenancy agreement an inspection was carried out by the landlord and a witness and that the tenant is to contact the landlord immediately with the contact number, email and address left for the tenant.

If the landlord had to change the locks the letter should state that access was only possible by changing the locks and a new set of keys can be obtained by contacting the landlord at any time on the details enclosed or any other arrangements put in place to provide the tenant with the new keys (such as it has been left with a neighbour).

If the landlord entered the property using their own key to the property, the letter should be left in a prominent place in the property. If the property was entered via a change of locks this letter should be attached to the front entry door as the tenant will not be able to go into the property and locate the letter if left inside.

On entering the property the landlord should take relevant pictures and note the following matters:-

- build-up of mail at the front door. If there is no build-up of mail have they been re-directed by the post office or is someone collecting them (mail should not be opened but be examined to note the date of the earliest post. This may indicate when the tenant last lived in the property);
- credit or debt on pre-pay electric and/or gas meter (if applicable);
- condition of or lack of food in the fridge, and the expiry date of packaged foods;
- property being empty (no tenant's furniture, fixtures and/or possessions);
- possessions been left behind and whether they are valuable;
- personal or sentimental items being removed (such as pictures);
- property damage (vandalism, uninhabitable, deliberate);
- pets no longer there;
- bathroom and kitchen been used or unused;
- keys left in the property;
- note or letter left to the landlord by the tenant;
- central heating not being used in the winter;
- sign or no sign of children living in the property; and
- any other relevant matters.

If the weather is cold the landlord should set the central heating to come on daily so as prevent frozen pipes from causing a flood.

If a landlord cannot be absolutely certain from their inspection and investigations that the tenant has abandoned the property, the landlord should not take any steps to resume physical possession of the property, but conduct further inspections and investigations in a timely manner until that certainty is achieved.

On further inspections a landlord can observe whether anything in the property has been interfered with since the last inspection, whether the letter left there has been moved, opened or otherwise interfered with, whether there is any fresh sign of someone living in the property, whether the pre-pay gas and/or electric reading has changed significantly, whether post has been moved, shopping done or any other relevant event. A landlord should be very careful NOT to assume abandonment in the school holiday periods as a tenant may have gone away for the holidays. It would be prudent for a landlord to wait until school resumes and see if the tenant returns.

If a landlord had to change the locks they should visit the property regularly if they have not heard from the tenant. The landlord should bring a further letter with them to be left outside the property for the tenant's attention. This letter should again explain that the locks had to be changed, the landlord has been seeking contact with the tenant and the landlord's contact details left for the tenant. On visiting the property the landlord should check if the original letter has been removed, and bear in mind that it could have been removed by someone other than the tenant, so it will be prudent to leave the second letter attached to the property. A landlord should check to see if the locks have been changed and whether entry has been gained to the property. If there is no change a landlord is best advised to continue their enquiries to contact the tenant as well as wait to see if contact is made as a result of the letter until some certainty as to whether or not the tenant abandoned the property is achieved.

If a landlord has doubts about whether or not the tenant has abandoned the property a landlord should recover possession through the courts rather than risk an action for unlawful eviction. For full details of this process see Chapter 21. Should a landlord have to go through the possession procedure, then the earlier it is started the better.

As a backup plan, a landlord should serve the relevant Notice Seeking Possession or Notice to Quit on the tenant at the very first visit to the property, when enquiries are being made about the tenant's whereabouts.

Whether and what notice can be served in respect of the tenancy will depend on whether it is in the fixed term or periodic. If the AST is in the fixed term a landlord will have to wait until a relevant ground for possession can be satisfied, such as rent arrears, to recover possession. If it is periodic a Section 21 Notice can be used. For full details of the processes see Chapter 21.

If it is a company let, a landlord should make company related checks to try to locate the tenant. If unsuccessful, a landlord will need to seek to recover possession during the fixed term via forfeiture whether based on non-occupation or rent arrears. If the tenancy is periodic a Notice to Quit can be served. The same will apply to non-excluded tenancies (see Chapter 5). After the Notice to Quit, served on a company let, has expired the contractual tenancy comes to an end and very limited statutory protection arises. As there is no one in occupation a landlord can walk in and take physical possession.

If it is clear that the tenant has abandoned the property the landlord should resume possession of the property and re-let the property to secure their rental income.

13.1 What should the landlord do about possessions left behind?

If there is a term in the tenancy agreement that allows a landlord to dispose of a tenant's possessions left in the property after the tenancy has ended, a landlord should follow that term precisely in dealing with those possessions. By signing a tenancy agreement a tenant has consented to the landlord dealing with the possessions left behind in accordance with the term.

If there is no term in the tenancy agreement dealing with possessions left in the rental property after the tenancy has ended, a landlord can follow the procedure in the Torts (Interference with Goods) Act 1977.

There are two main procedures that can be followed:-
1. where the landlord is able to trace and/or communicate with the tenant; and
2. where the landlord is able or unable to trace and/or communicate with the tenant.

13.1.1 Where the landlord is able to trace and/or communicate with the tenant

13.1.1.1 Impose an obligation on the tenant to collect or take delivery of their possessions

If a landlord is able to communicate with and/or trace a tenant, the landlord can impose an obligation on the tenant to collect or take delivery of their possessions. To do so a landlord will need to give the tenant a notice. The requirements of the notice are that it:-
*   is in writing;
*   is delivered to the tenant, left at or sent by post to their last known address;
*   has the name and address of the landlord;
*   gives details of the possessions and the address where they are kept; and
*   states that the possessions are ready to be delivered to and or collected by the tenant.

At the time of serving the notice placing an obligation on the tenant to collect or take delivery of their possessions, a landlord can serve a Notice of Intention to Sell the possessions. Should a landlord choose to do so it will save time, rather than serving this notice at a later date. Serving a Notice of Intention to Sell can be done at the same time only if the notice placing an obligation on the tenant to collect their possessions is being sent by post in a registered letter, or by the recorded delivery service.

13.1.1.2   *Notice of intention to sell*

A landlord serving a notice of intention to sell will need to fulfil the following requirements. The notice must:-

- be in writing and sent by registered or recorded delivery;
- state the name and address of the landlord;
- give details of the possessions and the address where they are kept;
- give a date on or after which the landlord proposes to sell the possessions; and
- allow a reasonable period of time between serving the notice and the date on or after which the possessions will be sold so as to give the tenant a reasonable opportunity to collect or have them delivered.

A landlord should not seek to claim any money in respect of the possessions as this will complicate and delay the procedure, such as requiring a period of three months to pass before making a sale.

13.1.2 Where the landlord is able or unable to trace and/or communicate with the tenant

13.1.2.1   *Selling the possessions*

A landlord can sell a tenant's possessions in the following circumstances:-

- where the tenant is in breach of an obligation to collect, take delivery of their possessions or give directions for their delivery. This obligation can be imposed by giving the notice mentioned above;
- where the landlord could impose an obligation on the tenant to take delivery, by giving notice to the tenant, but is unable to trace or communicate with the tenant; or
- the landlord can reasonably no longer expect to be required to safeguard the possessions on giving notice to the tenant but is unable to trace or communicate with the tenant.

The landlord must have either:-

a) given notice to the tenant of intention to sell and the period has expired; or
b) not been able to give such notice (cannot trace or communicate with the tenant) and can demonstrate reasonable steps been made to do so and is reasonably satisfied that the tenant own the goods.

The landlord will need to be able to show that they used the best method of sale reasonably available in the circumstances and hold for the tenant the proceeds of sale less the costs of sale. A landlord should hold any proceeds of sale less the costs of sale for the tenant for up to six years. After six years a landlord has a complete defence to any action by any person in respect of the monies, due to the Statute of Limitations.

13.1.2.2   *Obtaining the court's authority to sell*
In some situations a landlord may wish to obtain the court's authority to sell the tenant's possessions left behind in the property. This could be the case where the tenant has been located and the landlord tries to serve a notice of intention to sell, by recorded post, which is returned.

If the court's authority is being sought a landlord will need to demonstrate to the court that they:-
*   are entitled to sell the possessions because an obligation to collect has been imposed and a Notice of Intention to Sell has duly expired; or
*   would have been entitled to sell the possessions if an obligation to collect had been imposed and a Notice of Intention to Sell had been served.

If the court is satisfied that the above matters have been proven it may:-
*   order the sale of the goods subject to terms and conditions;
*   order the landlord to deduct the costs of the sale and any amount due to the landlord in respect of the goods; and
*   order the net proceeds to be paid into court on behalf of the tenant.

13.2 The tenant has abandoned the property and left other persons in occupation

A landlord may find that the tenant has abandoned the property and left other people in possession. They could be:-
*   strangers;
*   friends of the tenant;
*   family members of the tenant; or
*   people to whom the tenant has sublet part or the whole of the property.

A landlord cannot change the lock on these occupants or force the occupants to leave the property. To do so can result in civil and criminal penalties against the landlord under the Protection from Eviction Act 1977. They are not squatters who the police can now arrest for being in the property. Additionally, the tenancy of the original tenant will be continuing in most cases and the landlord could face a defence to any direct proceedings against the occupants.

A landlord should note that a tenant apparently abandoning the property does not end the tenancy. The law clearly sets out how a landlord or a tenant may end a tenancy and abandonment is not one of them.

TENANT ABANDONS PROPERTY

If the tenancy is a fixed term tenancy, a landlord may not be able to do anything about a tenant abandoning the property and leaving someone in there, in the short term. A landlord can seek possession on ground 12 of Housing Act 1988 Schedule 2, i.e. any obligation of the tenancy (other than one related to the payment of rent) has been broken or not performed. However, as this is a discretionary ground for possession court proceedings may be unsuccessful. However, if the tenant has genuinely abandoned the property a defence or court appearance is unlikely.

If the tenant has abandoned the property they will not be paying any rent. A landlord can seek possession on ground 8, 10 and 11 of Housing Act 1988 Schedule 2. All three grounds cover rent arrears but ground 8 is a mandatory ground which if proven must result in an order for possession (see Chapter 21). However, ground 8 requires that there be two month's rent arrears when the notice is served and at the date of the hearing. A landlord will therefore have to wait for arrears to accumulate.

If the tenancy is periodic a landlord can simply serve a Section 21 Notice and proceed to recover possession either by the accelerated or the normal possession procedure.

All proceedings should be commenced against the original tenant and not against anyone in occupation of the property. This is because until the landlord has ended the original tenancy, the landlord has no right to possession of the property against the occupiers.

Once a landlord has obtained a possession order against the original tenant the landlord should apply for a bailiffs' warrant enforced against the current occupiers (see Chapter 21 Recovering Possession).

However, if a landlord ends a superior tenancy and there is a lawful AST (sub-tenancy) the sub-tenant will become the assured shorthold tenant of the original landlord.

14 SURRENDER OF THE TENANCY

A surrender of a tenancy occurs when a tenant purports to give a landlord vacant possession of their property before their rights and obligations under the tenancy have come to an end and a landlord accepts this gesture by the tenant, thereby bringing the tenancy to an end.

There are therefore two acts to the process of surrendering a tenancy:-
1. the tenant seeks to give up their rights and obligations; and
2. the landlord accepts this act of the tenant to complete the process.

If a landlord does not complete the process, by acceptance, a tenant will remain responsible for their obligations under the tenancy, including payment of rent, until the tenancy comes to an end. A landlord cannot be compelled to accept a surrender of the tenancy. However, practicality should prevail.

14.1 Tenant seeks to give up their tenancy

A tenant can seek to give up their tenancy by an express or implied act:-
1. an agreement with the landlord to end the tenancy early. If this is achieved the tenant should provide the landlord with a deed or declaration of surrender. The tenancy will end in accordance with the provisions of the deed. This is an express surrender; or
2. the tenant can abandon the property. If a tenant abandons a property it can be interpreted as an offer to surrender the tenancy. If a landlord accepts this offer to surrender, the tenancy will come to an end. This is an implied surrender.

If the tenancy is a joint tenancy all the joints tenants must act together as one to surrender the tenancy. One joint tenant cannot surrender a tenancy and leave the other joint tenants obligated to the landlord, as there is no individual share of the tenancy that a joint tenant can relinquish.

14.2 Express surrender

Where a tenant and landlord agree to a surrender of the tenancy it is best to have evidence of this in writing. It protects a tenant against a landlord being able to enforce tenancy provisions for any event occurring after the date of surrender. It also protects the landlord by ensuring the tenant is not able to claim unlawful eviction following the surrender. It ensures no misunderstandings.

A landlord should therefore insist on evidence of any agreement to surrender in the form of a deed of surrender or a declaration of surrender. In any event any act of surrender where possible should be made in writing to provide evidence to the court should litigation follow.

SURRENDER OF THE TENANCY

When a landlord is contemplating agreeing to a surrender of the tenancy they should consider the following matters in any negotiation with their tenant:-

- notice period for surrender to occur (one or two months);
- time it will take to re-let the property depending on the market at the time of surrender;
- any anticipated void period;
- reason for surrender (if a tenant has lost their job there is no point holding them to a tenancy they may no longer be able to afford. However, they may be able to claim HB up to a maximum amount);
- whether the tenant has a guarantor;
- likelihood of securing a similar rent;
- any re-let costs such as agency fees;
- the checkout process as well as the matters set out in Chapter 1;
- the deposit; and
- access to the property during the notice period for viewings.

It is a far better situation for a landlord to agree a surrender with a tenant than to have a tenant in their property not paying any rent. Court action to remove a tenant who is not paying any rent can take several months.

14.3 Implied surrender

This usually occurs where a tenant abandons the property, thereby expressing an intention from their actions that they are giving up their rights and obligations under the tenancy and the landlord accepting this by resuming possession of the property.

In some situations the tenant's actions will give a clear indication that they are purporting to surrender the tenancy, such as a tenant removing their possessions from the property, terminating the utilities and posting the keys to the landlord. Other less clear examples are where the tenant has completely wrecked the property and left or, owes a lot of rent and has left.

If a landlord resumes possession of the property and re-lets or acts in a way inconsistent with the existence of a tenancy they will have accepted the purported surrender. The risk is in knowing exactly what the tenant intends from their action. If in doubt a landlord should read Chapter 13, which also sets out what actions a landlord can take in respect of possessions left by the tenant in the property.

15 MONEY JUDGMENT FOR RENT ARREARS

15.1 Why recover rent arrears without seeking a possession order

There are circumstances when a landlord may seek to recover rent arrears without seeking a possession order in the same proceedings. Examples of these circumstances are:-

- Where the tenant has abandoned the property and the landlord has resumed possession. If the landlord has obtained the documents mentioned in Chapter 2 from the tenant they may be able to trace the tenant's whereabouts and pursue a money judgment for rent arrears.

- A landlord may face a counterclaim for disrepair when seeking to recover possession based on rent arrears. If the counterclaim is successful a landlord could find that their possession claim has failed, the counterclaim has offset the arrears of rent and they have an order for repairs. A landlord in this situation who is determined to recover the rent arrears should seek independent legal advice. If they go ahead it is best to recover possession and rent arrears in separate proceedings. The possession should be recovered on a straightforward basis such as Section 21 Notice procedure (if available) and the rent arrears recovered as a money claim. This way any counterclaim to the rent arrears does not stop a possession order being made separately.

- Under the accelerated possession procedure a landlord can obtain possession of the property relatively quickly but cannot claim rent arrears. A landlord may therefore follow this procedure to recover possession and recover the rent arrears in separate proceedings.

- A tenant may be in a fixed term tenancy and accumulate arrears of rent. The landlord may not be able to satisfy the criteria to use ground 8 (mandatory ground for rent arrears) to recover possession at this stage. As ground 10 and 11 are discretionary grounds for possession based on rent arrears, a landlord may not wish to seek possession based on these grounds. A landlord may therefore decide not to seek a possession order but to recover the arrears of rent via a money judgment.

- A tenant may have valuable goods (plasma TV, X-box, Wii, playstation, furniture and other items of value) in the property which may be seized under a bailiffs' warrant to pay a money judgment for rent arrears. A landlord may therefore decide to pursue the rent arrears whilst leaving the tenant in possession so that there is a greater chance of satisfying the judgment. Obtaining an order for possession of the property based on rent arrears may result in the tenant leaving before any of their property can be lawfully seized.

- A tenant may not accept a rent increase whether via a rent review clause or a Section 13 Notice and may continue to pay the previous rent. A landlord may therefore, upon exhausting all other avenues, have no choice but to recover the arrears by court proceedings. A successful judgment would at least mean that the rent increase was ruled as lawful.

There are two aspects to a landlord recovering arrears of rent:-
1. obtaining a court judgment against the tenant, joint tenants or guarantor for the rent that is owed (money judgment); and
2. enforcing the money judgment so that a landlord has more than a piece of paper and actually receives some or all of the rent owed with any costs and interest that applies.

15.2 Things to do before starting court proceedings (pre-action matters)

From the commencement of and throughout a tenancy a landlord should:-
- closely monitor rent payments;
- keep an up to date rent statement; and
- most importantly deal with rent arrears swiftly and decisively.

A landlord should not allow rent arrears to accumulate before taking action. If rent arrears are allowed to accumulate a tenant can quickly find that they are unable to clear the arrears even if they want to. Some tenants may have decided not to pay any further rent and proceed to give their landlord the run around before the landlord actually realises that that is the case. Landlords should ensure that action is taken and delay on their part avoided if rent is not being paid. If a landlord ultimately has to accept a loss of rent, prompt action will minimise the loss.

If a tenant is in receipt of full or part Housing Benefit (Local Housing Allowance) and is not passing it on to the landlord, the landlord can contact the local Housing Benefit Office the moment a payment is late or not made and request direct payment. If granted it will ensure that at least some rent is being paid whilst action is being taken to deal with the arrears. For further details a landlord should read Chapter 22 on Housing Benefit (Local Housing Allowance).

In dealing with rent arrears a landlord should assume from the beginning that court proceedings may be necessary and ensure the actions they take can swiftly lead to the issue of proceedings, if it becomes necessary.

There is a *"Pre-Action Protocol for Rent Arrears"*[2]. However, this protocol applies mainly to social landlords and where the rent arrears are leading to possession proceedings. A private landlord does not have to concern themselves with this protocol and it is not referred to further in this book.

There is a general *"Practice Direction – Pre-Action Conduct"*[3] that the court expects parties to court proceedings to have followed before commencing those proceedings. If a party to court proceedings fails to follow the *Practice Guidance* the court can order sanctions or award costs against the failing party.

If a landlord discovers that the rent is not being paid the following steps should be taken immediately to limit and recover the arrears, protect their interest as a landlord and comply with the *Practice Direction – Pre-Action Conduct*. One major aim of the *Practice Direction* is to try to settle disputes without court proceedings and make unavoidable court proceedings proceed efficiently:-

- try contacting the tenant (phone, text, write letter, email) to discuss the arrears (keep records of the date and content of the text, letter, email, phone call and the response or lack of it from the tenant);
- if the tenant is not responding to the efforts to contact, visit the property in person or via an agent and preferably with a witness (carry a letter to leave at the property if there is no answer from the tenant). The landlord or agent should record the date and time of the visit(s) and the outcome i.e. contact, no contact and retain a copy of the letter;
- if there is no response from the tenant to a visit to the property, leave the prepared letter for the tenant. If the tenancy agreement allows for it the letter should notify the tenant of a property inspection at a particular date and time and let the tenant know that the landlord will access the property if they are not there;
- at the time/date given in the letter the landlord should visit the property with a witness, enter via keys and make a note of what the situation is, if it appears that the tenant has abandoned the property, follow the advice set out in Chapter 13 on abandonment;
- if contact is made and the tenant is willing, make an agreement in writing with the tenant to pay off the arrears. This arrangement should be affordable for the tenant otherwise the agreement will fail. Establish from the tenant how they will continue to pay current rent when due as well as the additional sum to reduce the arrears;
- if there is a guarantor for the tenant, they should be kept informed of these events and reminded that as a guarantor they are liable for the tenant's obligations under the tenancy;

---

[2] www.justice.gov.uk/courts/procedure-rules/civil/protocol/prot_rent
[3] www.justice.gov.uk/courts/procedure-rules/civil/rules/pd_pre-action_conduct

- advise the tenant to seek debt advice if this is relevant to their circumstances;
- if the tenant is not in receipt of Local Housing Allowance (Housing Benefit) advise them to make a claim if their circumstances allow; and
- take some payment from the tenant immediately, if they have it.

Taking the above action will allow a landlord to demonstrate to the court that court proceedings were a last resort. If there is no agreement to pay the arrears, if the agreement has been breached, if current rent is not being paid or there has been no contact with the tenant a landlord should send a "letter before action" to the tenant.

In the letter before action a landlord should set out the arrears that are owed and the period for which they are owed. This is best achieved by attaching a copy of an up-to-date rent statement. If the rent has increased by a notice or other agreement a landlord should refer to it and attach a copy. The letter should set out the steps already taken to contact the tenant and resolve the rent arrears. If a written agreement was made to pay the arrears, a landlord should refer to it in the letter, attach a copy and state if it has been followed.

A landlord should conclude the letter by letting the tenant know that court proceedings may be started if the arrears are not paid, that they should comply with the *Practice Direction – Pre-Action Conduct* and refer specifically to paragraph 4 which sets out sanctions the court can impose for non-compliance with the practice direction. The letter should request a copy of any relevant document the tenant has that the landlord might require for the case.

If the limitation period to recover the arrears of rent is about to expire (i.e arrears of nearly six years) a landlord should start proceedings immediately and then seek to comply with the *Practice Direction – Pre-Action Conduct* where they can.

A tenant should acknowledge the letter before action and respond to it in a reasonable time (usually around 14 days).

If the tenant has failed to respond to the letter satisfactorily a landlord should prepare to start court proceedings to obtain a money judgment for the arrears of rent.

A landlord should note that a tenant may respond to the letter and seek to make a counterclaim for a breach of the landlord's obligation under the tenancy agreement. This could be a counterclaim for disrepair or for not protecting the deposit under a deposit protection scheme. A landlord should weigh up the pros and cons before seeking to recover rent arrears and where required seek independent legal advice. This book does not cover the various counterclaims and defences that may be made and how they may proceed. This book simply shows the landlord the simplest route to recover arrears of rent. It is always important that a landlord complies with all their obligations under the tenancy agreement to protect themselves from possible litigation.

A court would expect a landlord before starting court proceedings to have taken reasonable measures to try to resolve the issue. A landlord should therefore document the details of the actions taken above, including telephone calls, letters, emails, texts, visits to the property and any agreement to pay arrears.

A landlord should *not* use threatening behaviour or harass the tenant to recover rent arrears. A landlord who does so could face prosecution for criminal liability under the Protection from Eviction Act as well as civil action for compensation to the tenant. The landlord could also be in breach of the covenant for quiet enjoyment.

15.3 Obtaining a money judgment for rent arrears (County Court judgment

There are two ways by which a landlord can seek a money judgment. One is the traditional method of obtaining and completing the court forms, submitting them to the court, paying a fee and possibly attending a court hearing. The other is commencing the process online at https://www.gov.uk/make-money-claim-online/ and possibly attending a court hearing.

From 19 March 2012 the majority of money claims now have to commence at the County Court Money Claims Centre (CCMCC). The postal address is Salford Business Centre, P.O. Box 527, Salford, Greater Manchester, M5 0BY. It is cheaper and quicker to commence the process online. If online court fees will need to be paid by debit or credit card, if by post the fees will need to be paid by cheque or postal order.

Proceedings for rent arrears should be brought in the county court if the value of the claim is under £100,000. Within the county court there are three procedures called "tracks" that can be allocated to an action for rent arrears. They are the small claims track, fast track and multi-track procedures. The procedure to be used will be determined by the court after a claim is made. The procedure or track that applies to a particular claim depends upon the amount being claimed and the complexity of the case:-

- claims of not more than £5,000 are usually dealt with under the **small claims track**;
- claims of not more than £25,000 are usually dealt with under the **fast track** if the trial is not more than a day; and

- claims above £25,000 and complex cases that will last more than a day are usually dealt with under the **multi-track**.

The procedural track to which a claim is allocated is very important. This book will only look at the **small claims track** for several reasons:

1. A landlord should monitor their rent payments and take action swiftly to ensure the arrears do not accumulate. If a landlord follows this advice claims for rent arrears should rarely exceed £5,000 and therefore a landlord will only be involved with the small claims track.
2. The small claims track is designed for straightforward claims. This book is not written to deal with expensive and/or complex claims. In those circumstances a landlord should consider getting independent legal advice.
3. The small claims track is the only track where solicitor's costs are not usually met by the losing party and so a landlord using this track is unlikely to engage a solicitor. This book aims to give advice to landlords in this circumstance.
4. The small claims track procedure is informal and designed for parties bringing a claim in person (i.e. litigant in person). Therefore, a landlord is more likely to need help with bringing a claim under the small claims track.

A landlord should start a claim which is solely for money in the CCMCC. The case will be transferred to the tenant's nearest county court if the case is defended. If not defended, the case can proceed to a conclusion at the CCMCC.

A landlord seeking to obtain a money judgment for rent arrears should follow the guidance below.

15.4 Complete form N1

Obtain the court form titled **N1** and the guide to completing the N1 form titled **N1a**;

The form can be downloaded from the Court Service website[4] and completed in type or printed and completed by hand in block letters with black ink. A landlord should read the guide before completing the claim form.

In the court proceedings the landlord is referred to as the claimant as they are bringing a claim and the tenant is referred to as the defendant as the claim is being brought against them, whether or not they actually defend it.

In the top box on the right of the form write the name of the county court at which the claim will be started. This will be the Northampton County Court as of 19 March 2012. This is the name to use when issuing proceedings at the CCMCC. If the claim is not started online the completed form, documents and

---

[4] www.justice.gov.uk/courts/procedure-rules/civil/forms

fees will need to be sent to County Court Money Claims Centre, Salford Business Centre, P.O. Box 527, Salford, Greater Manchester, M5 0BY.

The claim number and issue date will be completed by the court.

In the section headed "Claimant…" a landlord(s) full name(s) and address(es) should be entered.

In the section headed "Defendant(s)…" the full name(s) of ALL the tenant(s), and/or guarantor(s) depending on whom the landlord seeks the rent arrears should be entered. If there is more than one defendant, a claim form should be completed for each of them (see below).

In the section headed "Brief details of claim" the following should be written – The Defendant rented (*full address of rented property*) from the Claimant on (*date tenancy commenced*). The rent due under the tenancy is (*£xxx per week/calendar month/etc…*). The current arrears of rent are £xx. The Claimant seeks an order for the arrears of rent, costs and interest (if interest is sought). In the section headed "Value" write the amount of rent that is owed plus any interest, or if the arrears are on-going and the landlord knows what the value is likely to be by the time the court judgment is obtained write "not more than £5,000").

In the section stating "you must indicate your preferred court for hearings here" a landlord should enter the court where they would like a hearing (if there is to be one). If the hearing is defended the proceedings will be transferred to a local county court, otherwise it will proceed at the CCMCC.

In the section headed "Defendant's name and address…" write the title, name and address of the tenant/guarantor. If there is more than one tenant/guarantor copy the form and place a separate tenant/guarantor's name and address in this section until one form is completed for each of them.

If the landlord knows the exact sum that is being claimed this should be written in the box at the bottom right of the first page in the section "Amount claimed". The court fee should be written in the following box and the total amount in the final box. As the landlord is acting in person there is no Solicitor's cost. The amount of court fee can be found by contacting the CCMCC or online at www.justice.gov.uk/court/fees.

On page 2 answer "No" to the Human Rights Act 1988 question.

In the section headed "Particulars of Claim…" a landlord should write to the following effect:-

The Defendant rented [*address of property*] from the Claimant under a [*name the type of tenancy*] that commenced on [*give date*] at a [*weekly/monthly/quarterly*] rent of (*put amount*) [*copy of tenancy agreement attached – if available*]. (If the rent was increased write as follows) The rent was by *[agreement/notice]* increased on the *[nsert date]* to *[insert amount]* per *[week/month/quarter]*.

The defendant has not paid any rent for the period commencing *[date payment stopped]* and ending on *[date payment resumed or the tenancy ended]*. Or, the defendant has not paid any rent since *[date rent payment stopped]* and the arrears are £xx at the date of this claim and continues to increase at a daily rate of £xxx per day. Please see attached rent statement.

Efforts have been made to recover the rent by (phoning, writing, visiting) the tenant. An agreement was made to pay off the arrears (copy attached) but this has not been followed (if applicable). A letter before action was sent to the Defendant on (date) (copy attached) but despite these efforts the Defendant has not addressed the rent arrears satisfactorily.

The Claimant seeks an order that the Defendant pays to the Claimant the sum of (put amount) or the arrears that are outstanding at the date of the order (these arrears not being more than £5,000).

A landlord can also make a claim for interest to be paid on the debt that is owed. Interest can be claimed under a term of the tenancy agreement that provides for this or under County Court Act 1984 Section 69. If a claim for interest is being made under the County Court Act the following wording should be used:-

"The claimant claims interest pursuant to Section 69 of the County Courts Act 1984 at the rate of 8% per annum from *[insert date of when rent became due]* to *[date of issuing claim]* of £xx and also interest at the same rate up to the date of judgment or earlier payment at a daily rate of £xxx".

To work out the daily rate of interest take the sum that is owed multiply it by 8 divide by 100 and divide by 365 days = daily rate of interest. This daily rate should be multiplied by the number of days the debt has been outstanding up to the date court proceedings started.

In the section headed "Statement of Truth" the landlord should cross out the words "(The Claimant believes)", so that it reads "I believe that the facts stated in these particulars of claim are true". The landlord should cross out all of the second line and write their full name where indicated, leave blank name of claimant's solicitor and sign the form in the section marked "signed". Below the signature the landlord should cross out "(Litigation friend) and "(Claimant's solicitor)" so that it reads "(Claimant)".

In the last box on the left on page 2 a landlord should write the address to which documents should be sent to them if different from their address given in the first section of the form.

15.5 Starting a Claim

15.5.1 Starting a claim the traditional way (offline)

A claim is started by completing form N1 and submitting it to the court with supporting documents and the fee. A court case can involve a lot of documentation that will need to be referred to more than once. A landlord should therefore have their own filing system and keep copies of all documents, records of all communication and receipts.

A landlord should post three copies of each document to the court. This will be the completed claim form and the documents referred to in it (such as tenancy agreements, notices, rent statement and letters). If there is more than one tenant a separate form N1 would have been completed for each of them. Three copies of each tenant's form N1 and supporting documents should be sent to the court. One set of documents is for the court file, another set for each tenant/guarantor and a set for the landlord. The court will check that the documents are in order and if satisfied will stamp them with the court's seal, provide notice of issue, a claim reference and send a copy of the documents in the proceedings to the tenant and the landlord.

The landlord will be sent Form N205A by the court. This is called a "Notice of Issue". The Notice of Issue informs the landlord of:-

- the date that court proceedings began (i.e. court proceedings issued);
- the name of the court;
- the court reference number (claim number);
- title of the action;
- the address of the court;
- the date the proceedings is deemed to have been served on the tenant; and
- the date the tenant has to reply to the claim.

15.5.2 Tenant receiving notification of court proceedings

The court will send a copy of the claim form and accompanying documents to the tenant by first class post. It is deemed to have been received by the tenant on the second business day after posting. A landlord is notified of the date the tenant should respond to the court proceedings in Form N205A.

When the tenant is served with the court proceedings (i.e. documents) there are several actions they can take:-

1. provide the court with an acknowledgement of service (Form N9). This document confirms receipt of the court papers and notify the court and the landlord that the tenant will either defend all or part of the claim or contest the court's jurisdiction;
2. provide the court with a defence in Form N9B in which case the landlord will have to prove their case;

3. provide the court with an acknowledgement of service (Form N9) and then a defence in Form N9B in which case the landlord will have to prove their case;
4. do not respond at all to the court proceedings i.e. do not provide acknowledgement of service and do not provide a defence;
5. provide the landlord with a full admission in Form N9A in which case the landlord has won their case;
6. provide the landlord with an admission to part of the claim in Form N9A and/or provide a defence or counterclaim in Form N9B to another part of the claim; or
7. provide the court with a counterclaim in Form N9B.

15.5.3 The tenant/defendant has provided the court with an acknowledgement of service

The tenant has 14 days from the date the particulars of claim has been served on them, in which to respond to the court proceedings. The particulars of claim may have been served within the N1 claim form (as set out above in paragraph 15.4), by the landlord completing the section headed "particulars of claim" or it can be in a separate document which the landlord should serve on the tenant within 14 days after the claim has been issued.

The tenant's response can be an admission, defence, counterclaim in full or part or a combination of them.

If the tenant is unable to provide their defence within 14 days they can provide the court with an "acknowledgement of service" in form N9. Form N9 will notify the court and the landlord if the tenant is defending all or part of the claim or challenging the court's jurisdiction. If the tenant sends the acknowledgement of service to the court they have 28 days from the receipt of the particulars of claim to provide the court with a defence. The acknowledgement of service therefore extends the deadline to provide a defence.

Upon receiving the acknowledgement of service the court will send a copy to the landlord. This document should be kept with the landlord's court papers.

The acknowledgement of service also informs a landlord of the tenant's name, address for service and date of birth. Following receipt of the acknowledgement of service the landlord will have to wait for the tenant to make the next move. The acknowledgement of service will state what that move will be.

15.5.4 The tenant/defendant does nothing

From the time the tenant receives the particulars of claim, whether with the first court papers or at a later date, they have 14 days in which to respond to the court proceedings.

If the landlord and or the court has not had a response from the tenant within 14 days of the claim been served on them, the landlord can in some cases request a default judgment i.e. judgment without trial.

15.5.5 The tenant (defendant) has NOT provided a defence

The tenant has 14 days after receipt of the particulars of claim to provide a defence, or 28 days if the tenant returned the acknowledgement of service to the court.

If the tenant has not provided a defence within the 14 or 28 days' time limit as the case may be the landlord can in some cases request judgment by default (see below).

15.5.6 Admission to the whole of the landlord/claimant's claim

The tenant has 14 days from receipt of the particulars of claim, to admit in full or in part to the claim against them. If the tenant decides to admit to the claim in full they should complete and send Form N9A to the landlord.

Form N9A will notify the landlord of the following matters:-
- that the claim has been admitted in full;
- the personal details, employment details, bank account, savings, residence status, income, expenditure, other court orders and credit debts of the tenant; and importantly
- the form will state whether the amount admitted is to be paid in full and by what date or by instalments and the amount and frequency of those instalments.

Upon receipt of Form N9A the landlord should complete form N205A (Notice of Issue) if they received this form from the court or form N225 and return it to the court along with a copy of form N9A. This is to request judgment following the tenant's admission to the claim. The landlord should keep a copy of Form N9A for their records.

15.5.6.1 Completing form N205A to request judgment following a full admission
When a landlord has court proceedings issued for a specified amount of money, they will receive from the Court a Notice of Issue in form N205A. In addition to the matters mentioned in paragraph 15.5.1 form N205A deals with the following:-
- explains the actions the tenant can take when they have been served with the court papers;
- acts as a request form for judgment if the tenant has admitted the claim; and
- acts as a request form for default judgment (if the tenant has not provided a defence).

The bottom half of form N205A has a section a landlord can detach, complete and send to the court to request judgment.

In completing the detached section of form N205A, box "A" should be left unmarked as the tenant has admitted to the whole claim. To make a request for judgment box "B" which reads "the defendant admits that all the money is owed" should be marked. Below box "B" one of the following boxes should be marked to indicate:-

- that the landlord accepts the tenant's proposal to pay the amount admitted;
- that the tenant has not made any proposal to pay the amount admitted; or
- that the landlord does not accept the tenant's proposal to pay the amount admitted.

15.5.6.1.1   *Accepting the proposal to pay*

If the landlord accepts the proposal of the tenant to pay the amount admitted it should be indicated in the relevant box in section "B" of the form.

At section "C" the tenant's date of birth should be written, if known.

At section "D" the tenant's proposals to pay which have been accepted should be completed i.e. pay immediately, pay at future date, or by instalments indicating how much each month.

In section "D" the following should be completed:-

The amount the claim was for at the date of issue of the proceedings (i.e. how much rent was owed at that date) plus any interest claimed up to the date of issue ....

Any interest claimed from the date of issue to the date the request for a money judgment is being made. There is also a space below to specify the period for which interest is claimed and the rate e.g. 8% ....

The amount of court fees on form N1 (claim form) ....

The questions on solicitor's costs to be left blank as the landlord is a litigant in person ....

Write the subtotal of the above figures ....

Write amount, if any, paid since proceedings were issued

....

Write amount payable by the tenant ....

This will be the subtotal less any sum paid by the tenant since proceedings were issued.

15.5.6.1.2   *There has been no proposal to pay*

If the tenant does not make any proposal to pay in form N9A box "B" of form N205A should be marked to indicate that the tenant has admitted to the whole claim in full and then mark the relevant box to state that there has been no proposal to pay the amount admitted.

In section "C" the tenant's date of birth, if known, should be written.

Section "D" should specify how the landlord would like the amount claimed to be paid i.e. in full, immediately or by a specific date, or by instalments at a specified rate each month.

The remainder of section "D" as to amount claimed, interest and costs should be completed as set out above in paragraph 15.5.6.1.1.

15.5.6.1.3   *Rejecting the proposal to pay*

If the landlord does not accept the tenant's proposal to pay the amount admitted as set out in form N9A then the landlord should complete form N205A as follows.

Box "B" should be marked to indicate that the tenant has admitted to the claim in full and then mark the relevant box to indicate that the tenant's proposal to pay has not been accepted.

In section "C" the tenant's date of birth, if known, should be written.

In section "D" the landlord should specify how they would like the amount admitted to be paid i.e. in full, immediately or by a specific date, or by instalments at a specified rate each month.

The remainder of section "D" as to amount claimed, interest and costs should be completed as set out in paragraph 15.5.6.1.1.

Overleaf in the box titled section "E" the reasons why the tenant's proposal to pay is rejected should be stated. If there is no section "E", the reasons should be set out overleaf and the letters "PTO" put at the bottom of the first page. The rejection could be because the tenant's specific date to pay in full is too distant or because the amount of instalment is too low. Any objection should take into account the tenant's ability to pay (based on the information in form N9A) which will be affected by whether or not they are in employment and if so, how much they earn.

After the relevant sections of the form N205A have been completed the landlord needs to certify the form at the bottom of the front page. In the section of the form that reads "I certify that the information given is correct" the landlord should sign and date the form and cross out the words "(Claimant Solicitors)" and "(Litigation Friend)" in brackets so that it reads "(Claimant)".

A landlord should keep a copy of the form with their court papers and send the original to the court along with form N9A.

When the court receives forms N205A and N9A the information will be considered and an order made.

Alternatively, a landlord can request judgment following full admission by the tenant by completing form N225. This form is most likely to be used where the landlord has served the court documents on the tenant and/or where the landlord has served the particulars of claim on the tenant after court proceedings were issued.

The tenant would have made the full admission on form N9A. On receiving this form the landlord would have obtained from the tenant the information mentioned at paragraph 15.5.6 above.

15.5.6.2   Completing form N225
In the top right box the following should be written in the same order:-
* name of the court in which the case is proceeding (Northampton County Court);
* claim number (available from previous court correspondence);
* landlord's name and tenant's name in the relevant sections titled Claimant and Defendant respectively.

Part "A" of the form should be left blank.

The first box in section "B" should be marked to indicate that the full amount of the claim has been admitted.

15.5.6.2.1   Accepting the proposal to pay
If the landlord accepts the proposals of the tenant to pay the amount admitted it should be indicated in the relevant box in section "B" of the form i.e. "I accept the defendant's proposal for payment".

At section "C" if the tenant has stated their date of birth in form N9A this section should be left unmarked. However, if the tenant has not stated their date of birth in form N9A but the landlord knows it, this should be indicated by marking the first box and writing the tenant's date of birth in the space provided below. If the tenant has not provided their date of birth in form N9A and the landlord does not know it the second box of section "C" should be marked.

At section "D" of the form the tenant's proposals to pay which are accepted should be set out. This should be done by marking the relevant box if it is proposed that the amount admitted is to be paid immediately, by instalments (indicating how much each month) or in full by a specified date.

The remainder of section "D" should be completed as follows:-

The amount the claim was for at the date of issue of the
proceedings (i.e. as stated in the claim form)
plus any interest claimed up to the date of issue   ………………...

Any interest claimed from the date of issue to the date
the request for a money judgment is being made

There is also a space below to specify the period for
which interest is claimed and the rate e.g. 8%   ………………..

The amount of court fees on form N1 (claim form)   ………………..

*(The questions on solicitor's costs to be left blank as the
landlord is a litigant in person).*

Write the subtotal of the above figures   ………………..

Write amount, if any, paid since proceedings were issued   ………………

Write amount payable by the tenant   ………………

This will be the subtotal less any amount paid by the tenant since proceedings was issued.

15.5.6.2.2   *There has been no proposal to pay*

If the tenant has not made any proposal to pay in form N9A the first box in section "B" should be marked to indicate that the tenant has admitted to the claim in full and then mark the relevant box in section "B" to state that there has been no proposal to pay the amount admitted i.e. "The defendant has not made any proposal for payment".

At section "C" if the tenant has stated their date of birth in form N9A this section should be left unmarked. However, if the tenant has not stated their date of birth in form N9A but the landlord knows it, this should be indicated by marking the first box and writing the tenant's date of birth in the space provided below. If the tenant has not provided their date of birth in form N9A and the landlord does not know it the second box of section "C" should be marked.

In section "D" the landlord should specify how they would like the amount claimed to be paid i.e. in full, immediately or by a specified date, or by instalments at a specified rate each month.

The remainder of section "D" as to amount claimed, interest and costs should be completed as set out in paragraph 15.5.6.2.1 above.

15.5.6.2.3 *Rejecting the proposal to pay*

If the landlord does not accept the tenant's proposal to pay the amount admitted as set out in form N9A the landlord should complete form N225 as follows.

The first box in section "B" should be marked to indicate that the tenant has admitted to the whole claim and then mark the relevant box in section "B" to state that the tenant's proposal to pay is not accepted i.e. "I do NOT accept the defendant's proposal for payment".

At section "C" if the tenant has stated their date of birth in form N9A this section should be left unmarked. However, if the tenant has not stated their date of birth in form N9A but the landlord knows it, this should be indicated by marking the first box and writing the tenant's date of birth in the space provided below. If the tenant has not provided their date of birth in form N9A and the landlord does not know it the second box of section "C" should be marked.

In section "D" the landlord should specify how they would like the amount admitted to be paid i.e. in full, immediately or by a specific date, or by instalments at a specified rate each month.

The remainder of section "D" as to amount claimed, interest and costs should be completed as set out in paragraph 15.5.6.2.1 above.

On the back of the form the landlord should set out why they reject the tenant's proposal to pay. This could be because the tenant's specified date to pay in full is too far into the future or because the amount of instalment is too low. Any objection should take into account the tenant's ability to pay (considering the information in form N9A) which will be affected by whether or not they are in employment and if so how much they earn.

After the relevant sections of the form have been completed the landlord needs to certify the form at the bottom of the front page. In the section of the form that reads "I certify that the information given is correct" the landlord should sign and date the form and cross out the words "(Claimant Solicitors)" and "(Litigation Friend)" in brackets below so that it reads "(Claimant)".

A landlord should keep a copy of the form with their court papers and send the original to the court along with Form N9A.

When the court receives form N225 it will consider the information and make an order.

15.5.7   Admission to part of the landlord/claimant's case

If the tenant admits to part of the claim and wishes to defend the other part they can do this in two ways. The tenant can complete an admission form N9A in relation to the part of the claim they admit and complete form N9B in relation to the part of the claim they wish to defend. The other way is for the tenant to make payment in respect of the part of the claim they admit and submit a completed form N9B to the court in respect of the part of the claim they wish to defend.

If a part admission has been made by the tenant a landlord can respond in one of two ways. A landlord can:-
* reject the tenant's part admission; or
* accept the part admission in full satisfaction of the claim.

To do either of the above a landlord will need to complete form N225A (Notice of Part Admission). A landlord will receive this form from the court when a tenant has admitted to part of a claim. Alternatively it can be downloaded from the court service website (www.justice.gov.uk/forms/hmcts).

15.5.7.1   *Completing form N225A (Notice of Part Admission)*
In the top right box, if it has not been completed by the court, the following should be written in the same order from top to bottom:-
* name of the court in which the case is proceeding (Northampton County Court unless it has been transferred);
* claim number (available from previous court correspondence); and
* landlord's name and tenant's name in the sections titled Claimant and Defendant respectively.

If a landlord does not accept the tenant's part admission they should mark box A. If a landlord marks box A the claim will proceed as defended. For defended claims see paragraph 15.5.10 onwards.

If a landlord accepts the tenant's part admission in full satisfaction of their claim they should mark box "B". Below box "B" are three further boxes. A landlord should mark one depending on the proposal or non-proposal of the tenant for payment and how they wish to respond. If the tenant has made a proposal for payment of their part admission and the landlord accepts this they should mark the box headed "I accept the defendant's proposal for payment".

If the tenant has NOT made any proposal for payment the landlord should mark the box headed "The defendant has not made any proposal for payment".

If the landlord does NOT accept the tenant's proposal for payment they should mark the box headed "I do NOT accept the defendant's proposal for payment". In the space opposite to this section the landlord should set out why they reject the proposal for payment and continue on the back of the form if more space is needed plus indicate that there is further information overleaf (PTO).

At section "C" the landlord should mark the first box if the tenant's date of birth is not stated in form N9A or N9B and is known to them. The tenant's date of birth should be entered in the box below.

If the tenant's date of birth is not stated in form N9A or N9B and the landlord does not know it the last box in section "C" should be marked.

In the first part of section "D" a landlord should set out how they wish payment to be made. This part should only be completed if the tenant's proposal for payment is not accepted or none was made.

If no proposal for payment was made, or if made and is rejected, the landlord should set out in the first part of section "D" whether they would like the part admission to be paid in full immediately, at a future date, or in instalments and the rate of payment each month.

The second part of section "D" should be completed in all cases where the landlord accepts the part payment in satisfaction of the claim. It should be completed as follows:-

Amount of claim as admitted (this is the amount the
tenant indicate they would pay in satisfaction
of the claim)   ....

Court fees for the claim (i.e. set out in form N1)   ....

(There will be no solicitor's costs as landlord is acting in person)

The subtotal of the sums above is to be entered in the
subtotal box   ....

The box dealing with Solicitor's costs for the second
time should be left blank.   ....

If the tenant has made any payment this should be
entered where it states "deduct amount (if any) paid since issue"..................

In the final box the landlord should enter
the final sum payable by the tenant.   ....

The landlord should sign and date the form where indicated at the bottom of the page and send it to the court whilst retaining a copy for their records.

If the landlord does not accept the tenant's part admission the case will proceed as defended. If the landlord accepts the part admission and the proposals to pay an order will be made to that effect. If the part admission is accepted but no proposals were made for payment or the landlord rejects the payment proposals the court will look at the matter and make an order.

15.5.8 Tenant/defendant makes a counterclaim

A tenant can make a counterclaim against a landlord following the issue of proceedings. The counterclaim will usually be in the defence form N9B and is notified to the landlord by the court. The landlord will need to put in a defence or admission to the counterclaim.

This book does not deal with counterclaims. A counterclaim could be in respect of the deposit protection legislation, unlawful eviction, harassment, breach of covenant of quiet enjoyment, disrepair or any other cause of action the tenant may have. Depending on the amount counterclaimed and/or the complexity of the case, the case could be dealt with by the small claims track, fast track or multi-track. A landlord should seek independent legal advice in these circumstances.

15.5.9 The tenant/defendant has NOT provided an acknowledgement of service or a defence – application for default judgment

Default judgment is basically judgment without a trial.

If the tenant has not provided an acknowledgement of service, a defence or an admission, the landlord can apply for default judgment.

When a default judgment is applied for the court must be satisfied of the following:-
* particulars of claim were served on the tenant;
* the tenant has not filed an acknowledgement of service or a defence within the required time;
* the tenant has not paid/satisfied the claim; and
* the tenant has not returned an admission to the landlord.

In an application for default judgment the landlord can request interest on the sum claimed if a claim for interest was included in the particulars of claim.

Where there is a joint tenancy and an action is brought against several tenants the landlord can request default judgment against one of two or more tenants if the criteria above are satisfied and continue court proceedings against the other tenants if they have returned a defence.

An application for default judgment can be made by a landlord completing one of two forms and sending it to the court.

15.5.9.1   Completing Form N205A to request default judgment

When a landlord has court proceedings issued for a specified amount of money, they will receive from the Court a Notice of Issue in form N205A. One function of this form is to request default judgment.

The bottom half of the form has a section a landlord can detach, complete and send to the court to request default judgment.

To make a request for default judgment box "A", which reads "the defendant has not filed an admission or defence to my claim or an application to contest the court's jurisdiction", should be marked.

Section "B" should be left blank.

At section "C" the tenant's date of birth should be completed if known.

At section "D" the landlord should set out how they wish the tenant to pay the amount claimed. This should be done by marking the relevant box if the amount claimed is to be paid in full, immediately or at a future date or by instalments (indicating how much each month).

The remainder of section "D" is to be completed as follows:-

The amount the claim was for at the date of issue of the
proceedings (as stated in form N1) plus any interest
claimed up to the date of issue   ....

Any interest claimed from the date of issue to the date
the request for a money judgment is being made.
There is also a space below to specify the period
for which interest is claimed and the rate e.g. 8%   ....

The amount of court fees on form N1 (claim form)   ....

*(The questions on solicitor's costs to be left blank as the
landlord is a litigant in person)*

The subtotal of the above figures   ....

The amount, if any, paid since proceedings were issued   ....

Final amount payable by the tenant   ....

This will be the subtotal less any amount paid by the tenant since proceedings were issued.

In the section of the form that reads "I certify that the information given is correct" the landlord should sign and date the form and cross out the words "(Claimant Solicitors)" and "(Litigation Friend)" in brackets below so that it reads "(Claimant)".

A landlord should keep a copy of the form with their court papers and send the original to the court.

When the court receives the request for a default judgment it will consider the information before it and make an order.

Alternatively, a landlord can request judgment in default by completing form N225. This form is most likely to be used where the landlord has served the court documents on the tenant and/or where they have served the particulars of claim on the tenant after court proceedings were issued.

15.5.9.2 *Completing form N225 to request default judgment*
In the top right box the following should be written in the same order from top to bottom:
- name of the court in which the case is proceeding (Northampton County Court unless it was transferred);
- claim number (available from previous court correspondence);
- claimant (landlord's) name and defendant (tenant's) name in the relevant sections.

In section "A" mark both boxes. The first box is to confirm that there has not been an admission or defence to the claim and the second box is to confirm that the particulars of claim were served on the tenant.

Section "B" should be left blank as no admission has been received and a default judgment is requested.

At section "C" if a landlord knows the tenant's date of birth it should be inserted in the relevant box. If the landlord does not know the tenant's date of birth they should mark the final box in section "C".

At section "D" the landlord should set out how they wish the tenant to pay the amount claimed. This should be done by marking the relevant box if the amount claimed is to be paid in full, immediately or at a future date, or by instalments (indicating how much each month).

The remainder of section "D" is completed as follows:-

The amount the claim was for at the date of issue of the proceedings (i.e. as stated in form N1) plus any interest claimed up to the date of issue ....

Any interest claimed from the date of issue to the date the request for a money judgment is being made. There is also a space below to specify the period for which interest is claimed and the rate e.g. 8% ....

The amount of court fees on form N1 (claim form) ....

*(The questions on solicitor's costs to be left blank as the
landlord is a litigant in person)*

The subtotal of the above figures   ………………………..

The amount, if any, paid since proceedings were issued. ………………………..

Amount payable by the tenant   ………………………..

This will be the subtotal less any amount paid by the tenant since proceedings
were issued.

After the relevant sections of the form have been completed the landlord needs
to certify the form at the bottom of the front page. In the section of the form that
reads "I certify that the information given is correct" the landlord should sign
and date the form and cross out the words "(Claimant Solicitors)" and
"(Litigation Friend)" in brackets below so that it reads "(Claimant)".

A landlord should keep a copy of the form with their court papers and send the
original to the court.

When the court receives the request for a default judgment it will consider the
information before it and make an order.

15.5.10 The tenant (defendant) has provided a defence

The tenant would have been sent a defence and counterclaim form when they
receive notification of court proceedings against them (Form N9B). If the tenant
chooses to defend they will complete the form and return it to the court. The
court will send a copy of the form to the landlord.

The defence and counterclaim form will contain the following information:-
* whether the amount claimed is defended in full or part;
* if any amount admitted has been paid to the landlord;
* if an admission form is enclosed;
* if the claim is being defended because it has been paid in full;
* the defence; and/or
* the counterclaim.

A landlord will need to consider the defence and decide how to proceed with
their claim. Independent legal advice may be advisable at this point. The tenant
can dispute whether or not the rent is lawfully due, whether there are any
arrears at all or whether they are liable for the amount claimed.

A tenant can make a counterclaim for disrepair (which may include an element
of personal injury), deposit and/or breach of the tenancy. A landlord cannot
simply walk away from the proceedings if it gets difficult. If a tenant makes a
counterclaim a landlord will need to provide a defence to it otherwise the
tenant can get a default judgment on their counterclaim. This book does not

deal with counterclaims and landlords are advised to seek independent legal advice.

On the basis that the claim is only defended and there is no counterclaim, when the court receives the completed defence and counterclaim form the landlord will be sent a copy. The court will also send an allocation questionnaire to both the landlord and tenant. This form will specify the date by which it is to be returned to the court. The landlord may have to pay a fee when they return this form to the court.

The allocation questionnaire enables the court to manage the claim effectively as it provides information about the issues involved, the likely length of any hearing, witness and expert witness to be called, technical evidence to be presented, venue, IT requirements for the hearing and even if the parties are likely to reach a settlement.

15.6 Completing form N150 (Allocation Questionnaire)

The top right boxes of the form requiring the name of the court, claim number and date for returning form N150 to the court, is normally completed by the court before the form is sent to the landlord and tenant.

The top left box should have the landlord's name and directly below it the following numbers and also words in brackets should be crossed out [1st] [2nd] [3rd] [Defendant] [Part 20 Claimant] so that it reads [Claimant]. It is encouraged that the allocation questionnaire be sent to the tenant when completed and so this question in the form should be answered "yes" and a copy of the form when completed sent to the tenant.

In section "A" headed "Settlement" the first part for legal representatives should be left unmarked. In the second part headed "For all" question 1 should be marked "No". Question 2 should be left unmarked. In the box below question 3 the landlord should state the efforts made before starting court proceedings to settle the claim (such as phone calls, emails, letters, text, visits and responses or lack of it) and the efforts that have been made since court proceedings were issued and the tenant's response or lack of it.

At section "B" headed "Location of trial" if the claim needs to be heard at a particular court, such as a landlord being disabled and unable to travel, the "yes" box should be marked. In the box below, the particular court that a landlord wishes to hear the matter should be inserted along with the reason why.

In section "C" the landlord should mark the box "no" and state in the box below that no pre-action protocol applies to this claim.

In section "D" the landlord should indicate the amount of money in dispute at the first question. If the claim is for a £1,000 and the tenant challenges the entire claim then it is £1,000 which is in dispute. However, if the tenant admits to £600 of the claim then £400 will be in dispute.

The landlord should answer "no" to the question "have you made any application(s) in this claim" if none were made. If "yes" to this question a landlord should state what the application was for and when it is due to be heard. This book has not advised a landlord to make any application and such action is more likely when the matter is not straightforward.

On the question as to what witnesses will be called, the landlord should put their name in the left column and in the right column state that they are witness to the tenancy and rent arrears. If a letting agent, managing agent, other tenant, joint landlord is attending as a witness their name should be written in the left column and what they are a witness to in the right column.

As this is a simple rent arrears case where the landlord is not seeking more than the small claims financial limit (£5,000) there is no need for any experts and all the questions on experts should be answered "no" on the form.

On the question as to which track is suitable for the case the landlord should mark the "small claims track" box. There is no need to write anything in the box below as the small claims track would be the normal track for the claim.

The following section asking about electronic documents relate to the multi-track, as this track is not being used this section should not be answered.

At section "E" an estimate of the length of the trial will need to be given. This could be about 15 minutes if there are no additional witnesses and 30 minutes if witnesses are to attend. If there is any date that the landlord and/or any witness(s) is not available for the hearing the "Yes" box should be marked and their name should be placed in the left column and the date(s) to avoid in the right column.

A landlord should ideally attached proposed directions with the allocation questionnaire whether or not they have been agreed with the tenant. Directions are a list of instructions given by the court for each party to comply with, that should eventually lead to a hearing and the disposal of the claim. Either party can propose to the court what these directions should be in the Allocation Questionnaire (form N150). Typical directions include:-
- notification of the track to which the case has been allocated;
- each party being required to deliver to the other party(ies) and the court copies of all documents they intend to rely on no later than 14 days before the hearing;
- each party to bring the original documents to the court hearing; and

- a date and time allowed for a final hearing with at least 21 days' notice unless the parties agree to a shorter notice period.

A landlord should mark the "yes" box for the first question in section "F" and "yes" or "no" depending on whether or not the tenant agreed to the proposed directions.

Section "G" on costs should not be completed as indicated on the form as the case is being dealt with under the small claims procedure and/or the landlord is acting in person.

If the landlord's claim exceeds £1,500 as indicated on the form the landlord will need to pay an allocation fee and so "yes" or "no" will be indicated on the form accordingly. For details of the fees a landlord should see: www.justice.gov.uk/courts/fees.

In section "I" of the form the landlord should indicate "yes" to questions 1 and 2 as proposed directions will be submitted with the form and sent to the tenant. In the box below it should be stated when the tenant received them. This may well be a future date to indicate they have been sent with a completed allocation questionnaire. For the question "Do you intend to make any applications in the immediate future" the landlord should mark the "no" box.

The form should be signed, dated and below the signature the following words and numbers in bracket [Counsel] [Solicitor] [for the] [1st] [2nd] [3rd] [Defendant] and [Part 20 claimant] deleted so that it reads [Claimant]. Contact details for the landlord i.e. name, address, phone and email should be placed in the last section of the form.

When the court has considered the information in both parties Allocation Questionnaire it will send a Notice of Allocation to the landlord and tenant. A Notice of Allocation may contain standard directions or special directions.

Standard directions will usually include the following:-
- notification of the track to which the case has been allocated;
- each party being required to deliver to the other party(s) and the court copies of all documents they intend to rely on no later than 14 days before the hearing;
- each party to bring the original documents to the court hearing;
- a date, time and time allowed for a final hearing with at least 21 days' notice unless the parties agree to a shorter notice period;
- encouragement to both landlord and tenant to seek to settle the claim without a hearing and notify the court immediately if it is settled;
- notification that permission must be sought for an expert at the hearing by writing to the court immediately explaining why the expert's assistance is necessary; and

- notification of consequences for failing to comply with the directions.

Special directions may include the following:-

- require that a party clarify their case by providing a list of documents or other details relevant to the case;
- require that a party allow inspection of their documents by the other party by appointment within a time limit;
- state that the hearing will take place at a venue different from the current court;
- require a party to bring something to the court hearing;
- require signed statements of all witnesses;
- warn that failure to comply can result in certain evidence not being allowed or the claim struck out;
- give instructions about expert evidence;
- notify court of the use of video evidence and provide the other party with it;
- propose to deal with the claim without a hearing; and
- propose a preliminary hearing so the judge can explain certain things to a party.

15.7 Preliminary hearing

The court may hold a preliminary hearing in a claim. This may not occur in a straightforward case but could occur where the tenant has filed a defence with contentious issues. At the hearing the court may explain the special directions it has issued in a case or it may use that hearing to determine that one party has no chance of success in bringing or defending the case and conclude the claim at the preliminary hearing. If the case is continuing after the preliminary hearing the court may fix a date for a final hearing, state the time allowed for the final hearing and give further directions. Paragraph 5.6 sets out what a landlord should do on attending a court hearing.

15.8 Preparation for the final hearing

At the final hearing the landlord should be seeking to establish the following matters before the court:-

1. That the tenant is liable to pay rent to the landlord. This is usually established through providing a tenancy agreement signed by both parties. If there is no tenancy agreement, then by providing evidence of previous rent payments in the form of copy receipts or bank statements or in the form of a witness such as an estate agent.

2. The landlord may have to prove that they are indeed the landlord by showing a superior legal interest in the property such as the title deeds or mortgage statement.

3. Once it is established that the tenant is liable to pay the rent the landlord will need to prove how much the rent is. This may be via the original or renewal tenancy agreement, a rent statement, copy receipts for rent, bank statement showing payments, estate or managing agent witnesses, housing benefit correspondence or a Section 13 Notice if that has been used to increase the rent.

4. Address any defence the tenant may have raised, such as the rent has been paid or they are not liable to pay the rent.

The following should also be noted:-

1. Matters being put to the court should be set out in date order.

2. A landlord should have a list of all documents to be referred to which should already have been provided to the tenant and the court.

3. If a witness is reluctant to attend court, the court's help should be sought to issue a witness summons to force attendance.

4. If special equipment (such as video) is needed at the hearing the court should have already been informed and this should be confirmed before the hearing.

15.9 The hearing

In the small claims court a hearing is meant to be informal so that a party can present their case without having any legal background. Solicitors are not allowed their costs from the other party in small claims proceedings, therefore having legal representation may win a landlord's case but all the rent arrears recovered could end up going towards legal fees. This book intends to guide a landlord in making a successful claim themselves. The following are characteristics of a hearing in the small claims court:-

- the court can choose an appropriate method for conducting the hearing that they believe to be fair;
- the hearing is informal;
- strict rules of evidence do not apply;
- evidence does not have to be given on oath;
- cross examination may be limited;

- reasons are given for the court's decision; the hearing is usually held in public but can be held in private especially if details of a party's financial circumstances is being revealed;
- if the whole or part of the hearing is taking place outside of the court it will be in private;
- if the matter is being heard in court, the hearing will normally be in the judge's room (called chambers) or in a court room;
- judge may ask questions of witnesses before the parties do;
- judge may limit the time parties have to give evidence;
- a lay representative can speak on behalf of a party if the party is also in attendance at the hearing;
- interpreters are not provided;
- the hearing is recorded and transcripts can be made available;
- judgment is usually given at the end of the hearing, reasons may be given then or at a later date; and
- the claimant who wins will normally get their court fees, the amount claimed and certain expenses.

Paragraph 5.6 sets out what a landlord should do on attending a hearing.

15.10 Non-attendance of a party at a final hearing

A landlord or tenant may for one reason or another decide not to attend a final hearing. They may, however, wish for the hearing to proceed in their absence. In such a situation the non-attending party must do the following:-

- give written notice to the court and the other party at least seven days before the hearing of their non-attendance;
- serve on the other party all the documents given to the court at least seven days before the hearing; and
- request that the court decide the claim in their absence.

If a landlord does not attend the hearing and does not request it to be heard in their absence or adjourned to another date the court may strike out their claim effectively making there be no case.

If a tenant does not attend the hearing and does not request it to be heard in their absence or adjourned to another date and the landlord attends or request it to be heard in their absence the court may decide the claim on the evidence of the landlord alone.

If both parties agree the court can decide the claim without a hearing. A note of the reasons for the decision will be sent to both parties.

Obtaining a money judgment for arrears of rent does not equate to a landlord getting their money from the tenant. At this stage all a landlord has is a court document stating that the tenant is ordered to pay them a specified sum of money and may include an order to pay costs and also interest. A county court judgment will be registered against the tenant's name and will adversely affect their credit.

15.11 Enforcing a money judgment for rent arrears

If a tenant does not pay the money ordered to be paid in a judgment, by the time given in a judgment, the landlord will need to take enforcement action to recover the sum of money.

There are several enforcement actions that can be taken depending on the tenant's circumstances. They include:-

- attachment of earnings order (if they work);
- a warrant of execution (if they have valuable possessions);
- third party debt order (if their bank account is known and there are funds);
- a charging order (if they own property);
- bankruptcy (if the debt is greater than £750).

16 GETTING A TENANT'S EMPLOYER TO PAY RENT ARREARS FROM THEIR WAGES (ATTACHMENT OF EARNINGS ORDER)

16.1 Attachment of earnings order

If a landlord has obtained and keeps updated the employment information about their tenant, mentioned in Chapter 2 of this book, and the tenant remains employed, a landlord should be able to enforce a money judgment using an attachment of earnings order.

This is an order of the court served on the tenant's employer requiring them to deduct a sum of money from the tenant's salary/wages and pay it to the court until the money judgment, interest and costs are satisfied.

An attachment of earnings order can be applied for where a judgment order remains unpaid, or if it is being paid by instalments, an instalment due remains unpaid in full or in part.

There will be a fee with the application to the court. That fee will be recoverable from the tenant if there are sufficient funds. A landlord should contact the court or check the website (www.justice.gov.uk/courts/fees) for the correct fee to be paid.

The application may be made in the court for the area in which the tenant resides or the court where the judgment was obtained. If there is more than one tenant liable jointly under the judgment, the application can be made to the court in any of the areas in which any tenant resides if the judgment to be enforced was obtained in that court.

To obtain an attachment of earnings order a landlord will need to make an application to the court on form N337.

16.2 Completing form N337

In the top right corner of the form the name of the court in which the order is being applied for should be completed.

In section 1 the landlord's name, address and phone number are to be completed.

In section 2 the name and address for the person for service of court documents and receipt of payments if it is different from the details given in section 1 are to be completed. If the details are not different this should be left blank.

ATTACHMENT OF EARNINGS ORDER

The tenant's name, address and phone number should be completed in section 3.

In section 4 the name of the court where the judgment being enforced was obtained is to be completed, if that is not the same court being asked to enforce the judgment.

In the first box of section 5 the landlord should state the amount outstanding including unpaid warrant costs at the date of this application to court. In the second box of section 5 the issue fee which the court will advise of or can be found on the website and in the third box of section 5 the total amount now due (balance of debt plus issue fee) are to be included.

In section 6 the tenant's employer's name, address and phone number are to be completed. In the continuation of section 6 (on the right side of the form) the tenant's place of employment if it is different from the address given for the employer are to be completed. In the following box the occupation of the tenant should be written and in the final box of section 6 the works number or pay reference (which should be on the pay slip) should be completed.

In section 7 the landlord can state any other relevant information about the tenant such as the amount they earn, whether their position is senior and how long they have worked in the company, if known. The landlord should sign the form, cross out the words (claimant's solicitor) in bracket and insert the date.

When the application has been issued by the court (i.e. accepted with the relevant fee, stamped and dated) it will be served on the tenant with a reply form. The tenant will have eight days after receipt of the court documents to provide a reply in the relevant form. The tenant in replying to the court will be required to provide information of their employer, their earnings, resources and needs. The court may request earning details directly from the tenant's employer.

If the tenant pays to the landlord the outstanding sums due or any sums this should be notified to the court immediately. A copy of the tenant's reply to the court will be sent to the landlord.

If the court officer dealing with the application has sufficient information from the tenant's response, an attachment of earnings order may be made which will be sent to both parties and the employer. If either party wishes to object to the order they have 14 days to apply on notice (i.e. with the other party being notified) for the order to be reconsidered. The application will need to be made on form N244 and a fee will be payable. Following this the court will fix a date for a hearing. At the hearing the earlier order may be confirmed or a new order made.

If the court officer does not make an order upon receiving the tenant's reply, the case will be referred to a judge who may make an attachment of earnings order on the papers received or require that a hearing be fixed. If the judge made an order without a hearing either party may apply on notice for the order to be reconsidered giving their reasons. At the hearing the judge may confirm or reconsider the order made.

An attachment of earnings order will not be made for a debt less than £50 or for a sum outstanding on a debt which is less than £50.

If the tenant does not respond to the application issued by the court or fail to make payment to the landlord an order may be made in the following circumstance and to the following effect:-

- that the tenant provide to the court, by a certain time, a signed statement with the details of those who pays their earnings;
- how much are their earnings, resources and needs; and
- information to allow the tenant to be identified by the employer.

The order will:
- incorporate a notice warning the tenant of the consequences of non-compliance;
- be served on the tenant personally; and
- direct that future payments be made directly to the court.

If the tenant does not comply with the order the court office will issue a notice asking the tenant to show good reason why they should not be imprisoned and inform them of a further hearing date.

If the tenant fails to attend the adjourned hearing and a committal (for prison) order is made it may be suspended for the tenant to attend a hearing specified in the committal order, if the tenant fails to comply with the terms of the order a warrant of committal will be issued.

A landlord may be able to get their costs in these proceedings for:-
- a solicitor attending the hearing and serving the application;
- a counsel's fee; and
- the court fee to issue the application.

The costs may be fixed.

16.3 The order

The attachment of earnings order will be directed to a person (organisation) who to the court has the tenant in their employment. The contents of the order will:-

- instruct the employer to make periodical deductions from the tenant's earnings;
- specify the amount to be deducted and the period for which it is to be deducted and the time at which the payments ought to be made to the court's collecting officer;
- specify the protected earnings rate below which the tenant's earnings should not fall;
- have sufficient information for the employer to identify the tenant;
- specify the total sum outstanding as well as costs;
- state the tenant's full name and address;
- state the tenant's place of work, nature of their work and work number; and
- specify the application/allocation of the moneys by the collecting officer.

The collecting officer will deduct court fees if any and deal with the remaining monies to satisfy the judgment.

17 SEIZING A TENANT'S POSSESSIONS TO BE SOLD FOR RENT ARREARS (WARRANT OF EXECUTION)

17.1 A warrant of execution

A warrant of execution allows the court's bailiffs to seize goods belonging to the tenant from their home or business address, and sell them so that the proceeds can go towards satisfying the judgment debt.

A warrant of execution can be applied for when the tenant has failed to pay the amount they have been ordered to pay or have failed to pay an instalment they were due to pay. The application should normally be made to the court in which the judgment was obtained.

A landlord wishing to instruct the court's bailiff to seize a tenant's possessions needs to make an application on form N323.

17.2 Completing form N323

The form should be completed as follows:-

Section 1 of the form should have the landlord's name and address.

Section 2 should have the name and address for service of court documents and payment to the landlord if this is different to the details given in section 1.

Section 3 should have the tenant's name and address.

Section 4 should include:-

(4A) the amount of the judgment still owing at the date of the application to the court ....

(4B) the amount for which the warrant is to be issued (if the warrant is for unpaid instalment(s) then this figure will be different from the amount outstanding at 4A) ....

The issue fee ....

There will be no solicitor's costs as landlord is acting in person

The total amount for the boxes at 4B ....

In the last box of 4B the landlord should write the figure that will be outstanding after the warrant has been satisfied if the full amount of the money judgment is not been applied for at this stage e.g. where an unpaid instalment is being applied for.

In the top right hand box the court's name should be inserted. This will be the Northampton County Court if proceedings were not transferred from the CCMCC.

In the section of the form on the right headed by the words "I certify that the…" the landlord should sign the form and indicate below their signature that they are the claimant by deleting the words (Claimant's solicitor) then date the form.

At the final section of the form the landlord should provide the contact number for themselves or the name and contact number of someone else who they would like the bailiffs to contact about enforcing the warrant, and the tenant's contact number if known. The landlord should go on to state any difficulties the bailiffs may counter. This may include matters such as the number of people residing in the property, whether there is a dog or whether a resident has a criminal past that is relevant.

The warrant should be granted within two weeks of the application. A landlord should contact the court to find out if the warrant has been granted.

If the warrant has been granted the bailiffs will normally write to the tenant informing them that a warrant has been issued, the amount it was issued for and that they should pay within seven days. If no payment is made the bailiffs will normally visit the tenant's address within 15 days of the warrant being issued.

A bailiff can only enter the tenant's premises in the following situations:-
- they are allowed in by the person there;
- by a door left unlocked or a window left open;
- break into business premises which do not have living accommodation;
- enter if they have previously been allowed in and are returning to collect goods identified.

If the tenant ensures that the property is completely locked and do not open the door the bailiffs will not be able to fulfil the warrant. There may be a way around this. If the tenant is still living in the landlord's property a landlord may write to the tenant informing them of an inspection under the terms of the tenancy agreement. Most tenancy agreements allow a landlord to enter the property for the purposes of an inspection upon giving the tenant 48/24 hours written notice.

A landlord should then time their inspection of the property to coincide with the bailiff's visit. In doing so a landlord may be able to ensure that the bailiffs are able to enter the property and fulfil the warrant of execution by inadvertently inviting them in or allowing access through a door left unopened. The landlord would need to find out exactly when the bailiffs will visit to arrange this.

A bailiff can take possessions belonging to the tenant or jointly owned by them. The possessions should produce an income after their sale and removal costs have been deducted otherwise they are not worth removing.

The following items cannot be seized:-
- items needed for job or business;
- essential household items;
- items leased, rented or on hire purchase;
- possessions seized under another warrant.

A warrant of execution can be made for a full judgment sum or for outstanding instalment(s). The sum to be recovered by a warrant of execution should be no less than £50 or the amount of one monthly instalment or four weekly instalments whichever is greater.

There is a fee for obtaining a warrant of execution. The landlord should check the fee with the court or the court service website (www.justice.gov.uk/courts/fees). The fee for the warrant will be payable by the tenant if there are sufficient funds to satisfy it.

A warrant for execution is valid for 12 months and can be renewed after that period.

WARRANT OF EXECUTION

18 FREEZING A TENANT'S BANK ACCOUNT TO RECOVER RENT ARREARS (THIRD PARTY DEBT ORDER)

18.1 Nature of the order

If a landlord has collected sufficient information about a tenant as recommended in Chapter 2 of this book, a landlord may obtain a third party debt order.

A third party debt order is an order usually instructing a bank, building society or other institution holding funds on behalf of the tenant to freeze those funds at the time the order is served until the court decides whether the funds should be paid to the landlord.

A third party debt order cannot be made against a joint bank account unless all the joint account holders are also tenants against whom proceedings have been successful.

It is crucial that a landlord use informed and exact timing in serving a third party debt order. A third party debt order will only apply to the funds that a bank, building society or institution (i.e. a third party) is holding at the time the order is served. If a landlord serves the order on the third party when there are minimal funds being held, the order will only apply to those minimal funds and not to any subsequent funds that the third party may hold. The tenant is likely to take steps to ensure further orders recover minimal or no funds by ensuring no further funds are held by the third party on their behalf.

A landlord who has collected bank statements from a tenant at the commencement of the tenancy as recommended in Chapter 2 of this book should be able to deduce from those statements a pattern of when money goes in and out of the account e.g. wages, tax credits, maintenance, or other income.

On analysing this information the landlord can inform the court that they will serve the order when made. The landlord should then serve the order on the third party on the day they believe that sufficient funds will be in the account or when the maximum sum the tenant receives will be in the account to maximise the sum they can recover.

18.2 Making an application for the order

An application for a third party debt order will be made without the tenant being aware of it. It must be made in the court which made the judgment being enforced which will be the Northampton County Court (CCMCC) unless the proceedings have been transferred.

The application will be dealt with by a judge without a hearing. It is therefore essential that the paper work is completed fully and accurately.

An application for a third party debt order should be made on form N349.

18.3 Completing form N349

The name of the county court in which the application is being made should be put in the box at the top of the form with the heading "In the".

The "claim number" and "application number" boxes should be completed by the court.

The landlord's name should be written in the claimant's box.

The tenant's name should be written in the defendant's box.

The name of the bank, building society or institution upon whom the order will be served should be written in the third party box.

In the first part of the sentence below, the word "defendant" should be crossed out leaving "claimant" and "judgment creditor". In the latter part of the sentence the words "claimant" should be crossed out leaving "defendant" and "judgment debtor". Towards the end of the sentence the landlord should state the date the order being enforced was made, the court it was made in and the claim number of the proceedings in which it was made in the same order.

At section 1 of the form the name, address and postcode of the tenant (judgment debtor) should be stated.

At section 2 the following should be completed:-
- the amount the tenant was ordered to pay in the order/judgment being enforced and the amount due including further interest (if any) at the date the application is made;
- if payment was to be made by instalments the first box should be marked and the amount of instalment(s) that has not been paid should be stated; or
- the second box should be marked to indicate that the order was not to be paid by instalments.

The beginning of section 3 should be completed if the third party is a bank or building society. The bank or building society's name and address of its head office should first be completed. Below this the relevant box should be marked to indicate if the branch that deals with the tenant's account is known and if known the name of the branch at which the funds is being held and the address should be inserted. In the latter boxes, it should be marked whether the account number and sort code is known and, if known, they should be inserted. If the third party is not a bank or building society the last part of section 3 should be completed with the third party's name and address.

If it is known that someone else has a claim to the money owed by the third party this should be stated at section 4 with their name, address and any information known about their claim. It is likely that a landlord will not know the tenant's affairs in such detail to answer this question affirmatively. At section 5 the landlord should state how they know the information in sections 3 and 4 is correct i.e. their source.

At section 6 the landlord should mark whether or not they have made any applications for a third party debt order in respect of the judgment being enforced and, if yes, include the date of the application, the third party's name, address and postcode.

At the end of the form is the "Statement of Truth". In the first sentence the words in bracket "(the judgment creditor believes)" should be crossed out so that the sentence reads "I believe…" The second sentence which begins "I am duly authorised…" should be crossed out. The landlord should sign and date the form. In the sentence below the signature the words "Litigation friend" and "Judgment creditor's solicitor" should be crossed out so that it reads "Judgment creditor". The landlord should enter their full name below. In the final unnumbered section of the form the landlord should put the address to which documents should be sent to them and their postcode.

A fee will have to be paid when the application is made to the court. A landlord should check with the relevant court or their website for details of the fee (www.justice.gov.uk/courts/fees).

When the court receives the application, the court's staff will check the form, stamp it and send/give the landlord a reference. The application will then be referred to a judge who, if satisfied with the application, will make an interim third party debt order in form N84. Under normal circumstances the court will send a copy of the order to the landlord and the third party, upon the order being made, with the tenant being sent the order seven days later. However, the landlord can and should request that they serve the order on the third party themselves for the reasons given in paragraph 18.1.

Service of the order on the third party is crucial so as to ensure that the funds become frozen when they are at their maximum to ensure the landlord recovers as much as possible from the order as this may be their only real opportunity of enforcing judgment.

The interim third party debt order will not provide for any funds to be paid to the landlord at this stage. It only provides for the funds of the tenant held by the third party to be frozen. The interim order will include a hearing date where the judge can decide if the funds should be paid to the landlord by the third party. A landlord must attend the hearing or risk the order being dismissed and the tenant thereafter taking action to disperse their funds.

18.4 The interim third party order

A hearing date will be set in the interim order to consider the making of a final third party debt order (following which the funds may be paid to the landlord). The hearing date will not be less than 28 days from the making of the order.

The interim third party debt order will specify the amount of money which the third party must retain. It binds the third party as soon as it is served on them.

If the third party is not a bank or building society they must, within seven days of receiving the order, let the court know if they owe the tenant any money or owe less than the amount in the interim order.

If the third party is a bank or building society they must carry out a search to identify all accounts held by it for the tenant within seven days of being served with the order, and provide to the court and the landlord the following information:-

- the number of accounts;
- whether they are in credit;
- if in credit whether the balance is sufficient to cover the amount in the order;
- the amount of balance at the date the order was served, if less than the amount in the order;
- whether the bank/building society asserts any rights to the tenant's money and if so why; or
- that there are no accounts to which the order applies or the third party is unable to comply with the order for some reason and why.

18.4.1 Service of the order

A copy of the interim order, the application that was completed and supporting documents must be served on the third party giving them not less than 21 days' notice of the final hearing.

A copy of the interim order, the application notice and supporting documents must be served on the tenant not less than seven days after a copy has been served on the third party and not less than seven days before the final hearing.

If the landlord serves the order (as is recommended) they must provide a certificate of service to the court not less than two days before the hearing or produce a certificate of service at the hearing. A certificate of service is prepared by completing form N215.

18.4.1.1   What can the tenant/debtor do about the order?

A tenant who cannot withdraw any money from their account as a result of the order and is suffering hardship in meeting ordinary living expenses can make an application to the court, and an order can be made allowing payments out of the account, called a hardship payment order.

The tenant's application will be served on the landlord at least two days before the hearing.

18.4.2 The final hearing

The tenant and third party can object to a final order by providing the court with written evidence of their objections. If someone else has a claim to the money either the tenant or third party can inform the court of this. The landlord can dispute whether the third party has no money or less money than the judgment order if this has been asserted by the third party. This evidence must be provided to the court and all parties at least three days before the hearing.

At the hearing the court may make a final order, discharge the interim order and application, decide issues in dispute or direct a trial of the issues and give directions. Paragraph 5.6 sets out what a landlord should do on attending a hearing.

THIRD PARTY DEBT ORDER

19 SECURING RENT ARREARS AGAINST A TENANT'S PROPERTY (CHARGING ORDER)

19.1 Nature of a charging order

A charging order is an order registering a debt against the property (land, house or flat) a tenant owns. A charging order does not mean that a landlord will get the money sought when the order is granted. However, once registered it secures the money owed to a landlord against the property of a tenant so that when that property is sold or transferred a landlord should ultimately get their money. If a landlord collects the information about a tenant as recommended in Chapter 2 it may come to the landlord's attention that the tenant owns a property or has a share in a property.

Upon a sale/transfer of a tenant's property (with equity) the charge has to be paid before any remaining sums are paid to a tenant. However, a charging order does not place an obligation on a tenant to sell the property. For a sale to be achieved a landlord will need to apply to court for an order for sale. This process is not covered in this book.

A charging order, once made by the court, is by itself ineffective against a tenant's property unless it is registered against it. Earlier registered charges will take priority and have to be paid before subsequent registered charges. If there are no funds available because there is no equity in the property the charge may not be paid upon a sale.

19.1.1 Type of interest in a property

There are different interests that a tenant can have in a property. These include:-
- legal interest as a sole owner;
- legal interest as joint owner;
- beneficial interest as a joint owner; and
- beneficial interest without being an owner.

There are two main types of land ownership recorded in the UK. They are registered and unregistered title. Various rules govern registration of a charge against these titles and at what point a registration can be effected such as notice of proceedings, pending action and charging order.

There are volumes of books written on the various types of interest a person can have in a property and a single chapter in this book cannot convey that information. It is advisable that a landlord seeks independent legal advice and assistance in getting a charge registered against a tenant's interest in land. This chapter only deals with obtaining a charging order from the court.

19.1.2 Applying for a charging order

The application for a charging order is normally made without the tenant being aware of the proceedings (the term for such applications is a "without notice application"). A without notice application prevents the tenant disposing of the property before the order is made and registered.

An application for a charging order should be made to the court that made the judgment being enforced by the charging order, which will usually be the Northampton County Court unless it was transferred to another court. A landlord may obtain one charging order for more than one county court judgment against a tenant.

The application should be made on form N379 if it relates to land or N380 if it relates to other securities. This book will only deal with the application in relation to land.

19.1.3 Completing the application form N379

In the first box at the top of the form beginning with the words "in the", the name of the county court in which the application is being made should be entered.

In the claimant's box the landlord's name should be entered.

In the defendant's box the tenant's name should be entered.

The box for the claim number and the application number (appn. no.) should be left blank to be completed by the court.

In the sentence below at the first set of words in brackets "[defendant]" should be crossed out so that it reads "the (claimant) (the judgment creditor)" With the second set of words in brackets in the same sentence the word "[claimant]" should be crossed out so that it reads "the (defendant) (the judgment debtor)..." In the blank spaces of the sentence the date of the order being enforced, the court in which the order was made and the claim number of the proceedings should be entered in the same order.

At section 1 of the form headed "Judgment debtor" the name of the tenant, their address and postcode should be entered.

At section 2 of the form headed "Judgment debt" in the first part the amount the tenant was ordered to pay in the order/judgment being enforced and the amount due including further interest at the date this application is made should be entered. If payment was due by instalments the first box should be marked and the amount of the instalment(s) that has not been paid entered. If the judgment or order did not provide for payments by instalments the second box should be marked.

In section 3 the address of the land or property upon which the charge is sought should be entered. A search should be undertaken at the Land Registry website to ascertain if the property is registered and if so the title number should be entered here on the form. If the land is registered an Office Copy Entry of its details at the Land Registry should be obtained and attached to this form. If the property is unregistered, this should be written on the form.

In section 4 the interest of the tenant in the property, i.e. sole owner, joint owner or a beneficiary under a trust should be marked in the relevant box. If the land is registered this information should be included on the registered title and the box to say it is shown on the Office Copy Land Register entries attached should be marked. If this information was not obtained by Office Copies entries because the land is unregistered or it was obtained from another source the landlord should mark the box that states that "the judgment creditor believes it to be so because" and set out the source by which they got the information in the space below. This could be that it was provided by the tenant to the landlord at the sign up process.

In section 5 the landlord must indicate whether or not they are aware of other creditors of the tenant and if yes, their name and address, the nature of the debt and the amount. Some of this information may be available from entries on the registered title.

In section 6 the landlord should indicate whether they know if any other person has an interest in the land and if yes, their name, address and the nature of that interest. This will usually be indicated on the registered title of the property. If the property is unregistered a landlord will need to conduct a search in the Land Charges Register against the tenant's proper name to ascertain this information.

In section 7 the landlord can state any further information they would like the court to take account of.

Section 8 only needs to be completed where someone gives the information on behalf of a company, corporation or a firm.

The next section of the form is the Statement of Truth. At the first sentence the words in bracket (the judgment creditor believes) should be crossed out so that the sentence reads "I believe..." The sentence below which reads "I am duly authorised..." should be crossed out. The landlord should then sign and date the form and cross out the words in brackets below the signature that reads (litigation friend) and (judgment creditor's solicitor). The landlord should enter their full name below where indicated on the form.

In the final box the landlord should complete their address to which documents should be sent.

19.1.4 Presenting the application to the court

A fee will have to be paid when the application is made to the court. A landlord should make enquiries with the court where the application is being made or check online at www.justice.gov.uk/courts/fees for the fee.

When presented at court the staff will check that the papers are in order, collect the fee, give the application a court number and refer it to a judge. The application will initially be dealt with by a judge without a hearing. The initial application must be properly made, and all documents in order, to ensure success at this stage.

If everything is in order the judge will make an interim charging order in form N86 over the tenant's interest in the property and set a date to consider whether a final charging order should be made.

19.1.5 Service of the interim charging order

The tenant and other creditors (if known and directed by the court) will be served with copies of the interim charging order, the application for the order and supporting documents not less than 21 days before the final hearing. The documents can be served by the landlord or the court. It is best that the court serves the order so that a landlord avoids the additional work and obligations associated with serving the order themselves.

19.1.6 The final charging order hearing

If the tenant or any other person objects to a final charging order being made they will need to present their objections to the court and the landlord in writing not less than seven days before the hearing.

For the procedure of what a landlord/claimant should do when attending court for a hearing they should read paragraph 5.6.

At the hearing the judge may do any of the following:-
• make a final charging order;
• dismiss the interim charging order and its application; or
• give directions for and set a date for a trial on any issues raised.

The order made will be served on any person on whom the interim charging order was served. It is very important that the landlord gets the interim and final charging order registered against a tenant's property immediately when it is made. A charging order has no effect until it is registered against the property.

20 MAKING A TENANT BANKRUPT

Bankruptcy or the threat of it can be a very serious arsenal at the disposal of a landlord seeking to recover arrears of rent. If a tenant is made bankrupt, all the tenant's assets are taken to pay all the tenants debts. It is not just the rent arrears that are dealt with. It also results in future restrictions or prohibitions on the tenant performing in certain jobs, taking public and private offices and obtaining credit.

Sometimes threatening or initiating the process of bankruptcy can lead to a tenant abandoning the property therefore giving a landlord vacant possession without having to obtain a possession order. If a tenant abandons a property a landlord should follow the steps and procedures set out in Chapter 13 (Tenant Abandons Property).

Under the bankruptcy process the tenant's asset will be sold and the money used to pay off their creditors. However, some debts will take priority over others and if the proceeds of sale of the assets are not sufficient to cover all the debts that take priority over the rent arrears, a landlord could find themselves following an expensive process with no return.

To make a tenant bankrupt a landlord must prove that they owe them at least £750. If a tenant has rent arrears of £1,000 and a deposit of £500 (provided there is no other claim against the deposit) they will owe their landlord £500. This sum is below the threshold to make them bankrupt. There are three initial processes that can be followed before the bankruptcy petition (application) is put before the court. These are:-

- serve a statutory demand on the tenant. If the tenant fails to pay or agree payment, a landlord can proceed to make the tenant bankrupt;
- obtain a county court judgment then serve a statutory demand on the tenant; and
- seek to enforce a county court judgment and failing that proceed to file (present to the court) a bankruptcy petition (application) without using a statutory demand.

20.1 Statutory demand where no court order has been obtained

A statutory demand, where no court order has been obtained for the debt, is made by completing Form 6.1 which is available at the Insolvency Service website (http://www.bis.gov.uk/insolvency/about-us/forms).

20.1.1 Completing form 6.1

In the section headed "Demand" and the sentence starting with the word "to" a landlord should complete the tenant's title and full name. At the sentence starting with "Address" the tenant's full address and post code should be completed. This may be the address of the rental property or another address if the tenant has moved. This could be due to abandonment or because the tenancy has ended.

Below the sentence which reads "this demand is served on you by the creditor" at the sentence starting with the word "Name" the landlord should state their full name and at the sentence starting with the word "Address" the landlord should write their full address.

In the sentence below that reads "the creditor claims that you owe the sum of…" the amount of rent arrears should be entered. If there is a deposit and no claim against it for damage to the property, the amount of the deposit should be deducted from the rent arrears and the net sum inserted. This net sum should be at least £750.

At the bottom of the first page above the signature section the landlord should cross out the paragraph that refers to Minister of the Crown or Government Department.

At the section of the form that reads "signature of individual" the landlord's signature should be entered, followed by their name in block letters and the date. The remainder of the sentences on page 1 with the asterisk sign should be crossed out and the address, telephone number and reference left blank.

On page 2 under the section headed "Particulars of Debt" the landlord (creditor) should state to the following effect:

> An Assured Shorthold Tenancy/Company Let/Resident landlord tenancy (*delete as appropriate*) was granted to the tenant (insert tenant's name) which commenced on (*insert date*). The rent under the tenancy agreement is (£ *insert amount*) per calendar month/week (delete as appropriate). The tenant (*insert tenant's name*) has not paid rent from (*insert date*) to (*insert date or alternatively insert periods for which no rent has been paid*). To date the tenant owes (£ *insert amount*) in rent and (£ *insert amount*) in interest resulting in a total sum of (£ *insert amount*). Interest is payable as a result of term xx (*insert the number of the term as listed in the tenancy agreement*) of the tenancy agreement which states that (*insert wording of the term as set out in the tenancy agreement*).

If there is a deposit and no other claim against it the landlord should further write:-

> A deposit of £xxx is held as security by the landlord via a deposit protection scheme which reduces the arrears to £xxx which is the sum set out in the statutory demand.

If there is a deposit and a claim against it (such as damage to property) the landlord should further write:-

> A deposit of £xxx is held by the landlord via a deposit protection scheme. There is a claim against it for damage to the property, leaving £xxx towards the arrears/leaving no security towards the arrears. The final sum outstanding is £xxx.

At Part A of the form a landlord is required to put the details of the court where the tenant could present their own bankruptcy petition. For this purpose England and Wales is divided into insolvency districts that are administered by different courts.

A landlord needs to insert the details of the bankruptcy court that covers the insolvency district in which the tenant for the greater part of the last six months has carried on a business or if the tenant (debtor) does not carry on a business the details of the court that covers the insolvency district for where the tenant has lived for the greater part of the last six months. If the landlord cannot ascertain the insolvency district because it is unknown where the tenant lives or carries on a business then it should be presented in the High Court. The High Court and the Central London County Court covers the following areas as their insolvency district:-

> (a) Barnet; (b) Bow; (c) Brentford; (d) Central London; (e) Clerkenwell and Shoreditch; (f) Edmonton; (g) Lambeth; (h) Mayor's and City of London; (i) Wandsworth; (j) West London; and (k) Willesden.

It is advised that a landlord contact a court directly or search on the internet (www.justice.gov.uk/about/hmcts) to determine which court covers the insolvency district for where the tenant lives or has carried on a business as mentioned above.

In part B of the form the landlord needs to give details of to whom and where communication regarding the statutory demand should be sent. This includes name, address, telephone number and reference. This should normally be the landlord's details if they are acting for themselves.

It is unlikely that a landlord would need to complete part C. However, if a landlord has purchased a property with a sitting tenant and taken over the rent arrears of that tenant, then part C will need to be completed as the debt has been assigned from the original landlord to the current landlord. In this section the original creditor will be the former landlord and the assignee will be the current landlord.

20.2 Statutory demand where there is a court judgment or order for the debt

If a landlord has already obtained a county court judgment for rent arrears and wishes to make a tenant bankrupt the landlord can complete a statutory demand in form 6.2.

20.2.1 Completing form 6.2

Form 6.2 is quite similar to form 6.1. It should be completed in the same manner set out in paragraph 20.1 except for the following differences:

On the first page at the sentence that begins with the words "by a judgment/order of the" the name of the court should be inserted, following which the case or claim number should be inserted. Where the sentence reads "...between..."the landlord's name should be entered followed by the tenant's name in the next space. In the following spaces the landlord should enter the sum for which the judgment or order was obtained followed by the costs that was ordered to be paid. The remainder of the form should be completed as set out in paragraph 20.1 for form 6.1.

20.3 Serving a Statutory Demand

Under the Insolvency Rule 6.3 a landlord is required to do all that is reasonable for the purpose of bringing the statutory demand to the tenant's attention and if practicable to serve by way of personal service.

Personal service on an individual is effected by leaving it with them; on a company by leaving it with someone senior in that company; and on a partnership by leaving it with a partner or the person who has control or management of the partnership business at its principal place of business.

A landlord who has followed Chapter 2 in obtaining the required information/documentation from a tenant should have sufficient options to carry out personal service on a tenant and have a photograph by which the tenant can be identified. If the tenant is still living in the property at the time a statutory demand is to be served, a landlord will have a good opportunity for personal service.

The best way to ensure personal service is getting a process server to carry out service and provide the required evidence for future court proceedings i.e. affidavit of service. With the information a landlord should possess about their tenant, a process server should be able to carry out their instructions.

If a landlord wishes to carry out personal service themselves they should get a witness to accompany them and seek to place the statutory demand in the tenant's hand or leave it sufficiently close to the tenant whilst telling the tenant what it is. This could be on an occasion where a landlord carries out an inspection at the property in the presence of the tenant.

If it is impossible to effect personal service of the statutory demand on the tenant a landlord should note the efforts made to effect personal service, the time, date and the result of those efforts as this will be needed for future court proceedings. If a landlord fails in their attempt to effect personal service they will need to demonstrate another method of service by which they believe the statutory demand came to the attention of the tenant.

It is advisable for the landlord to seek an appointment with the tenant if personal service fails. If agreement is reached on an appointment the landlord should be prepared with the necessary documents to attempt personal service again.

If this fails a landlord should choose another method of service which it is believed will bring the statutory demand to the tenant's attention. This could include the following practical steps:-

- sending a copy of the statutory demand recorded delivery (marked private and confidential) to the tenant's place of work;
- leaving a copy of the statutory demand attached to the property address if the tenant still lives there and waiting to witness and record the arrival of the tenant and the statutory demand coming to their attention (this can be timed from the tenant working hours, school run or other routine);
- leaving a copy of the statutory demand attached to the windscreen of the tenant's car and recording it coming to their attention; or
- any other method that a landlord believes would bring the statutory demand to the tenant's attention given their particular circumstances.

If a landlord is unable to carry out personal service, and the attempts have been well documented, service may be effected by first class post or being hand delivered to the tenant's address. However, this method of service can cause a landlord difficulty in proving service in later court proceedings.

If a tenant sends written correspondence to a landlord, following posting of the statutory demand to the tenant, in which the statutory demand is mentioned a landlord can use that written correspondence as evidence that the statutory demand came to the attention of the tenant.

A tenant has a choice of actions on receiving a statutory demand:-
- make an application to the court to have it set aside;
- contact the landlord to make arrangements to pay the debt immediately or by instalments; or
- simply ignore it.

20.4 Tenant making an application to set aside a statutory demand

A tenant has 18 days in which to make an application to set aside the statutory demand (but can make a late application in some circumstances) or 21 days in which to comply with the statutory demand. An application to set aside is made to the court named in Part A of the form.

Following receipt of the tenant's application to set aside a statutory demand the court can either dismiss the application or set a date for the hearing of the application. If a date is set for the hearing the landlord will be notified of this and be sent a copy of the application and supporting documents submitted by the tenant.

At the hearing the court will listen to evidence from both parties and make a decision as to whether to set aside the statutory demand or allow the process to continue towards bankruptcy.

A tenant can apply to set aside the statutory demand on the following grounds:-
- a counterclaim against the landlord which equals or exceeds the debt in the statutory demand;
- the debt in the statutory demand is disputed on substantial grounds;
- the landlord has sufficient security for the debt; or
- the court is satisfied due to other reasons that the statutory demand should be set aside.

If no successful action has been taken or if no action at all has been taken following 21 days since the service of the statutory demand a landlord can present a bankruptcy petition to the court.

20.5 Making an application for the tenant (debtor) to be made bankrupt

A landlord should complete the following documents in sets of three, to be submitted on an application to make a tenant bankrupt (the landlord should also make a copy for themselves):-
- Form 6.7 if a statutory demand has not been complied with;
- Form 6.9 where there is no statutory demand but enforcement of a judgment has failed;
- Form 6.13A (witness statement) confirming that the contents of the bankruptcy petition are true; and
- Form 6.11 confirming that the statutory demand has been served.

If the statutory demand was not personally served a further witness statement setting out how the statutory demand was served on the tenant will need to accompany the court documents in order to obtain permission from the court to present the petition.

20.5.1 Completing form 6.7

At the first paragraph with the footnote (a) the full name(s) and address(s) of the landlord(s) should be entered and cross out "I" or "We" as appropriate.

At the second paragraph with the footnote (b) the full name, address and occupation (if any) of the tenant should be completed.

At the third paragraph with the footnote (c) the alias, if any, of the tenant should be completed.

At the fourth paragraph with the footnote (d) if the tenant carries on a business and the details are known it should be entered. The details are the trading name, whether the business is with others, business address and nature of the business.

At the fifth paragraph with the footnote (e) if the tenant resided at any other address(es) at the time of or after the debt was incurred it should be inserted.

At the sixth paragraph with the footnote (f) if the tenant carried on any other business at the time of, or after the debt was incurred it should be entered here with the same details as set out in the fourth paragraph.

At section 1 (for the average tenant) the second and third paragraphs are to be deleted as well as the second sentence of the first paragraph.

At section 2 the first paragraph is to be used if the bankruptcy petition is being presented in the High Court or Central London County Court and the relevant parts of the first paragraph are to be deleted to accurately describe the tenant's situation. In this instance the entire second paragraph ought to be deleted.

If the bankruptcy petition is being presented in a county court other than the Central London County Court the first paragraph should be deleted entirely and the relevant parts of the second paragraph deleted so that it accurately reflects the tenant (debtor's) situation.

In seeking to ascertain the county court in which to present the bankruptcy petition a landlord should contact the Court Service.

At section 3 the following should be stated: the amount of rent arrears; that they were incurred under a tenancy agreement dated xx/xx/xx (or if no tenancy agreement when the tenant began to occupy the property); when the rent arrears occurred; separately show the amount of interest, if any, and that the interest is being claimed under the tenancy agreement.

Section 4 should be left as it is.

At section 5 at footnote (k) the date the statutory demand was served is to be inserted and at footnote (l) the method of service of the statutory demand should be inserted. If a landlord has reasons to present the petition to the court before 21 days after service of the statutory demand has passed it should be inserted at note (m). This could be information that the tenant is disposing of their assets or seeking to leave the jurisdiction of the court.

At section 6 a landlord should leave paragraph one and delete the second and third paragraphs. As the sum the landlord is claiming is net of the deposit there is no security for the sum in the petition.

In the endorsement section a landlord should complete the date the petition is presented to the court and the tenant's name at footnote (n). The remainder of the endorsement will be completed by the court office.

20.5.2 Completing form 6.9

If no statutory declaration was served on the tenant, a landlord can seek to make them bankrupt after obtaining a money judgment and failing to enforce it by a warrant for goods. In this situation form 6.9 will need to be presented to the court.

Form 6.9 should be completed in the same way as form 6.7 and a landlord should refer to paragraph 20.5.1 when completing form 6.9 with the following exceptions:-

At section 3 at footnote (j) if any payment was obtained on execution of the warrant for goods, it should be included with the information required for this section.

At section 5 at footnote (k) the following should be entered in the same order:-
* the date of the money judgment;
* the name of the county court in which it was obtained;
* the title of the action (usually *the landlord name v the tenant name);*
* the claim number for the proceedings in which the judgment was obtained;
* the sum for which judgment was ordered;
* the name of the court in which a warrant of execution was obtained;
* the date when the warrant of execution was part enforced or attempted to be enforced.

The remainder of the form is completed as if it were form 6.7 as set out in paragraph 20.5.1.

20.5.3 Completing form 6.13A

Form 6.13A is a statement that the contents of the bankruptcy petition (application) are true. As is seen above the bankruptcy petition (form 6.7 and 6.9) does not provide for the landlord to sign it.

Form 6.13A is completed as follows:-

At paragraph 1 footnote (a) a landlord should complete their name, address and description (i.e. landlord of the debtor);

At paragraph 2 from footnote (b) the following should be inserted in the same order:-

- tenant's name as stated on the petition;
- at footnote (c) the date in the endorsement section of the petition when the petition is presented to the court;
- at footnote (d) the name of the court to which the petition is presented; and
- at footnote (e) the reference number of the court that issued the petition.

If the petition is following a statutory demand and the landlord has taken more than four months from serving the statutory demand to presenting the petition to the court, reasons should be given at paragraph 2, footnote (f).

If a landlord is an individual and is acting in person in presenting the petition the remainder of the form will not need to be completed. If the landlord is an organisation the remainder of the form will need to be completed with the person presenting the petition stating their capacity in the organisation, that they are duly authorised to make the statement of truth, that they have knowledge of the circumstances giving rise to the petition and that the contents of the petition are true to the best of their knowledge.

At the statement of truth the full name of the landlord or person signing in their capacity, their signature and the date should be entered.

20.5.4 Completing form 6.11

Form 6.11 is a certificate of personal service of the statutory demand on the tenant.

Form 6.11 is completed as follows:-

At the first sentence that reads "date of statutory demand" the relevant date should be entered.

At footnote (a) the name, address, description of person completing this certificate (such as landlord) and whether they are the creditor or someone acting on the creditor's behalf should be entered.

If the landlord completing the form did not serve the statutory demand, they should delete "[I]" and write the name of the person who served the statutory demand at footnote (b).

At footnote (c) insert the date the statutory demand was served and at footnote (d) insert 4 pm and delete before/after to indicate if it was served before or after 4 pm on a weekday. If the statutory demand was served on a Saturday 12 pm should be entered and before/after deleted to indicate if it was served before or after 12 pm. At footnote (e) insert the address at which it was served.

If an acknowledgement of service was received from the tenant, at footnote (f) the date of the acknowledgement should be entered followed by the method of the acknowledgement. If no acknowledgement was received, delete the entire sentence.

A landlord is required to produce a copy of the statutory demand marked "A" and a copy of the acknowledgement of service (if any) marked "B" with Form 6.11. The landlord should then where indicated enter their full name, sign and date the form.

When these documents have been completed (with three copies) a landlord will need to take/post it to the relevant court for the insolvency district in which the tenant lives for the petition for bankruptcy to be issued.

The process of making someone bankrupt is expensive and there is no guarantee of recovering the money owed to a landlord. A landlord (creditor) is more likely to use this as an effective threat rather than proceeding to make a tenant (debtor) bankrupt. The fees for bankruptcy at the time of writing this book are:-

- £220 in the county court;
- £465 in the High Court (it is unlikely that a landlord will need to use the High Court; and
- there is an additional fee to be paid to administer the bankruptcy of £525.

Some of these fees are recoverable if there are sufficient assets in the bankruptcy process.

Following presentation of the petition to the court the court will fix a hearing date and send a copy of the documents to the tenant usually giving them at least 14 days' notice of a hearing.

The landlord will need to serve a copy of the petition on the tenant by way of personal service. If this is not possible a landlord can apply to the court for other form of service such as post (i.e. substituted service).

Following service of the petition the landlord will need to provide the court with a certificate of service in form 6.17A or 6.18A. This should be provided to the court at least five working days before the hearing. If a tenant wishes to challenge the petition they should send a notice to the court and the landlord at least five working days before the hearing.

20.6 The bankruptcy hearing

A landlord (creditor) will need to prepare a list of people attending the hearing, for the court, on form 6.21. At the hearing the court will take evidence from the parties and other interested persons such as creditors. The court may make any of the following orders:-

- adjourn the proceedings to a future date;
- give directions for matters to be done before a further hearing;
- dismiss the landlord's application for bankruptcy;
- adjourn the proceedings with no future date; or
- make a bankruptcy order.

20.7 Make a bankruptcy order

A landlord may wish to instruct a solicitor in this process as it is one of the more complicated procedures to follow in this book. A landlord should not attempt this procedure unless he has read through the relevant contents of this book, reviewed the forms and feel competent to proceed.

If the bankruptcy application is successful a trustee will be appointed to collect and sell the tenant's assets and make payment to their creditors. The trustee will communicate with the landlord regarding repayment of the debt if sufficient assets exist.

A landlord should make detailed notes of all matters at the hearing and all parties attending. If the bankruptcy application is not successful a landlord may gain information from the hearing that may aid another method of recovery.

21 RECOVERING POSSESSION

The only way a landlord can lawfully recover possession of their property from a tenant who is unwilling to leave is by obtaining a court order for possession and then a bailiffs' warrant to evict the tenant.

A landlord is required to follow three stages when seeking to recover possession of an AST. The stages are:-
1. serve the correct notice (Section 8; 21(4)(a); 21(1)(b));
2. obtain a possession order (accelerated or normal possession procedure); and
3. obtain a bailiffs' warrant for eviction.

There are different procedures that can be used through the stages. What procedure a landlord can follow will depend on the type of tenancy, the ground(s), if any, being used for possession and the documents that a landlord has in their possession. Importantly, a landlord cannot get a possession order which is effective during the first six months of an AST when using the Section 21 Notice procedure. And it cannot be used to get a possession order during the fixed term.

It is advised that a landlord pursues the easiest and quickest procedure available to them to obtain possession of their property. The easiest procedure is one that is simple and does not allow a tenant a defence or counterclaim in the proceedings. Chapters 15 to 20 shows a landlord how they can obtain a separate money judgment for rent arrears and enforce that judgment against the tenant.

21.1 Procedures

There are different procedures that apply to the following types of ASTs:-
* fixed term AST with no break clause (Section 8 procedure);
* fixed term AST with a break clause (Section 8 & 21 procedure); and
* periodic AST (Section 8 & 21 procedure).

21.1.1 Fixed Term AST with no break clause

A landlord can only obtain possession during the fixed term if they have available to them and are able to satisfy the court of a ground for possession as set out in the Housing Act 1988 Schedule 2.

If a landlord does not have available to them a ground for possession during the fixed term or is unable to satisfy the court that possession should be made on an available ground under Schedule 2, the landlord will simply have to wait until the fixed term expires before they can regain possession through the courts. If a ground is not available for possession, comfort can be found in the fact that the tenant is complying with some terms of the tenancy.

21.1.2 Fixed term AST with a break clause

Here a landlord has two options to obtain a possession order:-

- obtain possession during the fixed term if they have available to them, and are able to satisfy a court of, a ground for possession as set out in the Housing Act 1988 Schedule 2; or
- obtain a possession order by ending the fixed term through the operation of the break clause and then using the Section 21 Notice (accelerated or non-accelerated) procedure to obtain a possession order.

21.1.3 Periodic AST

If an AST is a periodic tenancy because:-

- the fixed term has expired (statutory periodic tenancy); or
- there was never a fixed term to begin with (contractual periodic tenancy); or
- a contractual periodic tenancy was agreed at the end of the fixed term; then

a landlord can obtain a possession order by:-

- satisfying the court of a ground for possession under the Housing Act 1988 Schedule 2; or
- pursuing the Section 21 Notice (accelerated or non-accelerated) procedure.

21.2 Serving notices

Before a landlord can start court proceedings for possession a valid notice needs to be served on the tenant and the time period given in that notice expired. This is where landlords tend to make the most mistakes which can provide a tenant with a full defence to a claim for possession.

Paragraphs 3.1.4 and 5.3.1.3 set out in detail the issues around and procedures for serving a notice.

21.3 Section 8 Notice

If a tenancy is in the fixed term, which is not about to expire and there is no break clause to end the fixed term early, a landlord will have to satisfy the court of a ground(s) under the Housing Act 1988 Schedule 2 for a possession order to be made. In initiating this procedure a landlord will need to serve a Section 8 Notice on the tenant(s).

Within the Section 8 Notice a landlord will need to list one or more of the 17 grounds for possession stated in Schedule 2 which is available to them and satisfy the court of the requirements of that ground(s). A landlord should note the following with regards to the grounds:-

- not all grounds are available to a private landlord (grounds 2, 4, 14a);
- not all grounds can be used to recover possession during the fixed term (grounds 1, 3 to 7, 9, 16); and

- some grounds cannot be used to recover possession during the fixed term unless there is a term in the tenancy agreement providing for this to happen (ground 2, 8, 10 to 15, 17).

A landlord should carefully select the ground based on the above factors as well as being able to prove the ground to the court. If the landlord cannot prove the available ground(s) for possession the tenancy has to run the full course of the fixed term.

A Section 8 Notice may also be used when the fixed term is about to expire or has expired but as there is an easier and more successful procedure to obtain possession (i.e. Section 21 Notice) there is no reason for the landlord to rely on the Section 8 Notice procedure.

Landlords should use a proper Section 8 Notice as the notice need to contain certain prescribed information. If the prescribed information is not in the notice it will be held to be defective and court proceedings based on it may be dismissed.

21.3.1 Completing a Section 8 Notice

A proper notice will have the following information:-

The notice should be titled *"Housing Act 1988 Section 8 as amended by section 151 Housing Act 1996"*. It should be headed *"Notice seeking possession of a property let on an Assured Tenancy or an Assured Agricultural Occupancy"*. An AST is a version of an Assured Tenancy.

There should be instructions on how to complete the notice and the circumstances in which it should be used.

In the section of the form that says "To" the name of the tenant(s) should be written in the space provided and cross out the word "licensee(s)" in the sentence.

The form should state that *"the landlord /licensor (delete as appropriate) intends to apply to the court for an order requiring you to give up possession of...."*. The address of the property for which possession is sought should be entered here.

The form should go on to state that *"your landlord/licensor (delete as appropriate) intends to seek possession on ground(s) xx (insert the number of the ground(s) here) in Schedule 2 of Housing Act 1988, as amended by the Housing Act 1996, which reads as follows:* The full exact wording of the ground(s) as they appear in the Housing Act 1988 Schedule 2 should be entered here.

There are 17 grounds for possession. Below is a table of the grounds showing, whether they are available to a private landlord, whether they are mandatory or discretionary, whether they can be used in the fixed term and whether they must have been incorporated into the tenancy agreement to be used during the fixed term. A landlord should carefully check whether a ground is available to be used based on the criteria in the table below as well as whether the landlord can prove the facts to satisfy the ground.

Grounds for possession	Available to private landlords	Mandatory	Discretionary	Available if brought to tenant's attention no later than the beginning of the tenancy	Possession order available in the fixed term	Only available in fixed term if tenancy agreement says so	Length of notice
Ground 1 – owner occupier	Yes	Yes	No	Yes or court dispense with it	No	N/A	2 months
Ground 2 – possession due to a mortgage	No (mortgagee)	Yes	No	Yes or court dispense with it	See next column	Yes	2 months
Ground 3 – holiday let	Yes	Yes	No	Yes	No	N/A	2 weeks
Ground 4 – student let	No	Yes	No	Yes	No	N/A	2 weeks
Ground 5 – possession for minister of religion	Yes	Yes	No	Yes	No	N/A	2 months
Ground 6 – landlord intends to carry out substantial works	Yes	Yes	No	NA	No	N/A	2 months
Ground 7 – death of a tenant	Yes	Yes	No	NA	No	N/A	2 months
Ground 8 – two months or eight weeks rent arrears	Yes	Yes	No	NA	See next column	Yes	2 weeks
Ground 9 – suitable alternative accommodation is available for the tenant	Yes	No	Yes	NA	No	N/A	2 months
Ground 10 – rent arrears	Yes	No	Yes	NA	See next column	Yes	2 weeks
Ground 11 – persistent delay in paying rent	Yes	No	Yes	NA	See next column	Yes	2 weeks
Ground 12 – breach of any obligation	Yes	No	Yes	NA	See next column	Yes	2 weeks
Ground 13 – waste or neglect	Yes	No	Yes	NA	See next column	Yes	2 weeks
Ground 14 – nuisance or	Yes	No	Yes	NA	See next column	Yes	As soon as notice

annoyance or criminal conviction							is served
Ground 14A domestic violence	No	No	Yes	NA	See next column	Yes	2 weeks
Ground 15 – deterioration of furniture	Yes	No	Yes	NA	See next column	Yes	2 weeks
Ground 16 – employment let/tied property	No (employer)	No	Yes	NA	No	N/A	2 months
Ground 17 – induced to grant tenancy by false statements	Yes	No	Yes	NA	See next column	Yes	2 weeks

The form then requires a full explanation of why each ground is being relied on. In the example of a rent arrears claim based on ground 8 the wording could be *"the tenant is in £xxx rent arrears and has failed to pay rent between (date) to (date). The tenant is in more than two months or eight weeks rent arrears, see attached rent statement."*

The form should then set out prescribed notes on the grounds for possession, which should read as follows:-

If the court is satisfied that any of grounds 1 to 8 is established, it must make an order (but see below in respect of fixed term tenancies).

Before the court will grant an order on any of grounds 9 to 17, it must be satisfied that it is reasonable to require you to leave. This means that, if one of these grounds is set out in section 3, you will be able to suggest to the court that it is not reasonable that you should have to leave, even if you accept that the ground applies.

The court will not make an order under grounds 1, 3 to 7, 9 or 16, to take effect during the fixed term of the tenancy (if there is one) and it will only make an order during the fixed term on grounds 2, 8, 10 to 15 or 17 if the terms of the tenancy make provision for it to be brought to an end on any of these grounds.

Where the court makes an order for possession solely on ground 6 or 9, the landlord must pay your reasonable removal expenses.

The form should then require the date after which possession proceedings can begin to be inserted. This date is dependent upon the ground(s) being used and when the notice will be served (so as to give the tenant the minimum notice period). As seen from the table above there are three notice periods dependent on the ground being used. They are:-

- at the time the notice is served (i.e. immediately);
- two weeks; and
- two months.

However, if grounds 1, 2, 5 to 7, 9 or 16 are being used the notice cannot expire earlier than the notice period that would have been given in a Notice to Quit served on the same date. For a calculation of the notice period for a Notice to Quit see paragraph 5.3.1.

If more than one ground is being used with different notice periods, the longer notice period will apply except for ground 14. The notice period only begins to run from the time the notice is actually served or is legally deemed to have been served on the tenant. An allowance should be made, when setting the expiry date, for the time that will be taken for the notice to be served on the tenant (see serving notices at paragraphs 3.1.4 and 5.3.1.3). The form should contain the following prescribed information about the length of notice.

Where the landlord is seeking possession on grounds 1, 2, 5 to 7, 9 or 16, court proceedings cannot begin earlier than two months from the date this notice is served on you (even where one of grounds 3, 4, 8, 10 to 13, 14A, 15 or 17 is specified) and not before the date on which the tenancy (had it not been assured) could have been brought to an end by a notice to quit served at the same time as this notice.

Where the landlord is seeking possession on grounds 3, 4, 8, 10 to 13, 14A, 15 or 17, court proceedings cannot begin earlier than two weeks from the date this notice is served (unless one of 1, 2, 5 to 7, 9 or 16 grounds is also specified in which case they cannot begin earlier than two months from the date this notice is served).

Where the landlord is seeking possession on ground 14 (with or without other grounds), court proceedings cannot begin before the date this notice is served.

Where the landlord is seeking possession on ground 14A, court proceedings cannot begin unless the landlord has served, or has taken all reasonable steps to serve, a copy of this notice on the partner who has left the property.

After the date shown in section 5, court proceedings may be begun at once but not later than 12 months from the date on which this notice is served. After this time the notice will lapse and a new notice must be served before possession can be sought.

At the end of the form there should be a space for the landlord, agent or someone acting on the landlord's behalf to indicate who they are i.e. landlord, agent or other representative, insert their name, address, and signature, and to date the form. They can include their telephone number.

The notice should contain further prescribed information as detailed below, informing the tenant about the form and what the landlord and they can do. If there are joint landlords all of them must sign the form or agree for one to do so on their behalf.

What to do if this notice is served on you

- *This notice is the first step requiring you to give up possession of your home. You should read it very carefully.*
- *Your landlord cannot make you leave your home without an order for possession issued by a court. By issuing this notice your landlord is informing you that he intends to seek such an order. If you are willing to give up possession without a court order, you should tell the person who signed this notice as soon as possible and say when you are prepared to leave.*
- *Whichever grounds are set out in section 3 of this form, the court may allow any of the other grounds to be added at a later date. If this is done, you will be told about it so you can discuss the additional grounds at the court hearing as well as the grounds set out in section 3.*
- *If you need advice about this notice, and what you should do about it, take it immediately to a citizens' advice bureau, a housing advice centre, a law centre or a solicitor.*

There are mandatory and discretionary grounds for possession. If a mandatory ground for possession is being used, then if proven at court the judge has to make a possession order.

If a discretionary ground is being used for possession, not only does the landlord have to prove the ground, but the court has to be satisfied that it is reasonable in all the circumstances of the case to make a possession order. This can be quite difficult and it is not recommended that a landlord goes to court on a discretionary ground. If a discretionary ground is being relied on the court can make any order they see fit and a possession order may well be a last resort.

21.4 Section 21 Notices

There are two Section 21 Notices that a landlord can serve in relation to an AST before commencing court proceedings for possession. They are the section 21(1)(b) Notice to be used whilst the tenancy is in the fixed term and the section 21(4)(a) Notice to be used if it is a periodic tenancy.

No Section 21 Notice can be given in relation to an AST where a deposit has been paid if:-

- the deposit is not protected by a deposit protection scheme;
- the initial requirement of an authorised scheme has not been complied with within 30 days of receipt of the deposit;
- the prescribed information in the prescribed form or similar form has not been given to the tenant/relevant person within 30 days of the receipt of the deposit (A Section 21 Notice can be served when the prescribed information has been given); or
- the deposit given is not money (A Section 21 Notice can be given when the deposit is returned).

A Section 21 Notice can be served if the deposit has been returned to the tenant in full or with agreed deductions or an application has been made before the court by the tenant or relevant person, which has been judged on, withdrawn or settled between the parties.

A valid Section 21 Notice cannot be served where a property is subject to HMO, additional or selective licensing and is not licensed (see Chapter 11).

Under the Section 21 Notice procedure to recover possession a landlord does not have to prove a ground for possession as is required under the Section 8 Notice procedure. All a landlord needs to do to recover possession under the Section 21 Notice procedure is:-

- serve a valid Section 21 Notice (fixed term/ periodic);
- ensure the correct expiry date is given in the notice;
- commence possession proceedings after the notice has expired; and
- prove to the court that the tenancy is an AST; that the deposit has been dealt with correctly; that the property is licensed if it is subject to licensing; that the correct notice was served and that court proceedings commenced after the expiry date in the notice.

If a landlord complies with these procedural matters the tenant will not have a defence to the proceedings and the court *must* grant an order for possession. There is no discretion for the court to do otherwise.

21.4.1 Section 21(1)(b) Notice – fixed term tenancy

If a landlord wishes to serve a Section 21 Notice during the fixed term of the tenancy, a Section 21(1)(b) Notice *must* be used. The Section 21(1)(b) Notice can be served at any time after the tenancy has commenced. However, a landlord *cannot* commence possession proceedings until the notice period has expired which cannot be before the end of the fixed term and must give a minimum notice period of two months.

Some landlords serve a Section 21(1)(b) Notice at the same event where the tenancy agreement is being signed. However, to be on the safe side the landlord should get the tenant to note in any evidence of service that the tenancy agreement was already signed and the tenancy had commenced. It will then be difficult for the tenant to allege to the contrary in court. If the Section 21(1)(b) Notice is served before the tenancy agreement is signed and the tenancy commenced it will be void as at the time of serving the notice there was no actual tenancy to which it relate.

21.4.1.1 Completing a Section 21(1)(b) Notice
The Notice should be titled "Housing Act 1988, Section 21(1)(b) as amended by the Housing Act 1996".

The Notice should be headed "Notice Requiring Possession; Assured Shorthold Tenancy – Fixed Term".

The first section should require the name and address of the tenant(s) "To" whom the notice is to be given. The names of all the joint tenants should be entered as the tenancy cannot be brought to an end, for less than all the joint tenants.

The second section should require the name and address of the landlord(s). If an agent or representative is preparing the notice they should ensure that only the landlord or joint landlords name(s) are written in this section.

The notice should then have a sentence stating "I give you notice that I require possession of the dwelling house known as" following which the correct address of the rental property should be entered. The notice should then require the "expiry date". There are several rules to this date:-

1. the tenant must be given a minimum of two months' notice;
2. the notice must be given before or no later than the last day of the fixed term;
3. the notice must not expire earlier than the date the fixed term expires i.e. the earliest date it can expire is the day the fixed term expires.

June 2011

M	T	W	T	F	S	S
		1	2	3	4	5
6	7	8	9	10	11	12
13	14	15	16	17	18	19
20	21	22	23	24	25	26
27	28	29	30			

August 2011

M	T	W	T	F	S	S
1	2	3	4	5	6	7
8	9	10	11	12	13	14
15	16	17	18	19	20	21
22	23	24	25	26	27	28
29	30	31				

July 2011

M	T	W	T	F	S	S
				1	2	3
4	5	6	7	8	9	10
11	12	13	14	15	16	17
18	19	20	21	22	23	24
25	26	27	28	29	30	31

Using the above calendar if the fixed term of a tenancy ends on 8 June 2011 the last day a landlord can serve a section 21(1)(b) Notice is the 8 June 2011. On the 8 June 2011 the notice must have been actually served or legally deemed to have been served on the tenant. It will not have been served if it is posted to the tenant (first class or otherwise) on 8 June 2011.

The notice must give a minimum period of two months. One month from 8 June 2011 will be the 7 July 2011. The second month begins on 8 July 2011 and ends on 7 August 2011. The earliest the notice can end if served on 8 June 2011 is 7 August 2011. If the tenancy agreement specifies that a longer period should be given in the notice this should be followed. If the notice is served more than two months before the fixed term expires (i.e. more than two months before 8 June 2011) it cannot expire before the fixed term ends. Therefore the tenant will get more than the minimum two months notice. The notice can expire on or after 8 June 2011.

The form should then provide for the notice to be signed, dated and indicate the status of the person who signed the notice (i.e. landlord, agent or other representative).

21.4.2 Section 21(4)(a) Notice – periodic tenancy

A Section 21(4)(a) Notice is the version of the Section 21 Notice to be served on a tenant when the fixed term of the AST has ended and no further fixed term has been granted.

A Section 21(4)(a) Notice is invalid if served on the tenant during the fixed term, even, if the fixed term ends before the expiry date in the notice. If a Section 21 Notice is being served on the tenant before the fixed term has ended it must be a Section 21(1)(b) Notice.

21.4.2.1 Completing a Section 21(4)(a) Notice
The notice should be titled "Housing Act 1988, Section 21(4)(a) as amended by the Housing Act 1996".

The notice should be headed "Notice Requiring Possession; Assured Shorthold Tenancy – Periodic Tenancy".

The first section should require the name and address of the tenant(s) "To" whom the notice is to be given. The names of all joint tenants should be entered as the tenancy cannot be brought to an end, for less than all the joint tenants.

The second section should require the name and address of the landlord(s). If an agent or representative is preparing the notice they should ensure that only the landlord or joint landlords name(s) are written in this section. The notice should then have a sentence stating "I give you notice that I require possession of the dwelling – house known as" following which the correct address of the rental property should be entered.

The notice should then require the "expiry date". There are several rules to this date:-
1. the tenant must be given a minimum of two months' notice;
2. the notice must expire on the last day of a period of tenancy;
3. the notice must not end earlier than the date the tenancy could have been ended by a Notice to Quit. Therefore a quarterly tenancy must be given a minimum three months' notice period.

Below are examples of calculating the expiry date for a weekly and a monthly periodic AST for a Section 21(4)(a) Notice.

June 2011

M	T	W	T	F	S	S
		1	2	3	4	5
6	7	8	9	10	11	12
13	14	15	16	17	18	19
20	21	22	23	24	25	26
27	28	29	30			

July 2011

M	T	W	T	F	S	S
				1	2	3
4	5	6	7	8	9	10
11	12	13	14	15	16	17
18	19	20	21	22	23	24
25	26	27	28	29	30	31

August 2011

M	T	W	T	F	S	S
1	2	3	4	5	6	7
8	9	10	11	12	13	14
15	16	17	18	19	20	21
22	23	24	25	26	27	28
29	30	31				

Weekly tenancy – a tenancy started on Sunday 5 December 2010 and is a weekly tenancy. The end of a period of the tenancy is every Saturday and the beginning of a period of the tenancy is every Sunday (one week). If the tenancy was for a fixed term of six months the fixed term will end on Saturday 4 June 2011. After the fixed term expires, if no further fixed term is agreed, the tenancy will become a weekly statutory periodic tenancy.

If serving a Section 21(4)(a) Notice the first requirement is that a minimum period of two months' notice must be given. If notice is to be served on Friday 10 June 2011 a minimum period of two months' will end on Tuesday 9 August 2011.

The second requirement is that the notice must expire on the last day of a period of the tenancy. As a period of the tenancy starts on a Sunday and ends on a Saturday, the next Saturday after 9 August 2011 will be Saturday 13 August 2011.

The period given in the notice must not be sooner than the date the tenancy could have been ended by a Notice to Quit. The minimum notice period required for a weekly tenancy being ended by a Notice to Quit is four weeks and the current Section 21(4)(a) Notice gives at least two months.

A landlord can protect themselves from any error in the date the notice is to expire by using the following or a substantially similar saving clause in a Section 21(4)(a) Notice. It should read to the following effect and be inserted just after the expiry date *"or at the end of the period of your tenancy which will next expire after the end of two months following the service of this notice upon you"*.

If a landlord then gets the expiry date wrong but waits until he is sure that the correct period that should have been given in the notice expires he can commence proceedings for possession without fear that the notice will be found defective.

Monthly tenancy – Using the calendar above, a tenancy started on Saturday 5 December 2010 and is a monthly tenancy. The end of a period of the tenancy is the 4th of each month and the beginning of a period of the tenancy is the 5th of each month. Rent is due at the beginning of a period of the tenancy. The tenancy was granted for a fixed term of six months and the fixed term expired on Saturday 4 June 2011.

The first requirement is that a minimum period of two months' notice must be given. If the notice is to be served on Friday 10 June 2011 a minimum period of two months will end on Tuesday 9 August 2011.

The second requirement is that the notice must expire on the last day of a period of the tenancy. As the tenancy started on 5th of a month the last day of a period of the tenancy will be the 4th of a month. The next 4th of a month after Tuesday 9 August 2011 is Sunday 4 September 2011. Under this example a tenant gets nearly three months' notice for the expiry date to be valid.

The third requirement is that the period given in the notice must not be sooner than the date the tenancy could have been ended by a Notice to Quit. The minimum notice period required for a monthly tenancy being ended by a Notice to Quit is one months' notice.

If a tenancy is quarterly and is being ended by a Notice to Quit, three months' notice will need to be given for the landlord to comply with the third requirement above for the notice to be valid.

If a tenancy is yearly and is being ended by a Notice to Quit, six months' notice will need to be given for the landlord to comply with third requirement above for the notice to be valid.

The paragraphs above set out what a landlord should do if they have concerns about getting the expiry date in the notice wrong. If for some reason a landlord does not know when the tenancy began (e.g. property bought with an existing tenant and he does not have reliable documentation or tenancy is old and was agreed verbally) a landlord can serve a valid Section 21 Notice by giving an expiry date no earlier than two months after the notice is served, or no expiry date at all, and ensuring the notice contains the above mentioned saving clause.

The form should then provide for the notice to be signed, dated and indicate the status of the person who signed the notice (i.e. landlord, agent or other representative).

21.5 Obtaining a possession order

The next stage is obtaining an order for possession by starting court proceedings. If a landlord commences court proceedings for possession of a property before the Section 8 or the Section 21 Notice expires the proceedings will be found defective and the landlord will fail in getting a possession order. The landlord can start proceedings again when the notice period expires, relying on the same notice but with new court forms and a further court fee.

With the Section 8 Notice there is only one procedure to be used to obtain a possession order. For the purposes of this book it is called the "normal possession procedure".

With the Section 21 Notice there are two procedures to be used to obtain a possession order. For the purposes of this book one is called the "normal section 21 possession procedure" and the other is called the "accelerated possession procedure".

A possession action should be commenced in the court which has jurisdiction for the district (area) in which the property is located. The relevant court can be identified by checking the court services website (http://hmctscourtfinder.justice.gov.uk/hmcts/). Alternatively, if a possession claim is based solely on rent arrears the claim can commence online at www.possessionclaim.gov.uk/pcol/.

21.5.1 Section 8 – normal possession procedure

To start court proceedings a landlord needs to complete a Claim Form for Possession (Form N5) and a Particulars of Claim for Possession (Form N119).

21.5.1.1   Completing claim form for possession (Form N5)
In the court proceedings for possession the landlord is referred to as the claimant, as they are bringing the claim and the tenant is referred to as the defendant, because a claim has been brought against them whether or not they defend it.

In the top right box of the form the name of the county court in which proceedings are to be commenced should be entered. The court will complete the following box with the claim number.

In the section headed "Claimant" the landlord(s) full name(s) and addresses should be completed.

In the section headed "Defendant" the tenant(s) full name(s) and addresses should be completed. If it is a joint tenancy the names and addresses of all the joint tenants should be completed. An action cannot proceed against less than all the joint tenants.

In the section headed "the claimant is claiming possession of" the full address of the property for which possession is sought should be entered. In the sentence below which reads "which (includes) (does not include) residential property" the words in brackets (does not include) should be crossed out. If the claim for possession is not based on rent arrears, the words in the sentence below which reads "The claimant is also making a claim for money" should be crossed out.

The court will complete the section below by inserting a hearing date, time and venue.

In the box at the bottom left of the first page of the form the name and address of just one tenant should be entered. If there is more than one tenant a separate Form N5 should be completed for them and their individual name and address put in this box. This should be repeated until there is a separate form for each tenant. All the information in the forms will be similar except for this section where a separate tenant's details will be entered.

In the section at the bottom right of the first page the court fee to commence the claim for possession should be entered. A landlord should check with the relevant court or the court service website for details of the fee (www.justice.gov.uk/courts/fees). There is no solicitor's cost as these instructions are for a landlord acting in person. The total amount should be entered where indicated.

On page two at the top left in the section that reads "grounds for possession" the relevant box, based on the ground stated in the Section 8 Notice, on which possession is sought, should be marked.

A private sector landlord will either be using the boxes:-
- rent arrears;
- other breach of tenancy; and/or
- other (what constitutes other should be set out in the space provided and will include a ground where the tenant is not in breach of the tenancy).

The section at the top right of page two headed "anti-social behaviour" should be left unmarked.

The last three questions of this section should be marked "No". These are the questions on demotion of tenancy, suspending the right to buy and the Human Rights Act 1988.

At the "Statement of Truth" the landlord should cross out the words in brackets (the claimant believes) so that it reads "(I believe) that the facts stated in this claim form are true" The words "I am duly authorised by the claimant to sign this statement" should be crossed out. The landlord should then sign and date the form. An agent cannot sign and date this form on behalf of a landlord. One joint landlord can sign and date on behalf of the other landlords. Below the signature the landlord should cross out the words in bracket (Litigation friend) and (Claimant's solicitor) so that it reads (Claimant). The landlord's full name should be entered in the line below.

At the bottom of page two the address for the landlord where documents and payments are to be sent if different from the address given earlier in the form for the landlord should be completed.

Under the normal possession procedure a landlord will also have to provide the court with a completed Particulars of Claim (Form N119), with the Claim Form. If a landlord is unable to provide form N119 with the claim form they will have 14 days after court proceedings commence to provide the court and the tenant with the completed form.

21.5.1.2   *Completing particulars of claim for possession (Form N119)*
In this form the landlord is referred to as the claimant and the tenant is referred to as the defendant.

In the boxes at the top right of the first page the name of the county court for the district in which the property is located (as was completed on the Claim Form (N5)) should be entered in the box headed "name of the court". In the box below headed "name of claimant" the landlord's name(s) should be entered and in the box headed "name of defendant" the tenant(s') name(s) should be entered.

In paragraph 1 the full address of the property for which possession is sought should be entered.

In paragraph 2 the name(s) of the people living in the property should be inserted. If the tenant is not living in the property and the names of the occupants are not known a description of the persons such as "lady and two children" can be entered.

In paragraph 3(a) the type of tenancy i.e. Assured Shorthold Tenancy and the date when the tenancy began should be inserted. If the exact date the tenancy began is not known the month and year e.g. "around June 2000" can be inserted.

In paragraph 3(b) the amount of rent and the frequency at which it is paid should be completed.

In paragraph 3(c) insert the daily rent rate. This is calculated by taking the monthly rent multiplied by 12 months divided by 365 days or the weekly rent multiplied by 52 weeks divided by 365 days.

Paragraph 4(a) is to be completed if the claim for possession is based on rent arrears. If the Housing Act 1988, Schedule 2 ground 8 is being used to recover possession under a Section 8 Notice the words to the following effect should be written "the tenant was in eight or more weeks/two or more months' *(delete as the case maybe)* rent arrears at the date the notice was served and remains so.

RECOVERING POSSESSION

Possession is sought on ground 8 as set out in the Section 8 Notice. A rent statement is attached".

If grounds 10 and 11 of Schedule 2 (discretionary grounds for rent arrears) are being used with ground 8 (mandatory ground for rent arrears) or by themselves this should be set out, with the reasons why, and a rent statement attached. For reasons stated above (paragraph 21.3) it is not advised that a landlord rely on a discretionary ground for possession.

Paragraph 4(b) is to be completed if possession is sought on other breaches of the tenancy agreement except non-payment of rent, such as waste or neglect (ground 13). For reasons stated above (paragraph 21.3) it is not advised that a landlord rely on a discretionary ground for possession. However, if they do the ground and the reasons should be set out here.

Paragraph 4(c) is to be completed to list any other grounds for possession that does not include rent arrears and does not include the tenant being in breach of the tenancy such as the owner occupier ground 1, for possession of the property.

In paragraph 5 the actions that have been taken to recover arrears of rent should be set out. This will include things such as letters, emails, texts, phone calls, visits to the property and agreement to pay arrears of rent. Completing this is not necessary if ground 8 (mandatory ground for rent arrears) is being relied on as two months' rent arrears at the date the notice is served and at the date of the hearing (provided there is no counter claim for disrepair) will guarantee possession. However, if ground 10 and/or 11 (discretionary grounds) are being used to recover possession the above information should be entered.

Paragraph 6 requests details of the service of the notice. All notices listed in the sentence except "notice seeking possession" should be crossed out and the date it was served on the tenant entered. Although not specifically required, the space below this paragraph can be used to state how the notice seeking possession was served on the tenant and what proof there is of service i.e. left at property and there are pictures of this or recorded delivery which was signed for.

Paragraph 7 requests details about the tenant's circumstances. This can be completed if something is known about the tenant such as they are working, they are on benefits, they have somewhere else to go, but it is not necessary to do so. This paragraph is more relevant if possession is sought on a discretionary ground.

Paragraph 8 requests details about the landlord's circumstances, such as do they have a mortgage are they in financial difficulty and similar matters. If ground 8 is being used to recover possession it is not necessary to complete this paragraph. If the discretionary grounds 10 and 11 are being used a landlord should provide information about how they are financially affected by the non-payment of rent. If other discretionary grounds are being used not related to rent, the effects of the breach of tenancy on the landlord should be entered.

Paragraph 9 is to be ignored in its entirety as forfeiture is not being used and does not come under the Section 8 Notice procedure for possession.

Paragraph 10 is to be left as it is so that the court is being asked for an order including everything specified in this paragraph.

Paragraph 11 does not apply to private landlords and should be marked "no".

Paragraphs 12, 13, 14 and 15 do not apply to private landlords and should be left unmarked.

At the "Statement of Truth" the landlord should cross out the words in brackets (the claimant believes) so that it reads "(I believe) that the facts stated in this claim form are true". The words "I am duly authorised by the claimant to sign this statement" should be crossed out. The landlord should then sign and date the form. An agent cannot sign and date this form on behalf of a landlord. One joint landlord can sign and date on behalf of the other landlords. Below the signature the landlord should cross out the words in bracket (Litigation friend) and (Claimant's solicitor) so that it reads (Claimant). The landlord's full name should be entered in the line below.

21.5.2 Section 21 procedures for possession

It may not be universally known, but there are two court procedures that can be used to recover possession when a Section 21 Notice has been served on a tenant. They are the "accelerated possession procedure" and the "normal section 21 possession procedure". The procedure a landlord can use depends upon what documentation they have about the tenancy and whether they are seeking other orders in addition to an order for possession, such as rent arrears.

The criteria to use the "accelerated possession procedure" are:-
* a valid Section 21 Notice must have been served;
* the landlord must have a copy of all the documents referred to in the claim form;
* the landlord must only be seeking a possession order (no rent arrears or other damages); and
* if the property is a House in Multiple Occupation (HMO) it must be licensed or a licence must have been applied for.

If a landlord is unable to satisfy the above criteria (e.g. not having the tenancy agreements) the Section 21 Notice may be used to recover possession but under the "normal section 21 possession procedure".

Before starting court proceedings under either procedure a landlord must ensure that the notice period has expired. This will not usually be a problem where a Section 21(1)(b) Notice was served on the tenant during the fixed term as the expiry date can be calculated with certainty. However, where it is a periodic tenancy and a Section 21(4)(a) Notice was served with a saving clause (due to uncertainty regarding the end date of a period of the tenancy) a landlord will need to ensure that court proceedings do not start until the notice period has expired under the saving clause.

How to avoid starting court proceedings before the notice period has expired under the saving clause depends upon whether the tenancy is weekly, monthly or for another period. If the tenancy is weekly a landlord should:-
- give the minimum two months' notice; and
- wait for at least a further week (seven days) after the end of the two months' period so that the saving clause can take effect.

If the tenancy is weekly the last day of a period of a weekly tenancy will occur every seven days. Therefore as long as the landlord gives the minimum two months' notice and wait at least seven days, the expiry date will have occurred under the saving clause.

If the tenancy is monthly a landlord should:-
- give the minimum two months' notice; and
- wait a further month (up to 31 days) after the end of the two months' notice period so that the saving clause can take effect.

If the tenancy is monthly the last day of a period of the tenancy will occur every month. Therefore as long as the landlord gives the minimum two months' notice and wait at least a month the expiry date will have occurred under the saving clause during the one month waiting period.

The same principle applies for quarterly and yearly periodic tenancies.

21.5.3 Section 21 – claim form and particulars of claim for possession under normal Section 21 possession procedure

Under the Section 21 normal possession procedure a landlord will use the same court forms used under the Section 8 procedure noted at paragraph 21.5.1 i.e. complete a claim form for possession (Form N5) and particulars of claim for possession (Form N119).

21.5.3.1   Completing claim form for possession (Form N5)
In completing Form N5 the notes set out in paragraph 21.5.1.1 of this book should be followed with the following exceptions:

With the Section 21 normal possession procedure a landlord can make a claim for rent arrears. If so, at the section of the form on page one (below where the property address is inserted) the words in bracket (The claimant is also making a claim for money) should be left unmarked. If no claim for money is being made this sentence should be crossed out.

At the top left of page two in the section that reads "grounds for possession" the box beside "other" should be marked and in the space provided it should be written that "possession is sought under Section 21 Notice using the normal possession procedure".

21.5.3.2   *Completing particulars of claim for possession (Form N119)*

In completing Form N119 the notes set out in paragraph 21.5.1.2 of this book should be followed with the following exceptions:

Paragraph 4(a) is not to be used because although the proceedings may include a claim for money, possession is not sought on the grounds of rent arrears but on the basis of the Section 21 Notice procedure.

Paragraph 4(b) is not to be used as the claim for possession is not based on other breaches of the tenancy agreement.

At paragraph 4(c) the words "possession is sought under a Section 21 Notice using the normal possession procedure" should be inserted. The words "this procedure also includes a money claim for rent arrears/other breaches of the tenancy" should be inserted if this is being sought. If it is rent arrears a rent statement should be attached.

In paragraph 5 the actions taken to recover rent arrears (if this is being sought) should be inserted. This will include things such as letters, emails, texts, phone calls, visits to the property and agreement to pay arrears of rent.

21.5.4   Issuing court proceedings – Section 8 Notice or Section 21 Notice (normal possession procedure)

Issuing court proceedings is basically providing the court with the completed court forms, any documents relied on in the proceedings and paying the court fee. The following documents should be given to the court for proceedings to be issued:-

* Claim Form for Possession for each tenant x three (if there is more than one tenant then three copies of each Claim Form prepared for them);
* Particulars of Claim for Possession for each tenant x three (if there is more than one tenant then three copies of each Particulars of Claim prepared for them);
* Tenancy agreement, if any, to accompany each copy of the claim form;
* Proof of service i.e. recorded delivery slip/confirmation, pictures or other evidence to accompany each copy of the claim form;
* Section 8 or Section 21 Notice to accompany each copy of the claim form;
* Rent statement (if any) for each copy of the claim form; and

- Court fee.

It is good practice to have a covering letter with the court documents where a Section 21 Notice normal possession procedure is being used to recover possession to explain to the court that *"possession is not sought under the accelerated possession procedure but under the normal possession procedure because […]"* and give the reason why. This may be because rent arrears are sought, or the most recent tenancy agreement is not in the landlord's possession or there was never any tenancy agreement to begin with. Without such letter it has been known for the courts to return the papers and request that the accelerated possession procedure be used even though it is has never been compulsory to do so. This will temporarily delay a landlord getting a possession order.

These documents should be sent to the court by recorded delivery, or delivered by hand, to guarantee they are received.

The court staff will check that all the documentation are there as well as the payment, and, if in order the court staff will stamp the documents with the court seal and insert a hearing date. Proceedings have now been issued.

The court has to give the tenant at least 28 days' notice of a hearing. The hearing should be within eight weeks of the date the claim is issued.

The court will send the Claim Form, Particulars of Claim, Notes for Defendant, Defence Form and any relevant documents to the tenant not less than 21 days before the hearing. The tenant has 14 days in which to return a defence but can wait until the day of the hearing and give their defence to the court in person.

What defence the tenant can give depends upon the procedure being used. There are technical defences as well as substantive defences.

21.5.5 Defences to Section 21 Notice normal possession procedure

The defences a tenant may give to the proceedings may include:-
- the tenancy is not an AST;
- the notice is defective;
- the notice was never served;
- the Claim Form is defective;
- the Particulars of Claim Form is defective;
- the property is subject to licensing and is not licensed;
- possession proceedings were begun before the notice expired; and/or
- the deposit protection legislation has not been complied with.

If a landlord is also seeking a money judgment for rent arrears in the Section 21 notice normal possession proceedings additional defences by the tenant might include:-
- there are no arrears;

- the arrears are not as stated;
- the rent is not lawfully due; or
- there is a counterclaim for disrepair.

The defences to the money claim, if successful, should not stop possession being made under this procedure as the claim for possession is not based on rent arrears but the Section 21 Notice.

21.5.6 Defences to Section 8 notice normal possession procedure

With regard to the Section 8 Notice proceedings the following defences may be used:
- the tenancy is not an AST;
- the notice is defective;
- the notice was never served;
- the Claim Form is defective;
- the Particulars of Claim Form is defective; and/or
- possession proceedings begun before the notice expired.

If a landlord is also seeking a money judgment for rent arrears additional defences by the tenant might include:-
- there are no arrears;
- the arrears are not as stated;
- the rent is not lawfully due;
- a counterclaim under the deposit protection legislation; or
- a counterclaim for disrepair.

There may be additional defences and counterclaims in relation to the particular ground being relied on for possession as set out in the Section 8 Notice. Whatever the defence being used a landlord must be prepared to prove their case and show that any defence is not valid.

21.5.7 The court hearing

Paragraph 5.6 sets out what a landlord should do when attending court for a hearing.

The landlord should be prepared to state and prove the following:-
- type of tenancy;
- date tenancy granted;
- date fixed term expired (if applicable);
- date notice served;
- how notice was served;
- evidence of service;
- evidence to satisfy whichever ground is stated in the Section 8 Notice;
- the amount of rent arrears when notice served and at the date of hearing (if applicable) this should be shown via an up to date rent statement;

- evidence of deposit payment into scheme and provision of prescribed information;
- evidence of repairs e.g. receipts, invoice, reports and gas safe certificate;
- if a tenant has provided a defence or alleged a counterclaim a landlord should provide evidence to challenge this;
- evidence of the property been licensed if it is subject to licensing.

The judge will ask certain matters of the tenant, such as: -
- whether they received the notice;
- the quantum of arrears (if applicable);
- payments (if any) that have been made;
- details of any counterclaim; and
- any matters in dispute.

Depending on the issues in dispute the judge may make the following orders:-
- an order for possession;
- an adjournment with directions (i.e. scheduling a further hearing with matters to be done before that hearing); or
- dismiss the proceedings.

If the judge is making a possession order they will normally state the facts which they have found and then state the details of the order. The possession order can require the tenant to leave the property immediately, within 14 days, 28 days or where the tenant is likely suffer extreme hardship up to six weeks.

21.6 Section 21 Notice – Accelerated Possession Procedure

The criteria for using the accelerated possession procedure are set out at paragraph 21.5.2. If a landlord cannot satisfy the criteria in full this procedure should not be used as doing so will provide the tenant with a defence.

After a Section 21(1)(b) or Section 21(4)(a) notice has expired the landlord can use the accelerated possession procedure to obtain possession. The main difference between the accelerated possession procedure and normal section 21 notice possession procedure is that there is usually no court hearing with the accelerated possession procedure and there is no separate Particulars of Claim (Form N119) to be submitted with the court papers.

21.6.1 Completing Claim Form for Possession of Property – Accelerated Possession Procedure (Form N5B)

In the court proceedings for possession the landlord is referred to as the claimant, as they are bringing the claim and the tenant is referred to as the defendant, because a claim has been brought against them whether or not they defend it.

In the top right box of the first page headed "in the" the name of the county court should be completed. This will be the county court for the district (area) in which the let property is located. The relevant county court can be identified by checking the court services website at:
 http://hmctscourtfinder.justice.gov.uk/HMCTS/.

The landlord(s) full name and address(es) should be completed in the "Claimant" section.

The tenant(s) full name(s) and address(es) should be completed in the "Defendant" section. This may be different from the address of the let property in circumstances where a joint tenant is living elsewhere and this is known. If there are joint tenants the details should be entered for all of them.

In the section headed "the claimant is claiming possession of" the full address and postcode of the rented property should be entered.

The sentence requesting that the tenant pay the costs of the claim should be left unmarked.

In the section headed "Defendant's name and address for service" the details (name and address) for one tenant should be entered. If there is more than one tenant a separate form must be completed for each of them with their individual details entered here.

In the box headed "court fee" the court fee for starting the claim should be entered. The court fee can be ascertained through enquiries at the local county court or online at www.justice.gov.uk/courts/fees. There are no solicitor's costs as the landlord is acting in person. The total amount will therefore be the court fee. The court will enter the issue date i.e. the date court proceedings commenced.

On page two at paragraph 1 of the form the full address of the property for which possession is sought should be entered.

Paragraph 2 of the form should not be completed as it relates to a demoted AST.

At paragraph 3 the date the tenancy agreement was signed should be inserted and attach a copy of the first tenancy agreement to the form. If a further tenancy or tenancies was/were granted the date the most recent tenancy agreement was signed should be inserted in the second sentence of paragraph 3 and a copy of the further tenancy agreement attached to the form.

If the tenancy began on or after 28 February 1997 the words at paragraph 5 should be crossed out.

It is very unlikely that an AST for which a landlord is now seeking possession began before 28 February 1997 (i.e. more than 15 years old). However, if the tenancy began on or after 15 January 1989 but before 28 February 1997 the words at paragraph 4 should be crossed out.

At paragraph 5(c) the date the section 20 Notice was served on the tenant should be entered and in the space below details of how it was served should be stated. It is very unlikely that a landlord will need to complete this given that ASTs are not normally more than a year old much less being more than 15 years old. However, if this section is being used the date the Section 20 Notice was served should be entered and a copy of the Section 20 Notice must be available and attached to the claim form.

Paragraph 6 should be left unmarked.

At paragraph 7 the date the Section 21 Notice was served on the tenant should be inserted (this should be the date it is actually served or legally deemed to have been served on the tenant). In the space below details of how the Section 21 Notice was served on the tenant should be inserted, such as, being sent by first class post on (insert date of postage, recorded delivery or hand delivery). If the tenancy agreement provided for service to be executed in a particular way this should have been followed and referred to here.

In the final part of paragraph 7 the expiry date of the notice should be inserted. Where a saving clause is being relied on the wording of the saving clause should be inserted. A copy of the notice and proof of service are to be attached to the claim form.

At paragraph 8, if the rented property is not a HMO or is not subject to additional licensing as if it was an HMO, paragraphs 8(a) and (b) should be crossed out.

If the property is an HMO and is licensed under Part 2 Housing Act 2004 paragraph 8(a) applies, paragraphs 8(b) and (c) should be crossed out and a copy of the licence or application for a licence attached to the claim form. If the property is an HMO subject to additional licensing under Part 3 Housing Act 2004 paragraph 8(b) applies paragraphs 8(a) and 8(c) should be crossed out and a copy of the licence or application for a licence attached to the claim form.

At paragraph 9 if no cash deposit has been taken in relation to the tenancy after 6 April 2007 the "no" box of paragraph 9(a) should be marked. If a cash deposit was received on or after 6 April 2007 the "yes" box should be marked. A landlord should ensure that they have complied with the statement at paragraph 9(b) at the date the notice had been served.

If the landlord received a deposit which was not money i.e. property after 6 April 2007 the "yes" box should marked at paragraph 9(c). If no, the "no" box should be marked. If yes the landlord should be able to state that they complied with the sentence at paragraph 9(d) at the date the Section 21 Notice had been served.

A tenant can request that the court give a date for possession up to six weeks after the hearing date if they will suffer exceptional hardship if possession is granted any earlier. If a landlord accepts up to six weeks being given they should leave paragraph 11 unmarked. If the landlord objects they should cross out paragraph 11 in its entirety. Landlords should bear in mind when deciding on this paragraph that if the tenant does not leave the property on the date given in the possession order a landlord will need to apply to the court for a bailiffs' warrant for possession. The time involved in applying for the warrant and have it executed by the court's bailiffs can easily take four weeks.

Paragraph 12 should be left unmarked.

Paragraph 13 is the "Statement of Truth". The landlord should cross out the words in brackets (the claimant believes) so that it reads "(I believe) that the facts stated in this claim form are true" The words "I am duly authorised by the claimant to sign this statement" should be crossed out. The landlord should then sign and date the form. An agent cannot sign and date this form on behalf of a landlord. One joint landlord can sign and date on behalf of the other landlords. Below the signature the landlord should cross out the words in bracket (Litigation friend) and (Claimant's solicitor) so that it reads (Claimant). The landlord's full name should be entered in the line below.

In the final boxes of the Claim Form the address and contact details the court should use for the landlord should be entered if it is different to the details the landlord gave on the first page.

It is important that a landlord completes this form accurately so that a possession order can be made at the first attempt. The landlord must be able to attach the documents mentioned in the table below that relates to the paragraphs and information they completed in the form. The documents to accompany the claim form should be marked as set out in the table below on the front and subsequent pages.

Document	Letter to be written on the front and subsequent pages
First or only written tenancy agreement	A
Most recent written tenancy if more than one	A1
Section 20 Notice	B
Proof of service of Section 20 Notice	B1
Section 21 Notice	C
Proof of service of Section 21 Notice	C1
Evidence of HMO licence	D

21.6.2 Commencing court proceedings - Accelerated Possession Procedure

A landlord will need to provide to the court three copies of each Form N5B (there will be more than one Form N5B if there is more than one tenant i.e. joint tenants) each copy having the relevant documents attached to it. The Form N5B for the court to keep should have the original documents attached. The landlord has to pay a court fee (the amount to be paid can be obtained by contacting the court or checking online at www.justice.gov.uk/courts/fees). The court staff will check the documents and if satisfied that they have been completed, signed and dated, stamp the documents and insert a court issue date.

The court will serve on the tenant:-
* the Claim Form;
* accompanying documents;
* guidance notes and other information; and
* a defence form.

The court will send to the landlord a Notice of Issue. This document contains the following information:-
* the name of the court;
* the claim number;
* the name of the claimant(s) and defendant(s);
* issue fee;
* date claim was issued;
* date it was served on the tenant;
* time period for a defence to be provided;
* information about the proceedings; and
* tear off slip to request a possession order.

The tenant will have 14 days from service of the court documents on them to provide the court with a defence. The landlord should contact the court at the end of the 14 days period to find out if the tenant has provided a defence. If no defence has been provided the landlord should tear off the bottom section of the Notice of Issue, complete it and return it to the court (a copy should be kept by the landlord). This tear off slip is to request that the court make a possession order in the absence of the tenant providing a defence.

The Notice of Issue tear off slip should have had entered the details of the court, claim number, claimant and defendant's names as it appears at the top of the form. If this is not already entered the landlord should complete it. The last sentence in the Notice of Issue which reads "The defendant has given me possession of the premises. I ask the court to order the defendant to pay my costs" should be crossed out. The landlord should then sign and date the form and cross out the words "solicitor" and "litigation friend" below the signature.

A copy should be kept and the original Notice of Issue (tear off slip) sent to the court. On the court receiving this document, if the paper work submitted to the court to start the proceedings is completed correctly, with the necessary documents attached and a defence is still not received the court will make an order for possession. A landlord should make a request for a possession order within three months of the date when a defence should have been provided.

If a landlord:-
- has an AST;
- serves the correct Section 21 Notice;
- waits until the correct notice period expires to start court proceedings;
- accurately completes the claim form; and
- submits the claim form to court with all the accompanying documents

the tenant will not have a defence to the possession proceedings.

If the landlord does not get the above matters right the tenant can use that defect as a full defence to the possession proceedings. A landlord will then have to repeat the procedure from the point at which they made the error.

If the tenant submits a defence, a copy will be sent to the landlord and the proceedings will be referred before a judge for a decision. At that point the judge may:-
- make an order for possession (the court can do so without a hearing);
- set a date for a hearing where the court is not satisfied that the Notice was served or the landlord has not established that they are entitled to possession under this procedure;
- give case management directions; or
- strike out the claim if the claim form shows no reasonable grounds for bringing the proceedings.

If a hearing is fixed, the landlord and tenant will be given at least 14 days' notice of the date. Paragraph 5.6 explains what a landlord should do when they first attend court. By looking at the defence submitted by the tenant the landlord will know what their defence is and what they will need to prove at court to discredit that defence. A common defence is that the Section 21 Notice was not served. A landlord should be prepared to provide evidence to the court that the notice was served. At the end of the hearing the judge will make an order.

As noted above, the landlord must cross out or leave unmarked paragraph 11 of the form N5b that asks whether the landlord is against the tenant being given additional time to leave the property (up to six weeks). If the proceedings is dealt with without a hearing and the tenant requests additional time in their defence form the judge will make a possession order and may determine this request by a court hearing, if the landlord crossed out paragraph 11. If there is to be a court hearing it must be before the date on which the tenant is to give up possession. The judge will determine how much notice should be given to the parties of the date of the hearing. If the judge is satisfied that exceptional hardship exists at the hearing the possession date may be varied.

Once the date given in the order for the tenant to leave the property has passed, if the tenant remains in the property the landlord will need to apply for a bailiffs' warrant for eviction. Paragraph 5.7 set out details of how this application should be made.

PRIVATE SECTOR HOUSING BENEFIT
(LOCAL HOUSING ALLOWANCE since 7 April 2008)
TENANTS

BEING A LANDLORD

22 HOUSING BENEFIT/LOCAL HOUSING ALLOWANCE

22.1 What is Housing Benefit (HB)/Local Housing Allowance (LHA) and who can claim it?

HB/LHA is a payment made to or on behalf of a tenant to assist them in fulfilling their contractual obligation to pay rent.

There are two systems of HB in operation today:-

- the Local Housing Allowance system (LHA); and
- the Rent Referral system.

Although LHA came into effect on 7 April 2008, the old Rent Referral System is still in place for tenancies begun before this date where the tenant has been in continuous receipt of housing benefit and for certain types of properties regardless of when they have been rented. The Rent Referral System is being phased out for most properties. If a tenant of a qualifying property on the Rent Referral System stops and restarts their claim, the new claim will usually be under the LHA system.

HB/LHA is a means-tested benefit i.e. entitlement depends upon a tenant and their household's income, savings and/or capital. Tenants in receipt of Income Support, Job Seekers Allowance, Employment Support Allowance and Pension Credit will automatically be entitled to HB/LHA. Tenants can also get HB/LHA if they are working but on a low income. Tenants who receive HB/LHA are sometimes referred to in property advertisement as DSS (Department of Social Security) tenants.

Each local authority has a housing benefit office that administers HB/LHA for any applicant (tenant) living in their area.

The belief that tenants on HB/LHA are of a lesser reputation than tenants who are not in receipt of HB/LHA is far from the truth. There are good and bad HB/LHA tenants and good and bad non-HB/LHA tenants. Any tenant who is employed can lose their job and may find it necessary to claim HB/LHA to assist with their rent. This does not make them become a bad tenant.

It is now true that tenants on HB/LHA are and will increasingly continue to be less competitive than non-HB/LHA tenants in the rent they are able to afford in the private rented market. This is due to a series of changes that have reduced and will continue to reduce the HB/LHA tenants can get. However, the amount of HB/LHA still being paid will be competitive for a significant amount of properties in the private rental market.

Some of the advantages of a landlord accepting tenants in receipt of HB/LHA are:-

- it significantly increases the number of tenants to whom the property is marketed;
- shorter void periods;
- many local authorities operate a scheme that provides qualifying tenants with a deposit, rent in advance and other incentives and/or assistance to landlords that accept HB/LHA;
- tenants tend to want long term lettings;
- agents are not necessary to obtain a tenant; and
- in some instances HB/LHA is paid directly to the landlord on behalf of the tenant.

Some disadvantages of a landlord accepting tenants in receipt of HB/LHA are:-

- In a significant number of cases rent is paid 4 weekly and not per calendar month;
- HB/LHA is not paid on the due date in the tenancy agreement but on the local authority's payment schedule;
- It is more difficult to get insurance in respect of a tenant in receipt of HB/LHA;
- HB/LHA is paid in arrears;
- If a tenant has not got their own savings or is not assisted by a local authority scheme they may not have a deposit or rent in advance;
- Changes may occur to a tenant's HB/LHA payments during the tenancy and might lead to arrears;
- In some instances a landlord might be asked to repay HB/LHA;
- The HB/LHA rates or what the tenants can afford will gradually become more uncompetitive in the current property market;
- Rent increases are limited to what LHA will be paid;
- Rent arrears can be more difficult to recover.

22.2 What a landlord should do before renting to a tenant in receipt of LHA

In addition to the matters mentioned in Chapter 2 a landlord should carry out further checks before renting to a tenant who will be in receipt of LHA to ensure that they will be able to afford the property. These checks for affordability will answer the following questions:-

- will the maximum LHA cover the rent they seek?
- is the tenant eligible for the landlord bedroom size property under LHA rules? and
- will the amount of LHA the tenant is entitled to make the property affordable for them?

22.2.1 Ascertain the maximum LHA payable for the landlord's property

For every property there is a maximum LHA that will be paid. The maximum LHA rates for properties in England and Wales have been capped nationally at the sums set out in paragraph 22.13.1. However, the actual LHA rate for a property is set locally and may be lower than the capped rate.

A landlord should be careful about entering into a tenancy with a tenant in receipt of full LHA at a rent more than the LHA rate for their property. To do so will place the tenant at a high risk of rent arrears as they will have little or no disposable income to make up the shortfall between the LHA and the actual rent. The local housing benefit office will only top up the difference in limited circumstances and only for a short period. This decision is discretionary. It is unlikely that a top-up will be paid if the rent was higher than the LHA payable, from the beginning of the tenancy. A landlord therefore needs to know whether the LHA payable for their particular property will meet the rent at which they are marketing their property.

If the LHA is just below the amount of rent a landlord seeks for their property a landlord may want to consider lowering their rent to the LHA rate if this means a shorter void period and therefore a lesser overall loss of income.

Prior to April 2012 the LHA rate for a property was subject to fluctuation to match local market changes. The rate was reset monthly. A tenant who signed a tenancy in a particular month could sign at the maximum LHA for that month and the rate would apply to the tenancy for 12 months. However, since April 2012 LHA rates have been fixed for 12 months. To ascertain the LHA payable for a property a landlord should visit the directgov website at https://lha-direct.voa.gov.uk/search.aspx.

On the web page the landlord should enter the number of bedrooms and postcode for their property. The weekly LHA rate will be displayed. To work out the monthly LHA rate a landlord should multiply the weekly sum by 52 weeks and divide by 12 months.

The LHA rate is set independent of the local authority for the area in which the property is located and who will pay the LHA to or on behalf of the tenant. If a landlord ascertains that the LHA payable will be acceptable for their property they should continue to the next stage.

22.2.2 Ascertain if a proposed tenant is eligible for their size property under the LHA rules

Under the LHA rules there is a maximum bedrooms size property that a tenant will be eligible for. This will then determine the maximum LHA a tenant can get and whether they can afford the property. It is dependent on the makeup of their household. If a tenant is eligible for a two bedroom property under the LHA rules, their LHA calculation will be based on the two bedroom LHA rate even if they rent a three bedroom property.

It is important for a landlord to know whether a prospective tenant is entitled to LHA for their size property and can therefore afford the rent. In some cases a smaller property LHA rate may be high enough to pay the rent a landlord seeks for a larger property. If that is the case a landlord can sign a tenancy with a tenant in receipt of the smaller property LHA rate. In this instance a landlord should not sign a tenancy for multiple years as the tenant will not be able to afford an increased rent above the smaller property LHA rate that they are entitled to. A landlord will therefore be limited to what increased rent they can seek over the period of the tenancy.

The criteria under the LHA rules to determine the "bedroom size" property a tenant is eligible for are based upon the number of persons in the tenant's household, their sex and ages.

A landlord can ascertain what "bedroom size" property a tenant is eligible for by going to the directgov website at https://lha-direct.voa.gov.uk/search.aspx, selecting LHA bedroom calculator at the bottom of the page and completing the online form with the details of the tenant's household. A landlord will need to know how many persons are in the tenant's household, their sex and age to complete the form. Alternatively, a landlord can contact the local housing benefit office with the same information and they should be able to inform the landlord of the bedroom size property for the tenant.

Once a landlord has established that the prospective tenant is eligible for their size property, they should proceed to the next stage.

22.2.3 Ascertain the amount of LHA the prospective tenant will get

LHA is a means-tested benefit, therefore the amount, if any, that a tenant will get is subject to their means i.e. income, capital and savings. The more income, capital and savings a tenant has the less LHA they will get until they are no longer entitled. Some tenants in receipt of specific benefits that are already means-tested will automatically be entitled to LHA.

In order for a landlord to ascertain the amount of LHA a tenant will get they should visit the local authority website for the area in which the property is located. Most local authority websites have a LHA/benefit calculator. The tenant's information is completed on the online form which will calculate with a degree of accuracy the amount of LHA a tenant will get. This calculation will depend upon the accuracy of the completed online form.

Once a landlord knows the amount of LHA a tenant will get they can decide whether to enter into a tenancy. If the amount of LHA a tenant is entitled to will cover the rent the decision is straightforward. If the amount of LHA a tenant is entitled to is below the rent because of their income the landlord will need to discuss how and when the top up payments will be made and if it is affordable to the tenant. If a landlord is satisfied with the arrangement a tenancy can proceed.

22.3 Things a Landlord should do before the tenancy

Chapter 2 sets out the documents a landlord should obtain from and the checks to carry out on a tenant solely in receipt of LHA, and from a tenant who works as well as receives LHA. If a landlord obtains satisfactory documents and results to the checks they can proceed to rent to a tenant who is in receipt of or will be claiming LHA.

22.4 How does a tenant make a claim for LHA?

A claim for LHA must be made by the tenant to the local authority for the area in which the property is located. Some local authorities facilitate claims online and there is a general move in this direction. If that is not the case the tenant will usually need to attend the local housing benefit office or One Stop Shop and complete a claim form.

The LHA claim form will normally require the tenant to provide documents to verify the contents of their application. If a tenant does not have the documents at the time of the application they should still make a claim (and provide the documents at a later date) so that they preserve the date from which LHA will be payable, once the documents are provided.

A failure to provide the relevant documents to the housing benefit office can result in a delay in the claim being processed and put into payment or even the claim being cancelled. From time to time the housing benefit office will request documents from a tenant to verify changes in their circumstances, update their records, or satisfy an enquiry. If a tenant fails to provide the requested document(s) their claim will be suspended and ultimately cancelled.

22.5 Payment of LHA

A straightforward LHA claim should be put into payment within four weeks from the date of the claim. However, this may vary between local authorities. A landlord should normally get a letter from the housing benefit office when the claim has been put into payment.

LHA is paid in arrears and normally from the date the claim is made. It may be backdated in limited circumstances and for a maximum period so it is important that a tenant submits their claim before or no later than the date the tenancy commences, or if they are already in a tenancy from the date their circumstances changed to make them eligible for LHA.

Subject to limited exceptions LHA is only paid from the date a tenant has physically moved into the property even if the tenancy started earlier and the claim was made earlier. LHA is normally paid every four weeks. If the rent for a property is £1,000 per calendar month and the tenant is receiving full LHA the tenant or landlord will receive £923.08 every four weeks (£1,000 x 12 monthly payments divided by 52 weeks x 4 weeks = £923.08). Where LHA is paid four weekly a landlord will receive 13 four weekly payments for the year to account for the months that are longer than four weeks (£1,000 per calendar month x 12 months = £12,000 is equivalent to £923.08 every 4 weeks x 13 payments = £12,000.04). In some cases and dependent on local authorities' practices LHA may be paid per calendar monthly.

If a landlord does not receive payment from a tenant in receipt of LHA they should contact the housing benefit office as well as the tenant to find out why. It is likely that the housing benefit office will ask the landlord for authorisation to discuss matters with him. A copy of the form of authority should be sent to the housing benefit office. A landlord should retain the original. If it is the case that the LHA has been suspended because the tenant has not provided requested documentation a landlord should get the tenant to do so as soon as possible.

22.6 LHA being paid to the tenant or the landlord

LHA is generally paid to the tenant. The tenant should have in place arrangements to pay it on to the landlord. The best situation is for the tenant to have a separate bank account in which the LHA is paid and set up a direct debit to pay it to the landlord. Where a tenant only gets part of the rent as LHA they should pay the shortfall into this separate account to ensure sufficient funds are available to pay the landlord the full rent (monthly or four weekly rate) by direct debit.

Before LHA came into effect, landlords and tenants could arrange for HB to be paid directly to the landlord under the old Rent Referral system. This could be done at the tenant's request. However, that practice does not apply to LHA.

LHA can be paid directly to a landlord if the tenant's circumstances satisfy a certain criteria. If a landlord makes it a condition of their tenancy that the LHA is paid directly to them it will not be binding on the benefit service and the tenant has no power to make them comply with that provision.

Under the following circumstance the LHA **must** be paid to the landlord: -
* where the tenant is eight weeks or more in rent arrears.

Under the following circumstances LHA **may** be paid to the landlord:-
* where the tenant is having difficulty in managing their financial affairs;

- where the tenant is unlikely to pay their rent;
- where there is a history of rent arrears.

The circumstances listed below suggest that the tenant may have difficulty in paying their rent and may be used as evidence to substantiate a request for direct payment to a landlord:-

- severe debt problems;
- recent county court judgments;
- is an un-discharged bankrupt;
- unable to open a bank or building society account;
- some of their Income Support or Jobseeker's Allowance is paid direct to the gas, electricity or water company by the Department for Work and Pensions;
- is getting supporting people help;
- is getting help from a homeless charity;
- has learning difficulties;
- has an illness that stops them managing on a day-to-day basis;
- cannot read English;
- cannot speak English;
- addiction to drugs, alcohol or gambling;
- fleeing domestic violence;
- care leaver;
- prison leaver; or
- were homeless.

It is the housing benefit office that decides whether a tenant is likely to have difficulty in paying their rent. Evidence is needed to support a request from a tenant or landlord. Landlords should have details of rent payments and their efforts to resolve rent arrears with the tenant to present as supporting evidence, if rent arrears are claimed.

A landlord who has a tenant continuously in receipt of full LHA should never be owed more than one month's rent. As soon as the rent payment is a day late the landlord should contact the housing benefit office and make a request for direct payment. If granted, all future payments will come directly to the landlord. If there is no property damage at the end of the tenancy the deposit or deposit guarantee should cover the arrears. A request for direct payment should be in writing but does not have to comply with any formal requirements.

A tenant, landlord, letting agent and other interested party can request that LHA be paid directly to the landlord on the above criteria from the commencement of the tenancy. However, a landlord should make that request after the commencement of the tenancy if at any time the criteria apply, such as the tenant getting into financial difficulty.

If a tenant is being assisted in getting a property through a local authority's rent deposit scheme, a landlord might find it easier to get direct payment of LHA by liaising with the scheme.

22.7 Suspension of a tenant's HB/LHA

Tenants tend to receive HB/LHA over a lengthy period of time, usually years. In this period of time there are likely to be changes in the tenant's household and other circumstances. These changes may include:-

- family member leaving or joining the household (including partner);
- birth of a child;
- bereavement;
- commencement/loss of employment or pay increases/decrease; or
- changes with other benefits they receive.

Tenants are under an obligation to notify these changes to the housing benefit office and other benefit agencies but do not consistently do so. A landlord should notify these changes to the housing benefit office if he becomes aware of them. If no notification is provided there are various ways in which information about these changes may come to the attention of the housing benefit office. When notification occurs the housing benefit office will carry out a review of the tenant's claim (in light of the changes) to ensure that they are receiving the correct level of benefits. This normally means the tenant has to supply documentary evidence to the housing benefit office to verify the changes.

The housing benefit office will normally write to the tenant requesting the documents. If they are not provided further letters are sent which will eventually lead to the tenant's claim being suspended and even cancelled if the documents are not provided. When the documents are provided the suspension will be lifted subject to any adjustments. If the claim has been cancelled the tenant will need to make a new claim which may or may not be backdated to the date when the earlier claim stopped.

Landlords may find out that a tenant's HB/LHA has been suspended when they fail to receive any rent from the tenant because the tenant has no HB/LHA with which to pay it, or when the direct payments they have been receiving has stopped. At this point some landlords may find that the tenant is avoiding them and been difficult to get in contact with.

A landlord should seek to make contact with the tenant immediately and not wait days or weeks to take action. If the tenant is not answering the phone, responding to texts or email then visits should be made to the property and if necessary a landlord should be prepared to wait for the tenant. At the same time a landlord should contact the housing benefit office (providing their form of authority if not previously provided) and ascertain the reason why the HB/LHA has stopped.

A landlord should contact the tenant with this information and seek to get the tenant to engage with the housing benefit office in resolving their HB/LHA claim. If necessary the tenant may need to seek the assistance of an advice agency such as the Citizens Advice Bureau to deal with complicated matters. If the issues lie with the housing benefit office a complaint can speed up the process. The local authority should have and make available their complaint procedure.

22.8 Non–Dependant Deductions

A frequent occurrence with a tenant in receipt of HB/LHA, when their children grow up or adult relatives move in with them, is the application of a non-dependant deduction whether HB/LHA is paid direct to the landlord or to the tenant.

A non-dependant deduction is a deduction applied to a tenant's HB/LHA entitlement to reflect that a member of their household should now be contributing (the deducted sum) towards the housing costs as they are deemed to be no longer financially dependent on the tenant.

The amount of deduction is based on the non-dependant's income. Tenants are required to provide evidence of the non-dependant's income in order for the correct level of deductions to be applied. If this evidence is not provided the housing benefit office will apply the maximum deduction (currently £73.85 per week but this is due to increase). If the tenant does not make up the sum deducted by the housing benefit office rent arrears will occur.

If a landlord is receiving direct payment from the housing benefit office and a non-dependant deduction is applied to the tenant's HB/LHA entitlement they should receive notification of a reduction in the payment they are to receive. The landlord should immediately make contact with the tenant and the housing benefit office to ascertain the reason for and the amount of the reduced payment. If the landlord is informed that the HB/LHA has been reduced because of a non-dependant deduction they should inform the tenant how much the shortfall is (if they do not know about it) and make arrangements for it to be paid. If a tenant tells the landlord that the deduction is incorrect or should not be applied a landlord should advise the tenant to liaise with the housing benefit office or seek help from local advice agencies or the CAB.

The level of non-dependent deductions has remained constant for some 10 years up until April 2011 when they were increased. Further increases occurred in April 2012 and are planned for 2013.

22.9 Recovery of an Overpayment of HB/LHA from the tenant or landlord/agent

Some landlords and agents will not rent to a tenant in receipt of HB/LHA because of the rules on overpayment. An overpayment occurs where a tenant is paid HB/LHA to which they are not entitled. A tenant may not be entitled to all or some of the HB/LHA they receive because:-

- a change in the tenant's circumstances has not been notified;
- an official error (i.e. the housing benefit office makes a mistake); or
- a fraudulent claim or misrepresentation following a claim.

Overpaid HB/LHA can be recovered from the tenant, their partner, or the person to whom it was paid (landlord/agent). An overpayment of HB/LHA is recoverable under the following circumstances after April 2006:-

- An overpayment which **was** caused by a misrepresentation or failure to disclose information must be recovered from the person who has made the misrepresentation or failed to disclose the information. This can be the tenant, landlord/agent or both.

- An overpayment which was **not** caused by a misrepresentation, failure to disclose information or an official error can be recovered from the tenant, their partner or the person to whom it was paid (landlord/agent).

- An overpayment which is caused by an official error (i.e. local authority mistake by doing or failing to do something) must be recovered from the person who could reasonably have been expected at the time of the payment or notice of the payment to realise that it was an overpayment. This can be the tenant, landlord/agent or both. If it could not reasonably have been known that there was an overpayment it is not recoverable.

A landlord will **not** be required to repay an overpayment if **all** the following conditions apply:-

- HB/LHA was paid direct to the landlord;
- the landlord in writing notified the housing benefit office or the DWP that there might be an overpayment;
- the overpayment was not caused by the tenant moving out;
- the housing benefit office has identified a possible overpayment;
- there is belief that an offence of dishonest or false representation to obtain a benefit has been committed or there has been a deliberate failure to report a relevant change, in breach of the duty to notify a change of circumstances; and
- the housing benefit office is satisfied that the landlord did not participate in causing the overpayment, or acted/ neglected to act thereby contributing to the overpayment.

Most overpayments will arise from the tenant failing to notify the housing benefit office of a change in their circumstances and as such will be recoverable from the tenant. However, a landlord can be required to repay it if they knew of the changed circumstances and did not report it, such as a landlord getting direct payment knowing that the tenant has started work, or their partner moved in or a child has moved out. A landlord would normally expect that there would be a change to the direct payment they are receiving under these circumstances and if there is no change it is likely that it has not been reported.

A landlord will also be required to repay an overpayment where a tenant has moved out of the property or died and they continued to receive HB/LHA.

Usually when a tenant is required to repay an overpayment two steps will be taken by the housing benefit office:-

- the tenant's continuing entitlement to HB/LHA will be reduced or stopped as their benefit is adjusted to reflect the change in their entitlement which led to the overpayment; and
- the tenant's continuing entitlement, if any, to HB/LHA will be further reduced to allow the overpayment to be recouped usually by instalments.

A landlord with a tenant subject to an overpayment should immediately ascertain from the housing benefit office what sum will be paid and ensure that the tenant will make up the shortfall and monitor this arrangement.

Usually, when the housing benefit office becomes aware of an overpayment, HB/LHA is suspended whilst the matter is being investigated. In this period the tenant will normally be required to provide documentary evidence to verify any change in their circumstances. When this has been resolved a tenant (provided they have a continuing entitlement) will usually be owed a backdated sum from the time of the suspension. The housing benefit office will award a backdated lump sum to the tenant but withhold it in full or part to recoup the overpayment. This will ultimately mean a period when the landlord did not receive any payment (i.e. during the suspension). A landlord will need to make arrangements to recover the sum from the tenant, usually by instalments. Circumstances that can lead to a tenant being paid too much HB/LHA if not reported include:-

- tenant begins to work;
- tenant who is already working receives a pay increase;
- a member of the household has left the property resulting in the tenant being eligible for a smaller bedroom size property (under occupying);
- a partner who would make the tenant entitled to a lower HB/LHA moves into the property;
- a non-dependant deduction applies;

- in some circumstances where tenant has being away from the property for a longer period than 13 weeks; or
- any other changes resulting in an increase in income, capital or savings.

22.10 Discretionary Housing Payment (DHP)

DHP is a financial assistance that local authorities can provide, at their discretion, to tenants in receipt of HB/LHA. If successful in an application a tenant will normally receive top up payments to their HB/LHA usually to help with their housing costs. To be eligible a tenant must be entitled to HB/LHA and/or Council Tax Benefit.

DHP can be applied for where the:-
- HB/LHA cannot meet the full rent;
- application of non-dependant deductions means the tenant cannot pay their full rent;
- tenant needs to meet essential work costs;
- tenant needs rent in advance for a new letting;
- tenant needs a deposit for a new letting;
- tenant needs removal costs for a new letting.

Payments can be made to the landlord rather than the tenant. DHP will not be paid indefinitely and is only a short term solution to what may be long term housing problems.

The local authority has an application form to be completed by the tenant. The form will ask detailed information about the tenant's financial circumstances and their priority debts. The more information given will better enable a local authority to exercise their discretion in making a decision. If the tenant believes the decision is unfair they can always make a complaint to the local authority.

22.11 Third Party Deductions

The DWP can make deductions from a tenant's benefits to pay for certain debts, including rent arrears owed to a landlord from whom the tenant is currently renting a property, not a former landlord. If a landlord is seeking to recover rent arrears by this method they should do so during their tenancy. Third party deductions can be useful to vulnerable tenants who would otherwise be at risk of losing their home. Deductions must be in the best interest of the family.

Third party deductions can be made from a tenant in receipt of any of the following benefits:-
- Income Support;
- Income-based Jobseeker's Allowance;
- Pension Credit; or
- Income-related Employment and Support Allowance.

Third party deductions are applied for by completing an application form and sending it to the relevant DWP office. This form can be obtained from the local housing benefit office. For an individual debt a nominal sum will be deducted which will be under £5 per week. If there are several claims for different debts an order of priority will be applied to the debts. This means that an on-going debt payment can be stopped to allow a new debt with higher priority to be paid.

If a tenant is having deductions for more than one debt the maximum combined amount deducted from the tenant's benefits cannot exceed 25% of those benefits unless the tenant consents. Payments are normally made every four weeks to the landlord.

Where a tenant is on benefits and in receipt of full LHA, as soon as a payment is late a landlord should request direct payment to limit the arrears to one months' rent. If the tenant does not make satisfactory arrangements to pay the arrears or does not stick to an arrangement the landlord should request third party deductions.

On an application for third party deductions the DWP will need to know the following information:-

- name, address, NIS and date of birth of the tenant;
- landlord's name, address and bank details for payment;
- details of the benefit(s) which the tenant receives;
- details of other methods used to recover payment i.e. this must be a last resort;
- details of the amount of arrears;
- sums needed to be paid by the tenant to cover current rent commitments;
- other relevant information.

If third party deductions are agreed the landlord and tenant will receive a notification letter advising of the amount, the frequency of payment and how to notify the DWP of changes in their circumstances. If there is a cancellation of a tenant's benefit payments the third party deduction will stop. A landlord should notify the DWP when the debt has been paid in full. Any overpayment will be recovered.

22.12 What should a landlord do if a tenant in receipt of HB/LHA is not paying part or all of the rent?

A landlord should take the following action:-

- Make enquiries with the tenant to find out why rent payment has reduced or stopped. The tenant may not know, refuse to disclose, be difficult/impossible to contact, or may give a credible explanation.

- Regardless of what response a landlord receives to their initial enquiries with the tenant, contact should be made with the housing benefit office to confirm what the tenant has said or to obtain an explanation in the absence of a credible response from or if there has been no contact with the tenant (a form of authority will normally be required for this contact).

- If the landlord has received no payment from the tenant but the housing benefit office has confirmed that LHA (whether in full or part) has been paid to the tenant, a landlord should request direct payment of all future LHA payments.

- If there has been no LHA paid to the tenant or the LHA paid has been reduced, a landlord should find out why the payment has been stopped or reduced from the housing benefit office. This may confirm a response the tenant has provided. If the payments have stopped because the tenant is no longer entitled to LHA (such as the tenant and/or their partner are now working) a landlord should make arrangements with the tenant to pay the current and all future rent and arrears, if any.

- If the payments have stopped because the housing benefit office has requested information from the tenant which the tenant has not provided, a landlord should liaise with the tenant about the provision of that information without further delay.

- If the payments have been reduced because the tenant is no longer entitled to the full or amount of LHA they previously received (and the landlord has received the reduced amount whether from the tenant or direct payment), they should make arrangements with the tenant for them to pay the shortfall.

- If a tenant is facing difficulty in paying their rent due a reduction in LHA that is not related to an increase in their income or recovery of an overpayment, a landlord should ask the tenant to apply for a DHP.

- Refer the tenant to a local Citizens Advice Bureau or a Law Centre to receive advice and assistance with their LHA problems.

- Apply for third party deductions.

- If there is no improvement in payments, a landlord may well have to consider possession proceedings (Chapter 21) and proceedings to recover rent arrears (Chapters 15 to 20).

22.13 Changes to LHA

There are a number of changes that have occurred to LHA at the time of writing this book and there are further planned changes. Some tenants are already affected by the changes, some are subject to the changes but have a period of transitional protection before it takes effect and some will be affected by future changes. The table below sets out the changes and the date they have occurred or will occur. An explanation is given of the changes below the table.

Date	LHA change
April 2011	LHA cap. There is now a nationwide limit on the maximum LHA payable for different bedroom size properties.
April 2011	The 30 percentile rule.
April 2011	Non-dependant deductions increase (1st stage).
January 2012	Single persons over the age of 25 but below the age of 35 no longer entitled to LHA for a one bedroom flat but instead will get LHA for a room in a shared property.
April 2012	LHA rates which were previously set on a monthly basis to reflect local market changes will now be set for 12 months.
April 2012	Further increases in non-dependant deductions (2nd stage)
April 2013	Benefit cap will be piloted in four local authority boroughs (Haringey, Enfield, Croydon, Bromley).
April 2013	LHA rates to be increased in line with the Consumer Price Index
April 2013	Increase in non-dependent deductions (3rd stage).
Autumn 2013	Benefit cap introduced nationwide following above pilot.
October 2013	Universal Credit to be introduced with full transition to be completed by October 2017

22.13.1 Maximum LHA cap set for one to four bedroom properties

The caps set nationally are:-
- £400 per week for a four bedroom property;
- £340 per week for a three bedroom property;
- £290 per week for a two bedroom property; and
- £250 per week for a one bedroom property.

Where a tenant lives in a relatively cheap area the LHA cap will have minimum or no effect on the amount of LHA they receive as their local LHA is under the cap. The tenants most affected are those that live in expensive areas (e.g. Westminster, Kensington, Chelsea and other central London boroughs) and/or in large properties. The largest property the cap is set for is a four bedroom property. There is no longer any LHA rate for properties above four bedrooms. A tenant can rent a five or six bedroom property if they wish but the four bedrooms LHA rate will need to cover the rent.

The caps are applied to all new claims for LHA from April 2011. However, if there is an existing claim the cap will not take effect until the claim comes up for a review. A claim normally comes up for a review every 12 months, usually on the anniversary of the tenancy. However, a review can also occur at any time when there has been a relevant change in a tenant's circumstances that might affect the amount of LHA they get. Upon a review the tenant has a period of nine months, called transitional protection, where the LHA rate will not be reduced by the cap. After that if the LHA cap is lower than the actual rent the lower payment will take effect.

Therefore, if a tenant signed a tenancy on 28 March 2011 for a property with four bedrooms at £450 per week, the cap would not apply until the LHA claim came up for review a year later i.e. 27 March 2012 (a review may occur earlier if there is a relevant change in the tenant's circumstances). The tenant will have a further period of nine months where the level of £450 per week is maintained i.e. until 27 November 2012. Following this date the cap will apply and LHA reduced to £400 per week.

If the tenant is in a fixed term contract at this point they will remain liable to pay the contractual rent. Such a tenant can make an application for a DHP but this will be at the discretion of the local authority and will only be for a limited period of time.

22.13.2 The 30 Percentile Rule

Before April 2011 LHA rates were very competitive to market rates for properties. LHA rates were set at the 50 percentile rule. So, five out of every 10 properties were affordable at LHA rates.

From April 2011 the 30 percentile rule took effect. This means that only three in every 10 properties are affordable under LHA rates.

LHA rates are set against "local" market rates. There is no one set of rates for all of England & Wales. There is, however, a maximum cap for all of England & Wales. The 30 percentile rule will mean that for all properties that were rented at maximum LHA rate the tenants have experienced a reduction in their LHA payments from April 2011. Tenants will also face a reduction in the number of properties they can afford under the LHA rates.

The 30 percentile is applied to all new claims for LHA from April 2011. However, if there is an existing claim the 30 percentile will not take effect until the claim comes up for a review. A claim generally comes up for a review every 12 months usually on the anniversary of the tenancy. Upon a review the tenant has a period of nine months called transitional protection where the LHA rate will stay the same. After that if the LHA is lower the lower rate will take effect.

Therefore if a tenant signed a tenancy on 28 March 2011 for a property with four bedrooms at £380 per week, the 30 percentile for the local market area would not apply until the LHA claim came up for review a year later i.e. 27 March 2012. An LHA claim can come up for a review earlier if there has been a material change in the tenant's circumstances. The tenant will have a further period of nine months where the level of £380 per week is maintained i.e. until 27 November 2012. Following this date the 30 percentile will apply and LHA reduced to say £350 per week.

If the tenant is in a fixed term contract at this point they will remain liable to pay the contractual rent. Such a tenant can make an application for a DHP but this will be at the discretion of the local authority and will only be for a limited period of time.

22.13.3 Single Claimants under 35 years old

Under LHA rules (with limited exception) a single person under 25 years of age is only entitled to the LHA rate for a room in a shared property. From 1 January 2012 this age will be increased from 25 to 35.

There are single persons between the ages of 25 and 35 years who had been renting a one bedroom flat who will eventually have to rent a room in a shared property under the new rules, as that is all the housing benefit office will pay for.

It is unlikely that a landlord will be able to absorb the reduction in LHA rates and keep a single tenant under the age of 35 years in their one bedroom flat. Landlords will ultimately have to make arrangements with their tenant for them to vacate the property or take possession proceedings. Some tenants will have some protection from the new rule until December 2012.

The table below shows the date different tenants are affected.

Category of claimant	When affected
New claims	1 January 2012
Claims from 1 April 2011 for someone aged 25 to 34	Anniversary of claim
Claims between 8/4/08 and 1/4/11 and tenant is 25 years old on or before 31/12/11	12 months from 31/12/11
The above but 25 years old on or after 1/1/12	Anniversary of claim
Claims between 8/4/08 and 1/4/11	Review date (after 1/4/11) + 9 months

If the tenant is in a fixed term contract at this point they will remain liable to pay the contractual rent. Such a tenant can make an application for a DHP but payment will be at the discretion of the local authority and will only be for a limited period of time. This change is likely to result in an increased demand for rooms in properties with shared facilities such as HMOs.

22.13.4 The Benefit Cap

From April 2013 the government will be piloting a benefit cap on claimants of working age i.e. 16 to 64 (retirement age) in the boroughs of Haringey, Bromley, Enfield and Croydon. The benefit cap is intended to limit the total income a tenant gets from benefits to the average weekly income that someone of their status (single person or couples with or without children) who is working would earn.

Some websites offer a benefit cap calculator so that a tenant can put in their details and see if and how they may be affected.

A tenant in receipt of any of the benefits below will have the benefits added together and capped. These benefits are:-
* Bereavement Allowance;
* Carer's Allowance;
* Child Benefit;
* Child Tax Credit;
* Employment and Support Allowance (except where it is paid with the support component);
* Guardian's Allowance;
* Housing Benefit;
* Incapacity Benefit;
* Income Support;
* Jobseeker's Allowance;
* Maternity Allowance;
* Severe Disablement Allowance;
* Widowed Parent's Allowance;
* Widowed Mothers Allowance;
* Widows Pension; and
* Widows Pension Age-Related.

The cap is expected to be:-
* £350 per week for a single tenant; and
* £500 per week for tenants who are a couple, with or without dependant children or a lone parent with dependant children.

The cap will be implemented by adding all of the above benefits that a tenant gets and if the sum is over the cap their HB/LHA will be reduced until the capped figure is reached.

The cap will not apply to anyone receiving:-

- Working Tax Credit;
- Disability Living Allowance (subject to conditions);
- Personal Independence Payment (from April 2013);
- Attendance Allowance (subject to conditions);
- Industrial Injuries Benefits;
- Employment and Support Allowance, if paid with the support component;
- War Widow's or War Widower's Pension.

An extreme application of the cap can be seen in the following example. A family of four children receive the following benefits:-

- Child Benefit;
- Child Tax Credit;
- Housing Benefit; and
- Income Support.

Their housing benefit alone is at the maximum LHA rate of £400 per week. If the income from the other benefits total £350 per week their maximum income is £750 per week. When the expected cap of £500 per week is applied the tenant's LHA will be reduced to £150 per week (£350 per weeks in other benefits plus £150 reduced LHA = £500). If the tenant is to meet their contractual rent they will have to use money from their other benefits to make up the shortfall. A tenant subject to £500 per week cap having to pay rent of £400 per week will only have £100 left per week for all their other expenses. A tenant can avoid the effect of the cap by working and being eligible for working tax credits.

22.13.5 Universal Credit

This will be a new single payment to benefit claimants not in work or working but in receipt of a low income to replace several separate benefit payments. It will replace:-

- income-based Jobseeker's Allowance;
- income-related Employment and Support Allowance;
- Income Support;
- Child Tax Credits;
- Working Tax Credits; and
- Housing Benefit.

The following table sets out the starting schedule for Universal Credit:-

Claimant	When change takes effect
New claimants for the replaced benefits	October 2013
Claimants whose circumstances change e.g. birth of a child	October 2013
Existing claimants	April 2014 (phased in)
Remaining claimants	End 2015
For everyone	2017/2018

It is not anticipated that Universal Credit will reduce the tenant's income, as that would have already been achieved through the benefits cap. What Universal Credit will do is make tenants get their benefits in one monthly payment, like a salary and the sum of money will be paid directly to the tenant for them to then meet their living expenses. This will have significant impact on a landlord's ability to obtain direct payment of rent from the benefits service. This payment will not be administered by local housing benefit offices which may become defunct.

22.14 What should a landlord do about the changes?

As it is inevitable that some tenants will experience a reduction in the LHA they receive and might fall into rent arrears, a landlord with a tenant in receipt of LHA should take a pro-active approach.

Landlords should:-
- ascertain whether or not their tenant is in receipt of LHA (not all landlords will know this);
- ascertain if their tenant is in receipt of other benefits;
- ascertain other relevant personal details about their tenant;
- meet with their tenant;
- ascertain what changes may affect their tenant and when;
- check if any exemptions apply to the tenant;
- if tenant is affected, to what extent;
- see if tenant will be able to continue to pay their rent;
- if not, determine whether they will consider a reduction in the rent;
- if not, start taking measures to obtain vacant possession of the property i.e. serve notices in time to get vacant possession before the changes take effect;
- consider whether the rent they can get in the non-LHA market will be higher and what void period they will experience to achieve the wanted rent to see if it makes sense to keep existing tenant at lower rent; and
- encourage tenant to liaise with their local authority housing department if they are affected. Most local authorities are running projects to assist affected tenants.

22.15 Pre-Tenancy Determination System

Private rented sector tenants who have continuously claimed HB before the 7 April 2008 would not have received the LHA version of HB. Their claims are dealt with under the rent referral procedure, which also applies to the following whenever they are rented:-

- caravan;
- house boat;
- mobile home;
- hostel; and
- boarder.

Under this procedure the maximum rent payable under HB, for the particular tenant in the particular property, is determined by the rent proposed being referred to a Rent Officer. Rent Officers are employed by the Rent Service and are independent to the local authority in whose area the property is located. A rent will be referred to the Rent Officer when:

- a new claim for housing benefit is received for the lodgings mentioned above;
- there has been notice of a relevant change (e.g. number of occupiers, households members having reached 10 or 16, increase in rent and change in the property);
- a request is made by tenant or landlord for a pre-tenancy determination; and
- on the anniversary of the Rent Officer's decision.

The referral is normally made by the housing benefit office, but can be made by the landlord or tenant whenever they are negotiating an increase in rent or seeking to find out the rent at which they can renew the fixed term.

A referral is made by a landlord or tenant requesting a pre-tenancy determination. This is done by completing the relevant form with the tenant (as their household details are required) and submitting it to the Rent Service. The form asks details about the:-

- tenant;
- tenant's household (age, gender, relation);
- property;
- proposed tenancy (i.e. rent, rental period, length of tenancy); and
- landlord.

The form will need to be signed by the landlord and tenant before being submitted.

HOUSING BENEFIT

The Rent Officer sets the maximum housing benefit the tenant can get depending on the family size, property size and other details. The landlord and tenant can choose that the housing benefit be paid direct to the landlord.

Following the referral to the Rent Officer the landlord, tenant and housing benefit office will be notified in writing of the maximum housing benefit payable, from when it applies and for how long. If there is an issue with the level at which it is set a review can be requested.

Most of the other rules relating to a tenant in receipt of LHA apply to a rent referral claimant.

A tenant can convert their HB claim under the rent referral system to the LHA system. This can be achieved by the tenant stopping their rent referral claim for a period of a week and then restarting their claim by applying under the LHA system. The rent under the LHA system is usually significantly higher than that payable under the rent referral system. However, the landlord may need to forgo a week's rent to make the switch as it is likely that a tenant on HB is unable to afford to pay for the week when they do not have a claim for HB. The financial merit of this for the landlord will depend on the expected increase in rent.

23 COMPANY LETS

The term "Company Let" in the context of this book, describes a tenancy where a landlord lets a residential property (flat or house) to a company (the company is the tenant) for a residential use. The property, although rented by a company, is to be used for a residential purpose by a person associated with the company such as an employee, director, owner, business partner or guest.

Where a company rents a property to carry on a business or for a part residential part business use, this normally creates a business tenancy which is governed by the Landlord and Tenant Act 1954. This book does not deal with business tenancies.

The rights and obligations between a landlord and tenant under a company let, is mostly governed by the express terms of the tenancy agreement and the implied court-made (common law) rules that historically applied to most tenancies before legislation brought in greater control. It is therefore important for a landlord of a company let to have the right express terms in the tenancy agreement and to know the implied court-made rules that affect it.

It is not unknown for a landlord to use an AST agreement for a company let and to serve a Section 21 Notice to end such a let. However, a company cannot be a tenant under an AST as the tenant has to be an individual and not an artificial person. Even if an AST agreement is used for a company let, this will not make the tenancy an AST and serving a Section 21 Notice will have no effect. A company let is known as a "common law" tenancy and is without any main statutory protection built in.

23.1 Before starting the tenancy

Even if the company proposing to rent a landlord's property is well known and established it is advisable for a landlord to carry out certain checks before signing the tenancy agreement. This is important in the current economic climate following the demise of Comet, Woolworths, Jessops, Blockbusters and Republic to name a few.

Like individuals, a company can undergo a credit check. If the prospective tenant is a limited company in business for more than 12 months it should have filed trading accounts available to the public. If the prospective tenant is not a limited company or is trading less than 12 months there will usually be no public accounts available. In that situation background checks can be done on the company/business and county court judgments can be searched for.

It is recommended that a landlord use a reputable referencing agent that specialises in referencing companies to get a report upon which a decision can be made whether or not to let to the company.

Ultimately, if a landlord is not satisfied with the status of a company or, the referencing report obtained is of concern, a guarantor can be sought in the form of an individual such as a company director. As stated earlier in Chapter 2, checks need to be carried out on any guarantor to ensure that they would have been suitable as a tenant in their own right to rent the property. The guarantor should sign the tenancy agreement in the capacity of a guarantor.

23.2 Documents to be obtained

It is important that a landlord obtains as much documentation on a company proposing to be a tenant as is recommended to be obtained on an individual (as set out in Chapter 2). Doing so will put a landlord in the best possible position to deal with any problems that may occur during or at the end of the tenancy. It is recommended that a landlord obtain the following documents about a company, although the availability of the documents, the size and type of company will need to be considered. A landlord should use their judgement:-

1. company registration documents or the document that constitutes the company;
2. bank details (three months' bank statements);
3. previous landlord reference (if applicable);
4. form of authority;
5. up to three years trading accounts (if available);
6. a credible reference from an independent referencing agent. (This should include landlord's reference and financial background check);
7. an accountant's report (if available);
8. details of assets owned including property (if available); and
9. details of their liabilities (if available).

If the company has a guarantor a landlord should obtain the same documentation and carry out the same referencing as they would on an individual seeking to rent their property, as set out in Chapter 2. There is no point in having a guarantor against whom a landlord cannot enforce the obligations of the tenancy, either because the landlord has insufficient information about the guarantor to do so, or the guarantor was unsuitable.

23.3 The tenancy agreement

A company let agreement is governed more by contractual terms and common law rules rather than by legislation. The general rule is that if the agreement fails to mention something, there is no obligation on the landlord or the tenant to do or refrain from doing it. It is therefore important to get the tenancy agreement just right.

It is not unusual for a company to have their tenancy agreement and insist on it being used. A landlord may wish to negotiate the terms of the tenancy agreement with the company. In doing so a landlord should be aware of the matters discussed below.

23.3.1 Serving of notices

The tenancy agreement should explicitly set out:-
* how (by registered deliver, first class post, hand delivery or other method);
* when (at what date or on the occurrence of what event);
* where (at the branch, regional or head office); and
* on whom (company director, company secretary or company officer),
notices can be served on the company.

A landlord should ensure that Law of Property Act 1925 Section 196 is incorporated into the tenancy agreement to make it easier for notices to be served. This provision is explained in detail in paragraph 3.1.4.

23.3.2 Deposit

As a company let is not an AST, there is no statutory requirement to protect the deposit. The tenancy agreement should therefore specify:-
* how the deposit is to be held;
* what claims can be made against it;
* how a claim can be made;
* what is to happen to any interest accrued;
* how and when the deposit or the remainder of it should be returned;
* how disputes should be resolved; and
* that it should not be used as a substitute for rent.

23.3.3 Use of the property

It is important in the case of a company let (as well as any other residential letting) that the tenant is restricted from using the property for the purposes of carrying on a business either in part of or the whole of the property. Without such a term the tenant can use the property for whatever lawful purpose they wish and may cause a landlord to be in breach of their superior lease where applicable or create a business tenancy governed by a different set of rules.

23.3.4 Alterations and improvements

The tenancy agreement should have a term prohibiting the tenant from making alterations and/or improvements to the property or, in any event, requiring that the landlord's written consent is obtained before doing so.

23.3.5 Assignment

Without any restrictions in the tenancy agreement a company tenant can transfer all their rights and obligations in the tenancy to another person. This can create a problem where the new tenant may not have been referenced or not have a guarantor as was required of the original tenant. There should be a term prohibiting the tenant from assigning the tenancy or a term making such an assignment subject to strict requirements so as to protect a landlord's interest.

23.3.6 Rent

A strict interpretation of rent is the sum of money that is paid to the landlord for the use and occupation of the landlord's property. This does not include other charges incidental to renting the property. It is in the landlord's interest to include as many different payments that are associated with the tenancy as rent. If successfully done this gives a landlord the remedies available for rent arrears if there is a failure to pay those charges.

A landlord should note that rent is not lawfully due until a landlord has provided a tenant in writing with a name and address in England and Wales upon which notices can be served upon the landlord.

The rent clause should also state that the tenant is not allowed to make any deductions or set offs against the rent in respect of any obligation of the landlord under the tenancy. A set off is where a tenant claims that the landlord should give them monetary compensation for a breach of the terms of the tenancy and withholds an equivalent sum in rent.

23.3.7 Rent Review Clause

A landlord should give consideration to a rent review term if the tenancy is to continue beyond 12 months. Such a term should specify when or what event should trigger it and state clearly how the new rent is to be determined. The Section 13 Notice procedure to increase rent applies to ASTs, not company lets.

23.3.8 Sub-letting

When a company rents a residential property for a non-business use it is obvious that the property will be used to accommodate someone associated with the company. The tenancy agreement should specify the type of licence or tenancy that the company can grant to that person so as not to create a tenancy that may prove problematic to a landlord during the course of the company let or after it has ended. It is important that the sub-tenancy created is not an Assured Tenancy where it might be difficult to recover possession as opposed to an AST where it can be easier to obtain possession.

In any event, the type of tenancy a person will acquire depends more on the circumstances of the letting rather than the label put on the agreement. If a company sub-lets the property to an employee the default tenancy will be an AST if the criteria set out in Chapter 1 are satisfied.

When the first tenancy ends a sub-tenancy is usually also terminated and the original landlord is entitled to possession. However, if the first tenancy is ended

232   BEING A LANDLORD

by forfeiture or surrender the sub-tenant becomes the direct tenant of the original landlord.

If there is a sub-letting creating an AST and this is allowed under the tenancy agreement i.e. it is lawful, the assured shorthold tenant will become the tenant of the main landlord when the main tenancy ends.

23.3.9 Forfeiture and re-entry

It is important that the tenancy agreement contains a clause that allows the landlord to forfeit the lease for specified breaches and to have the right of re-entry. This will provide a landlord with a method of obtaining possession of the property during the fixed term as a result of breaches by tenant. The events leading to forfeiture should include bankruptcy, liquidation, receivership, rent arrears and other specified breaches. However, landlords should not take this clause literally and seek to re-enter the property and recover vacant possession.

If a landlord is seeking to use the procedure of forfeiture to recover possession of the property there is a strict process to follow and the tenant is entitled to seek relief in this procedure from the court. The services of an experienced professional should be used.

23.3.10 Break clause

It is important in a fixed term tenancy that a landlord includes a break clause. This will allow both parties to be able to terminate the agreement after a certain period of the fixed term has expired or on the occurrence of a specified event.

Whilst a fixed term tenancy gives a landlord the certainty of receiving rent over a fixed period, it also presents a lot of problems if a landlord requires vacant possession before the fixed term expires and cannot get it.

23.3.11 Repairs

The Landlord and Tenant Act 1985 Section 11 repairing obligation will apply to a company let as it is a letting of a residential dwelling, provided the letting is not for more than seven years. See Chapter 7 on repairs.

23.3.12 Renewal clause

A company tenant may want the option to renew the fixed term when it is due to expire and seek to have a term in the agreement to that effect. Such an option will usually mean that if the tenant fulfils certain criteria the landlord will have to renew the fixed term. The term usually requires that the tenant give the landlord notice at a specified time or on the occurrence of a specified event and that the tenant has not breached or is not currently in breach of the terms of the tenancy.

23.4 Recovering Possession of a company let tenancy

Recovering possession of a company let property is different from recovering possession of an AST. Obtaining a possession order of a company let is similar to that of a "Non-Excluded Tenancy" as they are both common law tenancies with minimum statutory protection. The procedure for recovering possession is set out in paragraph 5.3.

Before a landlord can recover possession of a company let property he will need to bring to an end the contractual agreement upon which that letting was created. How and when that contract can be brought to an end depends on whether it is a fixed term or periodic tenancy.

Once the contractual tenancy has been brought to an end, if someone remains in occupation of the property the landlord will need to obtain a court order for possession.

23.5 Bringing the contract to an end during the fixed term

23.5.1 Expiration of the fixed term

A fixed term company let will end automatically when the term expires. There is no legislation that provides for a statutory tenancy to come into existence. The landlord and tenant do not have to do anything for it to end. However, if the landlord and tenant act in a particular way at the end of the fixed term they may create a new periodic tenancy. These acts can include collecting rent and not insisting that the tenant leave when the fixed term expired.

A landlord wishing to recover possession at the end of the fixed term should advise the tenant in writing before the term expires that:-

- at the end of the fixed term they do not wish for a further tenancy to be created;
- should the property be occupied at the end of the fixed term a court order for possession will be sought;
- the tenant will be considered a trespasser if they remain in the property at the end of the fixed term;
- any payment taken from the tenant following the end of the fixed term will not be rent but will be considered as a charge for use and occupation; and
- any repairs carried out by the landlord after the fixed term has expired will not be under the landlord's repairing obligation and is not intended to create a new tenancy but is to protect the landlord's interest in the property.

A landlord should be absolutely sure that the fixed term has come to an end. If the contract has an option for it to be renewed and this process is successfully used a new fixed term tenancy will come into existence.

23.5.2 Break clause

A tenancy may end before the fixed term has expired if the tenancy has a break clause. The break clause should specify when, or upon the occurrence of what event, it can be exercised. A break clause is normally exercisable by both the landlord and the tenant.

A landlord should ensure that they fully comply with the requirements of the break clause. Once this is done the fixed term and the contractual tenancy will be at an end. Following this a landlord should not do anything which could be construed as creating a new tenancy.

23.5.3 Forfeiture and right of re-entry

If the company let agreement has a term allowing for forfeiture with a right of re-entry this can allow a landlord to bring a fixed term tenancy to an end if the tenant has committed a particular breach of the tenancy.

For forfeiture to operate there has to be a term in the tenancy agreement to that effect with a right of re-entry. The tenant must have done or failed to do something which allows the landlord to exercise the term. If the tenant has complied with the terms of the tenancy a landlord will not be able to rely on forfeiture. This is a complicated procedure and a landlord should seek professional advice. A tenant or sub-tenant can claim relief from forfeiture if they are able to remedy the breach.

23.6 Bringing a periodic company let to an end

Both the landlord and tenant will be able to end a periodic company let tenancy. Either party can serve on the other a Notice to Quit.

Paragraph 5.3.1 sets out in detail how to complete a Notice to Quit. A landlord should follow the same instructions when completing a Notice to Quit for a periodic company let tenancy.

A landlord should always check the tenancy agreement to see if there is a clause placing any particular requirements on the preparation and service of a Notice to Quit. Some tenancy agreements may specify the length of notice (subject to the minimum notice period) or how it is to be served on the tenant. Whatever is specified in the tenancy agreement should be strictly followed for the Notice to Quit to be valid and/or effectively served. Paragraph 3.1.4 sets out in detail how the Notice to Quit can be served on the tenant.

23.7 Obtaining a court order for possession of a company let

Paragraph 3.1.11 sets out the effect of a possession order on a sub-tenancy and against whom a landlord should seek a possession order and bailiffs' warrant. If the sub-tenancy is a lawful AST the sub-tenant will become the direct tenant of the landlord when the first tenancy has ended. This is also the case if a first tenancy (AST or not) was ended by surrender or forfeiture.

It is only when the contractual tenancy has ended that a landlord can commence court proceedings to recover possession. The contractual tenancy will end when the date in the Notice to Quit expires or when the fixed term comes to an end. Should a landlord commence court proceedings without ending the contractual tenancy the tenant will have a complete defence to the claim for possession.

A landlord should follow the steps set out in paragraph 5.4 onwards to recover possession of a company let tenancy. If doing so results in the landlord having a direct AST with a sub-tenant, the landlord will need to consider Chapter 21 in recovering possession of an AST. There are some differences in how the forms should be completed between a non-excluded tenancy and a company let which are highlighted below. Apart from those differences the form should be completed as if it was a non-excluded tenancy as set out in Chapter 5.

23.7.1 Claim form for possession (Form N5)

Paragraph 5.4.1 gives a step-by-step guide on how to complete Form N5 for a non-excluded tenancy. A landlord should follow those steps with regard to a company let subject to the following exception.

On page 2 of the Form N5 in the section titled "Grounds for possession" the landlord should mark "other" and write in the space provided "Possession is sought of a common law tenancy created by a company let that has been terminated by a Notice to Quit". If a Notice to Quit was **not** served as in the case where the fixed term has expired therefore ending the contractual tenancy the landlord should write "Possession is sought of a common law tenancy created by a company let that has ended when the fixed term expired with no new fixed term or periodic tenancy being agreed".

23.7.2 Particulars of claim for possession (Form N119)

Paragraph 5.4.2 gives a step by step guide on how to complete Form N119 for a non-excluded tenancy. A landlord should follow those steps with regard to a company let subject to the following exceptions.

At paragraph 2 of Form N119 the names of the people living in the property should be inserted. This will be different from the details of the tenant i.e. the company. The landlord can write to the following effect "the property was sub-let to Mr and/or Ms/Mrs Xxxx under an (insert type of tenancy, if known). They live in the property by themselves or with (provide details of other persons). If a landlord does not know the occupiers name(s) a description of the persons i.e. woman and two children can be inserted. If not known the landlord should state "not known".

At paragraph 3(a) the landlord should insert the type of tenancy i.e. "Common law tenancy" and the date when the tenancy began. If the landlord does not know the exact date the tenancy began, the month and year can be inserted such as "June 2012".

At paragraph 4(c) the landlord should write that "the tenant was granted a common law (company let) tenancy which has now been terminated by a Notice to Quit" or if the landlord is seeking possession after the fixed term has ended the landlord should write "the tenant was granted a common law (company let) fixed term tenancy and the fixed term has now ended with no further fixed term or periodic tenancy being agreed".

Paragraph 7 request details about the tenant's circumstances. The landlord can put the details of the company and problems it is known that the company may be experiencing, but it is not necessary to do so.

The remaining sections of Form N119 should be completed as set out in paragraph 5.4.2.

23.8 Issuing court proceedings

Paragraph 5.5 onwards sets out what a landlord should do to start court proceedings of a Non-Excluded tenancy. The same process should be followed to start court proceedings for a company let tenancy.

23.9 The court hearing

Paragraph 5.6 sets out the procedure to be followed in attending court and making the case for a possession order. A landlord should follow the same procedure subject to the following exceptions.

A landlord should be prepared with relevant documentation to prove the following matters:-
* the tenancy is a company let tenancy;
* the Notice to Quit has been prepared correctly;
* the Notice to Quit has been served on the tenant correctly;
* court proceedings were issued after the notice expired;
* or alternatively the fixed term has expired; and
* no new fixed term or periodic tenancy was agreed.

At the hearing a landlord will need to satisfy the court of the following matters:-
* The tenancy is a company let tenancy. This can be proved by showing the court the tenancy agreement and identity of the tenant.
* The notice has been prepared correctly. The judge will usually examine the notice to ensure that it is correct.

- The notice has been correctly served. The landlord may be able to do this via a witness who accompanied the landlord when the notice was been served, pictures of the notice been served, confirmation from the tenant that they received the notice on a particular date and any term in the tenancy agreement dealing with service of notice.
- Court proceedings were issued after the notice expired. This will normally be evident to the court from the documentation available.

On making a possession order the court will usually give the tenant two to four weeks to vacate the property. If the tenant can show that the time period would cause exceptional hardship the court can extend it to six weeks.

If the tenant fails to vacate the property on the date given in the possession order a landlord cannot remove the tenant from the property. To do so could amount to a criminal offence. A landlord will need to get a bailiffs' warrant for eviction. This is made by an application to the court on form N325 with the appropriate fee.

23.10 Completing Form N325

Paragraph 5.7 gives a step by step guide on how to apply for a bailiffs' warrant for eviction against a non-excluded tenant. The same process should be followed for a company let.

24 WHEN THE TENANCY HAS ENDED

A tenancy coming to an end can be the most contentious period of a letting for a landlord. A landlord would desire to part with the tenant having paid all rent and the property returned in as good a condition as when it was let. This is not often the case. There are matters a landlord should attend to before, when and after the tenancy ends.

24.1 Before the Tenancy ends

Under normal circumstances a landlord will know when their tenancy is going to end and when their tenant will be vacating the property. In anticipation of the tenancy ending the following matters should be attended to by the landlord and/or the tenant:-

- final utility bills (water, gas, electricity) and changing the name of the account holder with the suppliers;
- final bills for telephone, satellite or cable TV, broadband and any other paid services;
- notifying the Council Tax office of the tenant's intended departure and what will be happening with the property afterwards;
- re-letting the property;
- inspection of the property prior to the tenancy end date;
- ensuring the property will be cleaned and the furniture returned to its original position for the checkout;
- ensuring that if the locks were changed the landlord will get all the new keys and if not, all the original keys will be returned;
- ensuring that a copy of the inventory, tenancy agreement and photographs/video of the property are available;
- ensuring rent payments are up to date;
- arranging a date for the checkout; and
- have information about the deposit and scheme readily available.

The tenant should normally notify the utility company in advance (in accordance with the contract with their supplier) that the tenancy will be coming to an end and that they should be sent a final bill. The final bill will include standing charges up to the tenancy end date as well as a charge for any units used. This will not be necessary for prepayment meters for gas and electricity.

It is not uncommon for a tenant to have entered into a contract with a supplier for other services at the property such as satellite or cable TV and broadband. It is unlikely that a landlord will know who the suppliers are and the terms of the agreement. A landlord should inform their tenant that they should make arrangements for the final bill to be sent to them. Confirmation of these matters should be given to the landlord by the tenancy end date.

The Council Tax department of the local authority for the area in which the property is located should be notified of the tenant's intended departure so that a final bill can be settled. A landlord should bear in mind that students are not subject to Council Tax and some tenants on benefits would have been receiving Council Tax Benefit. The Council Tax department will want to know whether the property will be occupied or vacant after the tenant has left and what will be its future use so that appropriate future billing arrangements can be made. There are due to be significant changes to the administration and charging of Council Tax in 2013.

If a landlord has decided that they are going to re-let their property they should start to identify prospective tenants well in advance of the tenancy end date and arrange viewings at the property or get an agent to attend to this. This book does not deal with where and how a landlord can find tenants, but Chapter 2 sets out the matters that a landlord should attend to before the tenancy, when they have identified a prospective tenant. A landlord should ensure that they have sufficient time to carry out the checks mentioned in Chapter 2 so that they identify a suitable tenant to take the property when it becomes vacant.

A landlord should carry out regular inspections of their property throughout the tenancy. The frequency and intensity of those inspections will depend on what a landlord has discovered during the first or subsequent inspections. If the inspection shows that everything is fine a landlord may not inspect as often as when the inspection reveals concerns.

It is recommended that a landlord carry out a pre-end of tenancy inspection. This should be done as soon as it is clear that the tenant will be vacating the property and with sufficient time for any issues identified at the inspection to be rectified before the tenant leaves. An ideal time is at least two months before the tenancy ends.

The purpose of this inspection is to identify any breaches of the tenancy for which the tenant is responsible and to make arrangements for them to be put right. There should be a term in the tenancy dealing with such matters. If the tenant fails to put a breach of the tenancy right a landlord will need to seek deduction(s) from the deposit. At this early stage a landlord can get an idea of whether the deposit will be sufficient to cover the cost of putting the breach(es) right or whether further recovery action will need to be taken. A landlord who carries out a pre-end of tenancy inspection substantially reduces the chances of being surprised at what they discover at the checkout appointment.

A landlord should inform their tenant that they expect the property to be cleaned and furniture returned to its original position to aid the checkout process. This is subject to the tenant having a clean property at the start of the tenancy. A reluctant tenant should be reminded that deductions can be made from the deposit for cleaning (if the tenancy agreement allows) and professional cleaning of the property will be more expensive than the tenant doing or arranging it themselves.

An inventory and accompanying pictures and/or video would have been prepared with the furniture in a particular place in a room. A tenant may move the furniture during the tenancy for many reasons including hiding damage to the property and/or furniture. Returning furniture to its original position will make discovering missing items easier and aid better comparison with the way the property was at the beginning and end of the tenancy.

A landlord should notify their tenant that they are required to return all the keys which were given to them at the commencement of the tenancy. The keys that were given to the tenant should have been noted in the inventory. This will include communal door keys/fob, garage, window, garden shed, patio/balcony doors and entrance door keys. If a tenant has changed the locks they should give the landlord all the keys for the new locks. If a tenant is unable to comply with this request, the landlord may have to change the locks at the tenant's expense. This should have been set out in the tenancy agreement. If it becomes necessary, a landlord should put in place arrangements for the lock to be changed on the checkout date.

Nearer to the time that a tenant will be leaving the property a landlord should arrange a checkout inspection appointment. This appointment is for the tenant and the landlord/agent to inspect the property when the tenant has removed their possessions and cleaned it, if necessary. This will normally be on the date the tenant has vacated the property or shortly thereafter. A landlord should ensure that they have a copy of the tenancy agreement, the inventory and any photographs or video taken of the property to facilitate the checkout process (see below).

A landlord should always monitor rent payments carefully and take swift action to deal with rent arrears when they occur as set out in Chapter 15. If a tenant has significant rent arrears which they are seeking to satisfy out of the deposit, it may well leave a landlord with no deposit to cover any damage to the property. Damage to the property may have been discovered upon a pre-end of tenancy inspection. A landlord should inform the tenant of the final rent payments they will need to make up to the end of the tenancy and that these payments should be made in advance.

24.2 When the tenancy ends

A checkout inspection appointment should normally take place on the day the tenant vacates the property or shortly thereafter. At the checkout inspection the landlord should be prepared to do the following:-

- take meter readings if the property does not have prepaid meters;
- confirm that final utility bills have been paid;
- confirm that final bills for other services to the property has been paid;
- obtain tenant's forwarding address if not already done so;
- collect all keys from the tenant or have the locks changed if necessary;
- ensure all rent is paid up to date;
- carry out a thorough inspection of the property;
- have a document for the tenant to sign agreeing to what deductions, if any, should be made from the deposit;
- ensure there is sufficient time to deal with the checkout (a few hours); and
- have available the tenancy agreement, inventory/schedule of condition, photographs and/or video.

If a deposit was taken for the tenancy it ought to have been protected with a deposit protection scheme. A landlord should have the information about the scheme readily available. If following the checkout the parties cannot agree on any deduction sought, the dispute will be resolved under the procedure provided by the scheme. These procedures will have deadlines for matters to be attended to and so a landlord should be familiar with them, especially where a landlord is already aware that deductions will have to be made.

At the checkout a landlord ought to inspect every room and every item within the room to ensure that there has been no damage beyond fair wear and tear. In a bedroom this may involve more than looking at walls, ceiling, windows and doors. It may also entail moving furniture to check the flooring for carpet burns, pulling out drawers to check for any that might be broken and flipping mattress to check for stains. Nothing should be left unturned.

In the kitchen a landlord should check in the fridge/freezer for broken or missing shelves and cleanliness. The same checks should be applied to the washing machine, dryer, dishwasher, cupboards and cooker. Particular attention should be given to the oven and grill which if not in a clean state may require the attention of professionals. If the property has a garden it should be returned in the state in which it was let with the property. A landlord should take pictures/video of all damaged or dirty items for evidence to settle any disputed claims.

A landlord should not expect the property to be returned in exactly the same state/condition in which it was let. A carpet gets worn when walked on, walls may get slightly soiled when a property is lived in, appliances will experience wear and tear. The law allows for reasonable wear and tear to occur when a tenant rents a property. This needs to be taken into account when considering damages and deductions. Additionally, if an item was new it should normally be replaced with a new one, however, if it was used, dated and with wear and tear allowance should be made for this in the settlement figure.

If there are no deductions to be made from the deposit, following a thorough check, the landlord should give the tenant something to that effect in writing. If there are deductions to be made from the deposit the items to be deducted and the reasons for deductions should be listed, and the tenant asked to sign the document in agreement or acknowledgement. A landlord should refer to the tenancy documents during this process and seek to settle any disputes at an early and informal stage.

24.3 After the tenancy ends

Following the checkout a landlord may need to attend to the following matters:-
* reinstating the property to a condition where it can be re-let;
* repairing or replacing appliances;
* obtaining quotes for deductions from the deposit;
* keeping invoices/receipts for any expenditure;
* dealing with disputes about the deposit;
* letting the property;
* making insurance claims; and/or
* commencing litigation.

All deposits now have to be protected in/under a deposit protection scheme and all the schemes require issues around the deposit to be settled swiftly.

A landlord will usually need to get two proper quotes for all deductions sought and have a rent statement for any arrears of rent claimed. A landlord should not seek to make excessive claims such as quoting for a room to be painted when there was only damage to one wall or claiming to replace an entire fridge when just a door which is replaceable has been damaged. If a tenant agrees with the sums being sought, matters can be concluded swiftly with the deposit. If the tenant disputes some or all the items for which deduction from the deposit is sought, a landlord may need to present their case to whatever process is designated under the deposit protection scheme. A landlord should therefore ensure that they are familiar with the workings of the scheme under which the deposit is protected.

If a landlord has to make a money claim against the tenant for some above the deposit a landlord should follow a similar process to that set out in Chapters 15 to 20 for the recovery of rent arrears.

Index

BEING A LANDLORD